Rebel Dance, Renegade Stance

Rebel Dance, Renegade Stance

TIMBA MUSIC AND BLACK IDENTITY IN CUBA

Umi Vaughan

The University of Michigan Press
Ann Arbor

First paperback edition 2013
Copyright © 2012 by Umi Vaughan
All rights reserved

Published in the United States of America by
The University of Michigan Press
Manufactured in the United States of America
⊚ Printed on acid-free paper

2016   2015   2014   2013   5   4   3   2

A CIP catalog record for this book is available from the British Library.

Library of Congress Cataloging-in-Publication Data

Vaughan, Umi.
    Rebel dance, renegade stance : Timba music and Black identity in Cuba /
Umi Vaughan.
        p.   cm.
    Includes bibliographical references and index.
    ISBN 978-0-472-11848-9 (cloth : alk. paper) — ISBN 978-0-472-02869-6 (e-book)
    1. Timba (Music)—History and criticism.   2. Dance music—Cuba—History and criticism.   3. Dance—Cuba.   4. Blacks—Race identity—Cuba.
5. Blacks—Cuba—Social life and customs.   6. Cuba—Social life and customs.
I. Title.
ML3486.C82V38   2012
781.64097291—dc23   2012012837

ISBN 978-0-472-03575-5 (paper : alk. paper)

For Yasmeen

Preface

"¡Ivan, ven acá!" *Come inside, somebody yelled. He stopped his rap-ping, laughing, and dancing, quickly entered the house, and disap-peared into the* igbodú *(altar room). After improvising outside in all the latest styles of hip-hop and timba dance to the beat of a popular singer called El Médico de la Salsa, now, accompanied by a respected elder and a young apprentice, Ivan began to recite an ancient musical liturgy in honor of the orisha Changó on the batá drum.*[1] *Their percussive prayers echoed and explained the energy and complexity of the new, secular dances. The intricate arcs and turns of his salsa steps embell-ished and protected ancient information that lives at the center:* la raíz, *the root. This balance of modern and ancient continues to captivate me. Ivan and Cubans like him are time travelers and magicians. El Médico and Changó are one. This book tries to explain the connection.*

The Beginning

As I left for Cuba, many questioned why I would expose myself to what seemed to them a dangerous situation in a "far away," "communist," "poor," "Third World" country, and for such a long time. I especially re-call the playful, yet serious teasing of my grandfather who would say, "We want you to be done with Cuba so you can hurry up and get a job! Don't fool around and can't get back!" As in the Buena Vista fever that took hold of the United States and the Elián fiasco that brought the is-land into view as well, perceptions of Cuba are made of fear and fantasy. People of the African Diaspora who travel and dwell throughout its many frontiers and communities need to tell our stories. Through these encounters much can be learned to advance academic knowledge, improve living conditions, and expand life opportunities for people of the diaspora in various contexts from local to global. Too often, as with Zora Neale Hurston, Katherine Dunham, or St. Clair Drake, the work gets lost somehow, and never reaches the scholarly canon or any wide audience. I want to tell our stories so that everyone may hear.

Finally, after much dreaming, anticipation, and sacrifice by my family and me, I traveled to Cuba many times, between 1999 and 2002, staying two or three weeks around Christmas and New Year's or a few months during the summer, welcomed by my friend's mother and officially hosted by Olavo Alén at the Center for the Investigation and Development of Cuban Music or Alberto Granado at La Casa de África. Each of these experiences was building familiarity as well as personal and professional connections, working up to a longer stay. Moving through Havana City, I was convinced that I had to be there to learn something, though I was still unsure what.

Over the course of several trips and an extended residency, I truly caught the rhythm of the place. Sometimes people refused to believe that I was American and not from Cuba! They say *cubanizao* or *aplatanao* about foreigners who have "become Cuban." In Havana, they thought I was a *guajiro* or *palestino* from Oriente. In Oriente, they thought I was from some other *monte* or maybe from the Dominican Republic or Puerto Rico. I watched the *telenovelas*, saw a Cuban interpretation of world politics nightly on *la mesa redonda* or roundtable, I drank sweet coffee in the morning and at night, ate *caldosa* stew on July 26 and *comida de cajita*, the delicious meals in a box found throughout Havana. I tossed my dreams to the wind at the edge of Havana's seawall. I sang to the orishas and learned to play Changó's drums. I rode up close and personal with humanity on the P1 bus and the infamous *camello* or camel bus. I went from Havana to Santiago by train, I was mistaken for a Rastafarian and a pimp, and signed as a witness in the counting of votes for representatives in the Havana municipality of Marianao. There and in neighborhood of Los Sitios, we told stories to pass the time during *apagones* or blackouts.

Fui a buscar los mandados (I ran errands). Family, the grandmother in the home where I lived, died and we grieved. I went to the cockfights with my friend Pedro. I cruised around the perimeter of the U.S. military base in Guantánamo and felt the unity and the power of Cuban patriotism and, dare I say, Revolutionary spirit, as I lifted a bus along with other men, women, and children. I danced with all the best orchestras at clubs, on patios and *balcones* (balconies), at weddings, *cumpleaños* (birthdays), and Carnival, and talked with many of their directors, musicians, and fans about music and Cuba.

Despite being a foreigner, I was rarely a complete outsider. I came with a great friend, my *ecobio*, who helped me and taught me many things about Cuba right from the start, a gesture for which I will always be grateful to him and his family. I am an African person and that too facilitated my connection with Cuba. Many of the "ancient African organizing principles of song and dance" (Thompson 1984, 2) that I had come to study—though expressed in unique ways on the island—were already familiar to me. My connection to Africa, both culturally and by my dark skin color, identified me with the Afro-Cubans who were primarily responsible for the music that interested me. I also believe that an unknown ancestor of mine was among the rebellious blacks expelled from Point Coupee, Louisiana, to Cuba in 1795 (Gomez 1998, 53), or one of those that came to New Orleans from Cuba after abolition on the island in 1886 (Acosta 1989, 28), and that their spirit binds me to Cuba and is responsible for my Cuban accent! Thus my fieldwork in Cuba was about history in a personal as well as a diasporic sense.

Dance anthropologist Katherine Dunham describes an instance in Haiti where her separation from the group—her outsider status, exemplified by her inability to eat a sacrificial food she found disgusting—was erased (or at least mitigated) by her dancing. "I danced more than I have ever in my life, before or after," she writes, "and for the first time the ground at my feet was kissed" (1994, 234–35). Lévi-Strauss writes of Dunham in the foreword to her book *Dances of Haiti:* "To the dignitaries of the vaudun who were to become her informants, she was both a colleague, capable of comprehending and assimilating the subtleties of a complex ritual, and a stray soul who had to be brought back into the fold of the traditional cult" (Dunham 1983, xvi).

Though I am no Katherine Dunham, I dared to take on the task of writing about Cuban music precisely because I can dance, and only under this condition—having lived the music and experienced its meaning through movement, catching *the common beat*—could I forge words that swing. Like dance scholar Barbara Browning writes of her experience in Brazil, in Cuba I learned many things with my body (1995, 167), both dancing and just being. Through this ethnography of music and dance I explore the economic, social, and ideological constraints under which social classes and racial groups interact, focusing especially on Afro-Cubans. In my work, Afro-Cuban voices (to use Sarduy and Stubbs's term) and bodies speak.

Acknowledgments

There are many people to recognize for their help in bringing this work to fruition. Thanks to my editor at the University of Michigan Press, Ellen Bauerle. Thank you to Kim Butler for opening doors and to Yvonne Daniel for her generous suggestions. Thanks to Barbara Polcyn, Lauric Marx, Carol Jacobson, Ed West, Vicky Veenstra, Bruce Mannheim, Jennifer Roberts, Janet Hart, Stuart Kirsch, Ifeoma Nwankwo, Judith Becker, Glenda Dickerson, Evans Young, Don Sims, Elizabeth James, Kevin Gaines, Rebecca Scott, Fernando Coronil, Kelly Askew, Maxwell Owusu, Conrad Kottak, and my mentor Ruth Behar at the University of Michigan, Ann Arbor.

At California State University Monterey Bay, thanks to all of my colleagues in the Division of Humanities and Communication. Special recognition goes out to the students of my class "Afro Cuba Hip Hop: Music and Dance in the Black Atlantic" who read excerpts from this volume and were a sounding board for many of the ideas I present here.

In Cuba, thanks to all my teachers and friends at the Center for the Investigation and Development of Cuban Music (CIDMUC), Olavo Alén, Liliana Casanella, and Raimundo Villaurrutia, and to the library staff, Tamara Sevila Salas, Eloisa Marrero Sera, and Sara Martínez García. At the Fundación Fernando Ortiz thanks to Miguel Barnet, Trinidad Pérez, María Teresa Linares, Jesús Guanche, Hildemar, and David. Thanks to Alberto Granado and Esther Pérez at La Casa de África. Modupe to Tomás Fernández Robaina. Mil amores to Nancy Morejón and thank you very much to Gloria Rolando. Thank you to Eduardo Rosillo, Jorge Petineaud, and Rolando Zaldívar. Gracias/thank you/muito obrigado to Carlos Moore.

Thanks of course to all the musicians who shared their time and their tumbao with me: Fito Reinoso, Pancho Quinto, Carlos Aldama, Papo Angarica, Manolito Simonet, David Calzado and La Charanga Habanera, José Luis Cortés, Pedro Pablo and his Orquesta Rebambaramba, Paulito F.G., Cándido Fabré, Elio and Orderquis Revé, Angelito Bonne, Aramis Galindo, Yvette Porras from Orquesta D'talle, La Charanga Forever, Yoel Driggs, Pedro Fajardo, Mario "Mayito" Rivera, Boris Luna, Edmundo "Mundele" Pina, and Yenisel "Jenny" Valdés from Orquesta Los Van Van, Pedro Calvo, José Luis Quintana "Changuito," César "Pupy" Pedroso, Lázaro Valdés and Bamboleo, Tirso Duarte, Luis Abreu Hernández of Los Papines, and Joaquin Betancourt.

Gracias to Miriam Viant, my godmother, who taught me so much of Cuba, and to her son Francisco who brought me to her. Thanks to Alexis, Amor, Amexis, Anilexis, Aniel, Inocente, Ángela and Yvonne, *el familión*. Thank you to Haníbal, Maida y José, Armando, La China, El Moro y todos del barrio.

Contents

CHAPTER I
Introduction: Dancing & Being

It makes sense to study Cuban culture through music and dance because in Cuba they are everywhere; the two are as elemental as water and air. Particularly popular dance music, with contributions from all of Cuba's ethnic components (African, Hispanic, Chinese, indigenous, Haitian, Jamaican, etc.), has penetrated every fiber of the society. By looking at the musical form timba and various dance spaces in Havana where it is performed, *Rebel Dance, Renegade Stance* recounts social crisis and transformation and the role of music/dance as a mirror, medium for, and an active element in the creation of national culture. During the moment of timba's birth, development, and boom the 1990s the Cuban phrase *seguimos en combate* (we are still at war) was particularly poignant; and a new music/dance developed to express the times. Like other genres and rhythms have been in the past, timba is now the music/dance style that is most cultivated in Cuba (Sarduy 2001, 171; Pérez 2003, 130; Perna 2005).

Its borrowings from Cuban *son*,[1] and from other national and international genres, make it so that almost everyone can enjoy it. Its popularity in Cuba and abroad has sparked debate among academics and intense media promotion, created new dance spaces, inspired musical creativity and output, and influenced government policy. At the same time, timba faces criticism and rejection from some sectors of the Cuban public (1) because of its identification with marginal black identity and (2) for perceived hedonistic, capitalist tendencies inside its performance. In spite of its detractors, timba is impossible to ignore. Its presence as an important cultural phenomenon is indisputable. My own wish to visit Cuba was inspired by timba, which I discovered through discs of El Médico de la Salsa.

Theoretical Perspectives: Music and Dance are One

As in many cultures of the African Diaspora, music and dance in Cuba are inseparable. Students of Africa and its diaspora, especially the Caribbean and Cuba, consistently describe a zone of "musical ferment where people love to dance . . . individuals become passionately attached to the dances they do, [and] assert their identity through movement" (Sloat 2002, ix). Throughout the Black Atlantic we find names that refer to music-dance complexes and/or gatherings that feature music and dance by necessity. In this way, *samba* from Brazil, *zouk* from Martinique and Guadeloupe, *rumba* and timba from Cuba (among countless other genres) reiterate and emphasize the unity of music and dance. Throughout the African Diaspora "music is almost always music for dancing," and "dancing is an intense listening state" (Sublette 2004, 57).

Pioneers in the study of African cultures in the New World, like Fernando Ortiz, have given detailed attention to music and dance for good reason. Their work affirms that music and dance data "make significant contributions to African Diaspora studies" (Daniel 2005, 1). Some, like dance anthropologist Yvonne Daniel, refer to the complex whole as "dance/music" due to particular disciplinary interests; still music and dance are recognized as inseparable. Other scholars approach from the music side but similarly cannot avoid the importance of dance. For example, most of the contributors to the edited volume *Music and Black Ethnicity* (Béhague 1994) actually examine music *and dance* in relationship to the efforts of various African Diaspora communities to define and identify themselves. Speaking of Panama, one of them writes, "The core from which energy flows during performance consists of song [music] and dance. . . . There is rarely dance without song or song without dance" (Smith 1994, 239). In fact, "there exists a symbiotic relationship between them" (240). More recently, the contributors to *Rhythms of the Afro-Atlantic World* take as a basic premise that music and dance are inextricably linked. Collectively the essays consider music and dance *together* as "critical arenas in which Afro-Atlantic subjects have continuously represented and reinvented their multiple bases of identity" (Diouf and Nwankwo 2010, 1).

Rebel Dance, Renegade Stance: Timba Music and Black Identity in Cuba begins with the acceptance that music and dance are one. I sometimes use the term *music/dance* to emphasize this unity but not always. Still, whenever one of these aspects of performance (music or dance) is described or discussed, it is always with the other in mind. For example, outlining the history and examining the sound and structure of Cuban music are preparations for my arguments about the use and meaning of dance. Music is inspired by dance, as in the case of the famous *chachachá* rhythm that derived partly from musicians interpreting the sounds made by dancers' feet in 1950s Cuba. Dance in contemporary Cuban spaces is fraught with meaning precisely because of the history of the music that animates it and the people who create that music.

Maroon Aesthetic

Because it taps into the spirit of struggle and creativity, I refer to timba as "timba brava" (García Meralla 1997) and, furthermore, call it "maroon music." The *American Heritage Dictionary of the English Language* defines *maroon* as "a fugitive black slave in the West Indies in the 17th and 18th centuries; the descendant of such a slave; plantation slaves who had run away to live free in uncultivated parts" (1992). "Brava"—brave, ferocious, wild, splendid—refers to the anger, unpredictability, and excellence in rebellion that are associated with maroons and timba. What might at first seem odd connections allude to continuing systems of racial inequality and the relationship between marginalized communities and the powers that be.

Both timba and maroon life in the Caribbean colonial period are based on "outsider identity," unique language, "raiding," and the use of old principles to improvise new styles in emergent social circumstances, which Amiri Baraka calls "the changing same" (Jones 1967). Maroons "stress individual style and dramatic self-presentation, openness to new ideas, and value innovation and creativity" (Price 1999, 285). Puerto Rican sociologist and salsa authority Ángel Quintero-Rivera offers a definition of the Taíno-Caribbean root word *símaran*.

> Stray or "runaway" arrow . . . from there it took on the meaning of "gone," "up in arms," or "mad" used to describe domestic animals that took to the hills, and to men—first Indians then later blacks—who rose up and sought their freedom far from the dominion of their masters. (1998, 265)

Generally, the maroons were enslaved indigenous and African peoples throughout the Americas who escaped from bondage, established viable communities, and fought to maintain their hard-won freedom (Agorsah 1994, 2). As a response to socioeconomic oppression, cultural colonialism, and racism, *marooning* is a common strategy throughout the Black Atlantic—linking Latin America, the Caribbean, and North America (Depestre 1984, 261). Often we think of Cuba in terms of its uniqueness—called Cuban exceptionalism—as the largest and historically "whitened" Caribbean island, its huge international musical influence, its communist revolution under Fidel Castro, and so on. The maroon aesthetic, however, helps to rightly situate Cuba as part of a region, "a historic family" shaped by similar events and circumstances (Depestre 1984, 260; Mintz and Price 1985; Mintz 1989; Benítez-Rojo 1996).[2]

On Cuba's sister island, Puerto Rico, maroons "sought to live on the margins of the state" (Quintero 1998, 276). This distance was not due to any opposition to the state per se but rather to the maroon aversion to subordination under state regime. To safeguard their positions, maroons sometimes fought on behalf of the colonial masters or signed treaties that pitted them against fugitive slaves. Scholars acknowledge maroons as "frontline fighters in the struggle against slavery in all its forms," but also emphasize maroons' "strong ideas of *self*-sufficiency, *self*-help and *self*-reliance" (Agorsah 1994, xiv; emphasis added). It is this concern with self-preservation that motivated maroon communities to act in ways that compromised the struggles of other oppressed groups under slavery, or indeed aided the colonial system. While sociocultural "marronage" certainly entails transforming the anguish of the black condition and the status of servitude through "creative explosion" (Depestre 1984, 271, 258), the relationship between maroon communities and the dominant society remains complex and at times contradictory. In fact, the maroons who had been the "chief opponents" of slave society, at times became "its main props" (Bilby 1994, 83). In a similar way, the maroon aesthetic—and timba—exist in conflict and complicity with the state and mainstream culture.

In his book *Afro-Creole: Power, Opposition, and Play in the Caribbean*, Richard Burton develops an argument that helps explain the contradiction within the maroon aesthetic. Following Michel de Certeau (1980) by eschewing the common use of the word *resistance* to mean *all counteraction* against a hegemonic power, Burton explains the relationship between a newly defined "resistance" and what is called "opposition" to describe the liberating cultural explosions of New World blacks. In this conception, "resistance" refers to "those forms of contestation of a given system that are conducted from *outside* that system, using weapons and concepts derived from a source other than the system in question"; while "opposition" refers to "those forms of contestation of a given system that are conducted *within* that system, using weapons and concepts derived from the system itself" (Burton 1997, 6).

Burton echoes Foucault (1978, 95–96) stating that instances of true "resistance" are rare in human history, in the case of the Caribbean happening perhaps only in Saint Domingue between 1791 and 1804, and in Cuba in the late 1950s. Burton contends, for example, that in most Caribbean contexts, once island-born slaves began to outnumber those of African origin, contestation took the form of "opposition," because the enslaved and oppressed drew heavily on materials (like language and religion) that were furnished by the dominant culture (Burton 1997, 6). In the process, oppressed peoples not only oppose the dominant group on the latter's own ground but are themselves drawn further into the dominant group's worldview. I apply Burton's concepts to timba as maroon music. *Resistance* is a word that could express timba as a kind of marronage or cultural counterattack; however, "opposition" (in the sense that de Certeau and Burton use it) is more accurate because it acknowledges the contradictory aims of those acting through timba, as well as the origins of some of their greatest "weapons" (like conservatory musical training or U.S. designer fashion) within dominant Cuban or so called Western society.

Performance

Black Atlantic performance "[poses] the world as it is against the world as the racially subordinated would like it to be" (Gilroy 1993, 36). In order to study "the power of music in developing black struggles by communicating information, organizing consciousness, and testing out or developing the forms of subjectivity required by political agency, whether individual or collective, defensive or transformational," it is necessary to consider both the formal attributes of performance and the moral bases of expressive culture (36). "Comprehending them necessitates an analysis of the lyrical content and the forms of musical expression [which I discuss in chapter 2] as well as the oft hidden social relations [which I decipher in chapters 3 and 4] in which these deeply encoded oppositional practices are created and consumed" (37). Paul Gilroy is talking about Erving Goffman's "linguistic and expressive" messages in the service of social transformation: "Politics . . . [is]

played, danced, and acted, as well as sung because words can't express [an] unsayable claim to truth" (37). The struggle for justice inspires the music, so naturally its messages and delivery are hotly contested.

In *Rebel Dance, Renegade Stance*, I interpret "politics . . . [as it is] played, danced, and acted, as well as sung" in the context of Black Atlantic cultural expressions (Gilroy 1993, 37). I take special note of distinct patterns of language, dramaturgy, enunciation, and gesture. I read the contours of an ongoing performative call-and-response that encompasses the intimate relationship of performer and crowd and all other possible trajectories of communication within the dance space. That is to say, I examine many kinds of interaction in the dance space, not only in the form of dance but also in other kinds of encounters. For example, signification by drinking at a table with friends is readable too. Dance spaces are important *espacios de sociabilidad* that contribute to the elevation of one or more national cultures; they are situated where diverse and particular identities are constructed, imagined, and interact (Marful 2002, 12).

I kept copious field notes mostly every day, moving between Spanish and English, using various text strategies: narrative, poetry, quotations from news and conversation, personal reflections, anthropological theory. Lyrics to songs from studio-recorded and live performances were transcribed by myself and analyzed by myself. I studied dance as symbolic and representative body expression that highlights and encourages individual achievement, reaffirms "conventional behavior" or "established patterns" (Dunham 1983, xvi), and allows humanity to momentarily transcend the mundane and access infinite possibility.

My efforts to insert myself in these spaces—dance, academic, and others—where I conducted my investigations entailed "ethnographic high jinx," which reveals a lot about my various identities and the perceptions of me in Cuba. Cubans are accustomed to being studied by anthropologists due to their rich culture, which is so characteristic of the process of transculturation that marks the meeting of cultures everywhere. Even still, swallowing an investigator like me seemed to be a challenge. When I arrived at the José Martí International Airport in Havana on my first trip in 1998, I already spoke Spanish, but not Cuban Spanish, and so I fumbled to understand when Cubans communicated to me as if to another Cuban, "Hey, citizen, you're in the wrong [customs] line!" Awkward familiarity and distance were to come up time and again as I got to know Cuba better and as I moved through different kinds of spaces on the island.

A Note on Photographs Included in the Text

As an artist as well as an anthropologist, making photographs is part of the way I go about understanding the world. If it is true that the eyes are the windows to the soul, then when gazes meet and hold one another the result is sublime and totally human. The images included in this book capture the embrace of the eyes, the expanse of space, the swinging release of dance—allowing images to speak along with the text. In doing so, they enrich the description of music and of the Afro-Cuban experience, which are my foci.

Using a simple, all-manual Nikon FM2 camera I developed a relationship with my surroundings. At first the camera seemed too large, too intrusive. I felt that this appendage, this eye, made me a permanent outsider, an unwelcome voyeur. As time went on, however, the camera seemed to shrink and disappear among my community consultants. Eventually not only was I able to capture delicate moments without disturbing them, I was also able to act through photography and dialogue with Cubans about Cuba, especially about issues of race and color. The series of photographs included in chapter 3, "Afro Cuba," is a prime example. In this approach I talked with people about names used to refer to various racial classifications, wrote those words out on the city itself (walls, staircases, doors, etc.), and then juxtaposed the same people with the words/ideas they had used to explain complex issues to me. The result was several beautiful images that dramatize race—identity, terminology, and relations—in Cuba. When I returned to Havana several years later, many of the graphs and drawings remained on the walls where people continued to comment on and discuss them.[3]

W

The experience of interacting with people through photography helped me understand that timba was born in the face of challenges posed by a radically changing Cuban society that was in crisis throughout the decade of the 1990s. We will see how timba is an important voice for Afro-Cuban people. Inasmuch as it creates/constitutes a space for particularly Afro-Cuban social/cultural/economic development, timba is "maroon music," in both dialogue and tension with Cuban society. U.S. American journalist and political analyst Eugene Robinson explains that the difference between salsa and timba is "a matter of stance,

power, and lethal intent—the difference between a debate and a riot"
(Robinson 2004, 70).

The photographs help to show that it is important to understand just
what is meant by the aggressiveness, the fragmentation, and *mal gusto*
(bad taste) among other characteristic elements that many students of
timba have noted. What or who has brought these elements into being?
At what or whom are they directed? Photographs support text in revealing what these musical developments have to do with the social environment in Cuba from 1990 to the present. What is meant by the term
Afro-Cuban? What is the historical development and significance of
(Afro) Cuban music from the end of the nineteenth century to the dawn
of the twenty-first? How are concepts of race, class, and gender performed around music in distinct spaces within the context of Cuban society? How does Cuba fit into the notion of diaspora? How did my identity as African (American), man, anthropologist, dancer, photographer,
santero, *negro prieto* (dark-skinned), and so forth affect and effect my
experience in Cuba? Focusing on Havana, the capital, as emblematic of
the nation as a whole, these are the main questions my fieldwork attempted to answer. There is a glossary at the end of the book with
meanings for words and phrases that might be unfamiliar.

Outline

Cubans of color (blacks and *mulatos*) use timba in various ways to identify, impugn, and transgress social boundaries—both literally and figuratively—through music, dance, and other kinds of performance.
Within their music, inside their physical bodies, and throughout various spaces, Cubans of color reaffirm their sense of belonging and importance inside the culture and social structure of Cuba. The aggressive
sounds, marginal themes, vulgar coded lyrics, and at times the eccentric
or "ghetto" self-representations are but affirmations of identity that in-
tend not to destroy Cuban society but rather to find a just position
within it. This has been the case in the fight of Cuban blacks and mulatos since colonial times.

Just as Afro-Cubans had complex, sometimes contradictory, relationships to oppressive power in the past, whether as maroon communities, combatants in the Ten Years' War and the Independence War, or
as supporters of the 1959 Revolution, their continuing struggle for
equality in the present has taken unexpected forms and used new strate-

gies. The case of timba is not a simple case of black or African resistance through music, because various sectors of Cuban society—including the state—have claims on timba as well.

Chapter 2, "Timba Brava: Maroon Music in Cuba," examines the music, its history and cultural context. It lays out various definitions of timba, traces the development of Cuban music before timba, describes the music and dance style, and examines critiques of timba and some of its most important proponents to date. As "maroon" music, timba is briefly compared to salsa and other forms of dance music from the Black Atlantic. The maroon aesthetic—for example, improvisation, "raiding," and struggle   highlights timba as the continuance of old ways of surviving and making culture. The maroon aesthetic contests a system, in this case, the Cuban state apparatus and cultural mainstream, with tools (like Western fashion and top-notch musical training) that are derived from that same system. Thus, I use Burton's notion of "opposition" to explain and emphasize the continued integration and marginalization that have been extant for black folk in Cuba from colonial times down to the Castro era.

Chapter 3, "Afro Cuba," explores social and historical factors that have shaped Afro-Cuban identity. It discusses Cuban racial categories and relations, describes important black social organizations and publications that have contributed to the fight for social justice in Cuba, explores the process/cycle of rejection, acceptance, commodification, and recontextualizing of Afro-Cuban culture, and provides evidence from the life experience of Cubans of various social milieus in the form of stories, jokes, and my photographs. In this way, Afro-Cuban voices and bodies speak on their own about the social circumstances under which timba developed, extending the work of scholars who accept that Cuba has made significant progress toward racial equality, yet remains imperfect. This chapter argues that today's timba music and timba dance spaces take on the function of organizations and publications that no longer exist, as the voice and open space for black expression.

Chapter 4, "Doing Identity," describes day-to-day living conditions during the special period, later economic reforms, and the self-presentation (performance) of Afro-Cuban youth. A social type called "the especulador" is analyzed and used as a metaphor for Afro-Cuban youth in dialogue and tension with the Cuban state, mainstream Cuban culture, and "the world outside." The especulador is considered in the context of exclusive dollar-only clubs and discos whose very existence contradicts the socialist ethic and highlights the shortcomings of state policy vis-à-vis Afro Cuba. Here the focus on performance is a unique perspective and reveals a portrait of contemporary Cuban culture.

Chapter 5, "The Joy Train: Dance Spaces in Havana," continues to examine those spaces where timba is the medium for the performance of identities. I provide thick descriptions and analyses of dance events within free open-air public dances, expensive dollarized clubs, and an "intermediary dance space" called La Tropical. While all share timba music as the medium for social (inter)action, each represents a space with different characteristics. Building on previous chapters, I consider the demographics, spatial arrangements, and the action—what happens—in these spaces. I show how the public dance—in the absence of cabildos, associations, and societies—takes on some of their functions. Dancing and being within these spaces, real people participate in the ongoing evolution of Afro-Cuban identity and Cubanness through performance.

Chapter 6, "Around the Iroko Tree: Fieldwork in Cuba," situates my fieldwork methodology and theory. It explains how my own identity in Cuba was shaped by the notion of Afro Cuba, and what happened when that played out in various kinds of spaces—from the public dance, to research institutes, sacred ceremonies, and private homes. It also challenges anthropologists to do ethnography in a way that promotes the liberation of those we study, considering them as collaborators and important audiences for our work. This chapter also provides another window into the everyday lives, values, and aspirations of Cuban people on the island at a critical moment in their history.

Chapter 7, "Conclusion: Keep Dancing," summarizes my argument, highlights the original contributions of this research to the literature, and points out new directions for future research.

In the "Epilogue: Remembering Manolín," I discuss developments in Cuba after my fieldwork was completed. I trace the career of the emblematic timba singer Manolín, El Médico de la Salsa, since his arrival in the United States, questioning the relevance and viability of timba outside of Cuba.

CHAPTER 2
Timba Brava: Maroon Music in Cuba

Yo traigo la verdad, pa' tí y pa' tu mamá . . .
I bring the truth, for you and your mother too . . .

—JOSÉ LUIS CORTÉS EL TOSCO
(a chorus from his song "Masca la cachimba")

Nowadays all musicians and close observers of Cuban culture acknowledge the boom of Cuban popular dance music that occurred at the opening of the 1990s and maintained itself until the closing of that decade. The sound that was born during that period—the musical practices, instrumentation, treatments of traditional themes, and all-new thematic content based on emergent realities (having, of course, roots in previous epochs)—formed a legitimate and new kind of popular music, first called "Cuban salsa," then "timba." This chapter describes timba and argues that it is an important Cuban phenomenon where several processes and social debates intersect. Specifically, I look at economic policy, identity formation, gender roles, and especially at race struggles. Definitions of the term *timba* itself give clues to its nature both as a musical genre and as a form of social action.

Fernando Ortiz suggests that the word *timbá* is onomatopoeia—like *batá* or *tambó*—replicating the sound of drums (1994, 8). *Timba* was an old word that used to mean a group of gamblers in the Spanish army—deriving from the word *timbal*, because they would use the kettledrum as a card table (Sublette 2004, 272). In the *solares* (tenements or ghettos) of Havana and Matanzas during the nineteenth century, a meeting of men with drums and rum was synonymous with *rumba de solar*, one of the roughest, "of the people" (*del pueblo*) manifestations of rumba; "*¡La timba se ha puesto buena!*" (This joint is jumpin') (García Meralla 1997). Here, we understand *rumba* or timba as a kind of fiesta or social activity that would always include food, drink, song, dance, drums, invited guests from the neighborhood, and so on (Acosta 2004, 40; Sublette 2004, 272). Journalist and scholar of Cuban music Maya Roy tells

1. Timba Brava, 2003.

us, "Timba and timbero are expressions that appear frequently in the context of the rumba, exclamations with which one called out to the drummers, to encourage them" (Roy 2002, 180). Not only does timba imply sound, but also it implies people (especially marginalized people) and collective action.[1]

Guava paste eaten with bread as an inexpensive snack called "pan con timba" is another common usage in Cuba. Timba also means "belly" (vientre) and refers, some say, to the feminine energy of the drum, pregnant with sound and power; thus it is delicious and full of possibilities. Los Papines first recorded the term; "I like to hear a bolero, guaracha, or son montuno if it has timba, bonkó" (Luis Hernández Abreu, interview, 2003). Timba is Arsenio Rodríguez and Benny Moré (García Meralla 1997). There is timba in the swaying stride of Cuban women, in any neighborhood sidewalk, and even in the desire of foreigners to imitate the way Cubans dance (García Meralla 1997). These references to El Benny, Arsenio, and the swaying hips of Cuban women invoke notions of essential Afro-Cuban male and female energy, and issues of race, class, and gender are worked out through timba music-making and dancing.

Timba is also a jam session with percussive piano and horns, mixing jazz, a great deal of son, and, to round it all off, bass guitar that takes on the voice and musical vocabulary of rumba. Many Cuban musicians, including Ángel Bonne, David Calzado, and César Pedroso refer to occasions when they played this way during breaks while studying at the Escuela Nacional de Arte (ENA) or Instituto Superior de Arte (ISA). They agree too that timba is Cuban dance music in its highest degree of development, made contemporary by incorporating popular music (rhythms or songs, instrumentation, ways of playing) from around the world. Timba is the transposition and extension of Cuba's musical roots to a new era, accentuated by different harmonic concepts and different technologies (Roy 2002, 200). Some identify timba with abstract values like "strength" (Bamboleo, interview, 2003), referring on one hand to its sound but also to the way Cubans rely on music as sustenance ("strength") to carry on under difficult circumstances.

One of the best timba bands is Manolito y su 'Trabuco'—which literally means a firearm from the times of the Independence War of 1895 and figuratively refers to anything forceful or strong (Manolito Simonet, interview, 2003). According to Roy, "Originally timba designated the marginalized neighborhoods of large cities" (2002, 180). La Timba is a working-class neighborhood in Havana, evolved from a shantytown on the outskirts of prosperous Vedado (Scarpaci, Segre, and Coyula 2002, 73). The famous *rumbero* Chano Pozo, who played with Dizzy Gillespie and brought Latin jazz to the fore, was born in a *solar* called Pan con Timba (Cluster and Hernández 2006, 146). Timba is a "Cuban attitude toward music and dance" (García Meralla 1997), and a social movement or subculture (Perna 2005). Leymarie calls this music "nueva timba," and identifies it as an expression derived "from the word timba designating a conga" (Leymarie 2002, 253). Whether she means the conga drum itself (*tumbadora*) or the drum rhythm and procession from eastern Cuba, the connection makes sense. The term was recontextualized by Juan Formell as Cuba's answer to *salsa*, which had long been rejected by many on the island as an imperialist product. Timba is the "convergence of politics and pleasure" (Aparicio 1998, 92).

As a musical style or genre, timba helps to mark identity and is closely related to associated cultural features such as recreational activities, use of language, attitudes toward sex, and so on, which similarly contribute to forming and maintaining group identity. Timba is intrinsically related to the social context in which it has developed and in which it takes place. The discernible patterns that distinguish timba from other types of dance music reflect cultural meanings shared (and possibly contested) by all those who participate in a communicative event such as musical performance. These meanings are related in fundamental ways to conceptions of identity—the way people perceive and define themselves, especially in relation to other groups. The corollary to this is that social change is reflected in stylistic change. These alterations will reveal survival strategies as well as the perceptions and values of the social group that is experiencing the change (Pacini-Hernández 1995, 18).

Considering both journalistic and academic writings about timba, one perceives the surprise, frenzy, scandal, rejection, and passion that the timba movement has aroused, and also the acceptance—still contested—that it finally seems to have earned. The discourse on timba places it as a brash music, threatening for various reasons, but at once respected for its virtuosity, daring, and success. Like Caliban (Retamar 2000) timba appropriates language (both spoken and musical) to express its subaltern perspective. It is a musical performance that has created "a resistant space beyond the realm of politics in which rebelliousness of various sorts or identifications with alternate ideologies may be emphasized" (Moore 2006, 8). It is part of an "unruly musical wave that exploded in Havana in the late 1980s" (Sublette 2004, 272). The uneasy relationship of popular music and the state has existed since colonial times and has only assumed new details after the triumph of the revolution. The tension is caused by the fact that popular music is made by individuals and groups (to some extent) independent of the state, "and in some cases in opposition to it" (Sublette 2004, 272).

Virtuoso musicians often come from, and are still rooted and producing in, the marginal barrios of Havana. Few people would dare attack the skill of timba musicians, trained as many of them are in the country's best schools. Nevertheless some lament the use of skills that were developed through study at state-run schools to make music that is perceived as vulgar, shamelessly commercial, or simply too black. (Imagine if the architects of early hip-hop were conservatory trained!) As we explore timba and social action in Cuban dance spaces, it is important to recall José Martí's claim that to be Cuban is more than black, white, or mulato. He insisted that there is no such thing as race; that it was merely a tool used locally to divide the anticolonial effort and globally by men who invented "textbook races" in order to justify expansion and empire (Ferrer 1999, 4). One aim of Martí's work was to persuade white Cubans to drop their fear of blacks (Brock and Castañeda 1998, 128). Cuba's mulato poet Nicolás Guillén extended Martí's ideas about racial unity in Cuba claiming that, "Cuba's soul is mestizo, and it is from the soul, not the skin, that we derive our definite color. Someday it will be called 'Cuban color'" (de la Fuente 2001, 182). We will see how timba is survival music that emanates from Cuba's black communities and is inspired by Martí's and Guillén's ideal of racial equality and fusion. Timba seeks integration, not separation, through sound.

A Long Tradition of Mixed Music

Timba is *música mulata,* as Puerto Rican sociologist Ángel Quintero Rivera would say; a fusion of multiple elements in which it is difficult to distinguish and separate the ingredients, so well integrated are they in the final product. Cuban music specialist Danilo Orozco has coined the term *intergénero,* or "between-genre," to describe timba: "a concrete hybrid that has been nourished by a very dynamic and specific mixture of juxtaposed elements in constant tension, which does not permit untangling the components" (Orozco n.d., 4). Musical "alchemists" (García Meralla 1997) blend many influences: rumba, son, Afro-Cuban ritual music, jazz, songo, Puerto Rican bomba, North

American folk music, reggae, Caribbean and New York salsa, hip-hop, rock, funk, samba and European classical music (Orovio 1998). Cuban pianist Gonzalo Rubalcaba, who is renowned as a jazzman but also participates in important popular dance music projects (very notably with Issac Delgado), says that "of all the music in the world Cuban music is among the most capable of assimilating influences of other cultures and sounds without losing its own authenticity, rather enriching it" (Gonzalo Rubalcaba, interview, 2001).

In general, popular dance music of Cuba has a long tradition of fusion, demonstrated by hybrid forms and mulato styles. *Danzón*, for example, melded derivations of the English country-dance, French *contredanse*, and Spanish *contradanza* with contributions from Afro-Cubans and black Haitian immigrants to create the first truly Cuban music/dance form. In his novel *Cecilia Valdés*, Cirilo Villaverde describes the "moaning" character of danzón as "from the heart of a people enslaved" even without the congas, clave, cowbells, and so on that would enliven later genres (Cluster and Hernández 2006, 55). (*Danzón* is mentioned as the traditional Cuban dance par excellence in Cuba's constitution.) The fusion that makes timba is equally dramatic and diverse of sources.

Figuratively, timba is what happens when various worlds make contact—local and foreign, high and low class, socialist and capitalist, black and white. Timba, like salsa and other music from the Black Atlantic, is a "sociomusical practice claimed by diverse communities for radically diverse purposes" (Aparicio 1998, 67). Specific factors affecting the content and performance of timba, its development and boom, include a long tradition of black popular music in Cuba, excellent musicians trained under the Revolution, economic and social crises during the special period, new approaches to international visitors and trade markets, and revitalized debate on race relations.

The Evolution of Cuban Dance Music before Timba

The earliest forms of uniquely Cuban music were enriched by African and European sources (Carpentier 1946; Alén 1999), which merged on the island to create totally new creole forms through an ongoing process of transculturation (Ortiz 1995; Morejón 1988, 188). For example, nourished by Yoruba, Bantu, Fon/Ewe, Calabar, and Spanish roots, Cuban rumba evolved by the mid-1800s as a popular music/song/dance complex among poor urban blacks (Daniel 1995; Alén 1999, 47–60). Rumba functioned as a site where oral histories were constructed, protests raised, and diversion from life's hardships found. Many Cubans rejected rumba because of its African sound—the musical ensemble consisting of clave, three drums or boxes, a lead singer (el gallo), and a chorus—and the overt sexual references within the dance. Although it was a form created and developed primarily by black Cubans, because rumba took place in marginalized spaces some poor whites participated too.

Haitian colonists and their slaves, who had fled the aftermath of the Haitian Revolution of 1791, stimulated a craze for the French con-tredanse in Cuba. The Cuban version of Spanish contradanza and French contredanse added African percussion instruments—güiro (a ser-rated gourd scraped with a stick) and timbal, plus a slower cadence that gave it a different, decidedly Caribbean feeling. Cuban contradanza re-ceived severe criticism during its early days. This fits musicologist Maya Roy's description of Cuban music as the "creolization" of a Euro-pean musical foundation under the influence of musicians of African origin (2002, 2).[2] After Miguel Faílde—a black man and devotee of Afro-Cuban religion "invented" danzón in 1879, commentaries in Cuban newspapers attacked it also as "diabolical" and "contrary to Christian-ity" because of its association with "prostitution and improper race mixing" (Carpentier 1946, 27). It was not until later in the 1920s and 1930s that mestizaje (race mixing) would be accepted as a root of Cuban culture, though that reality was already long present on the island.

Though it was played before, perhaps as early as the 1800s, son came to Havana from eastern Cuba in the early twentieth century, and by the 1920s it emerged as a genre of international importance (Alén 1999, 27–28). Like earlier forms, it was criticized as too wild and barbaric. The dance step was described as "lascivious" and dangerous! Ethnomusicol-ogists Robin Moore (1997) and Leonardo Acosta (1989) remind us that both danzón and son were initially repudiated for being black and then later appropriated by the dominant white classes that had rejected them. Danzón and son were eventually used to represent Cubanness and to defend the national culture against the influences of U.S. jazz and Europeanized tango, which invaded the island in the 1920s. In their day, when Arcaño y sus Maravillas mixed danzón and son, and Arsenio Ro-dríguez developed the orchestra format called "conjunto" (incorporat-ing the conga drum), both were criticized for their "música negra" and relegated to play in marginal spaces due to the color of their skin. Even still, son remains the strongest reference point for all Cuban dance music that has been produced since. The Cuban love-hate relationship with black music and black people has helped to shape timba, which, like any good son of *son*, has grown and claimed its space despite initial rejection.

The influence of African American jazz started to appear in Cuban music during the 1930s when Latin jazz bands began incorporating instrumentation and arrangement ideas from Count Basie, Duke Ellington, and others (Moore 1997; Roberts 1979). Jazz strongly influenced Cuban musicians—such as the López brothers, Armando Romeu, Pedro "Peruchín" Justiz, Chico O'Farril, Bebo Valdés, and El Niño Rivera—who through their work in the Cuban jazz band format mixed North American jazz with Cuban flavor. These bands played all genres of dance music (*guaracha, lindy hop, son,* etc.), and introduced Cuban percussion to jazz, opening the way for Afro-Cuban or Latin jazz, led by Dámaso Pérez Prado in Mexico and Frank "Machito" Grillo, Mario Bauzá, Chano Pozo (all Cubans), and Dizzy Gillespie (African American) in New York in the 1940s and 1950s. Cuban music and bebop became "cubop . . . a marriage of love" (Leymarie 2002, 2). In the 1940s, riding the wave of the big band sound, *mambo* emerged, also led by Pérez Prado, spawning a craze that swept the United States and Western Europe. Cuban popular dance music since that time has cultivated the jazz root, cubanizing it in the process to develop the musical language of timba. The sassy horn licks of the past became the *mambos* and *champolas* (horn phrases) that make timba so rich and exciting today.

In the 1950s, Enrique Jorrín created *chachachá*, a derivative of *danzón* that was based on the rhythm he heard in dancers' footsteps (López 1997). This style was so popular that it remained current into the 1960s, inspiring a North American version of the dance, as well as cha interpretations by North American artists like Nat "King" Cole. Despite the popularity of Cuban music in the States, its continued development was largely hidden from North American listeners due to the U.S. trade embargo imposed on Cuba in 1962. Revolutionary policy on the island affected the development of music in significant ways as well.

Focusing on ending crime and prostitution, the Revolution curbed much of Havana's nightlife, which had supported the development of dance music (Acosta 1999, 9). As a result of the closure of most clubs and theaters, musical innovation languished. Also many musicians put down their instruments to take on other important work of the Revolution—like cutting sugarcane (Armando Valdés, interview, 2003). During the 1960s several rhythms were introduced but none with the mass appeal or longevity of *son*, *mambo*, or *chachachá*. Each incorporated elements of conga and iyesá, while keeping elements of *son* and mambo (Acosta 2004, 141). The *pachanga* by Eduardo Davidson, *pa' cá* by Juanito Márquez, *pilón* by Pacho Alonso and Enrique Bonne, *dengue* by Pérez Field and Roberto Faz, and *Mozambique* by Pello el Afrokan each made a splash but failed to achieve international, or even extended national, popularity (Acosta 1999). Each was a rhythm with its own dance step. Despite their limited success, they exemplified the tight link between music and dance that has been inherited by the timberos.

In the 1960s a new generation of Cuban singer-songwriters endeavored to create music that was "different from [popular dance music] produced before the Revolution." In their view, Cuban music had been too focused on "love, dark cafes, bars, etc." and had not given enough attention to meaningful lyrics (Sarusky 2004, 10). They wanted to counteract what they perceived as banality and commercialism in Cuban music of the 1950s (Benmayor 1981, 14). They took inspiration from turn-of-the-century *trovadores* (troubadours) like Sindo Garay, who pioneered a style called *canción*, known for beautiful, socially engaged lyrics sung to guitar accompaniment. The new movement came to be called Nueva Canción or Nueva Trova. Its mission was to create new, poetic music of the future, as opposed to what was considered "bar music" of the past (Sarusky 2004, 18).

Singer-songwriters like Pablo Milanés, Silvio Rodríguez, Sara González, and Amaury Pérez recorded prolifically and toured widely throughout Latin America. They collaborated with rock and jazz musicians and composers like Leo Brouwer, Sergio Vitier, and Leonardo Acosta. Their records were the first in Cuba *not* to specify a particular dance rhythm (Sarusky 2004, 53). By the end of the 1960s the pioneers of Nueva Canción founded Grupo de Experimentación Sonora with the specific mission of analyzing and transforming the Cuban musical repertory. They criticized popular music as too "imitative" and static, because untrained musicians made it and transmitted it by ear. Rhythms and melodies were overly dominant, while texts "did not exist." Despite instances of state censorship (Sarusky 2004), the musicians of the Nueva Trova became "cultural ambassadors of the Revolution . . . a voice for new values" (Benmayor 1981, 11, 13).

Nineteen sixty-eight was a turning point. In that year all the nightclubs and parlors of Havana closed for at least one year (as if acting on the critiques by the Nueva Trova movement). Nevertheless several dance orchestras were born that would be important for the new musical language they elaborated, and which would later be taken up and extended by the timberos. Elio Revé y su Charangón was founded in 1968 and gained popularity based on changes imposed by then-member Juan Formell, modernizing *changüí* (a proto-son rhythm from Guantánamo) under the influence of jazz, *filin* (a melancholy U.S. American-styled ballad deriving its name from the English word *feeling*), the son compositions of Benny Moré and Chapottín, and the rock and roll of the Beatles.

In 1969 Juan Formell split with Revé and founded Los Van Van. They introduced a new style called *songo* and were among the first and definitely the most successful in incorporating rock and roll, synthesizers, drum machines, sound effects, and new harmonic concepts in Cuban dance music (González 1999, 51–52), making an early step toward today's timba sound. Los Van Van reinterpreted tradition with rock and roll–styled breaks on the snare drum, jazz electric flute alongside traditional five-hole flute, and a violin section that emphasized rhythm over harmony (González 1999, 51–52). Perhaps their best-known instrumental innovation has been the incorporation of trombones to the charanga format.

Speaking of Los Van Van and its contributions, Orozco mentions a peculiar way of combining violins and flutes, subtle harmonic approaches based on the blues, vocal renditions that evoke something of the American vocal quartets of the 1960s and the ethos of the soul singer, overtones of pop-rock, and a dynamic, varied sense of rhythm and time. According to Cuban music scholar José Loyola Fernández, Van Van's rhythmic-harmonic interweaving of percussion, bass guitar, and piano with freer, more figurative interpretation of *tumbaos* and polyrhythmic percussion was definitely a precursor of today's timba. In the case of Los Van Van and their *songo*, perhaps due to the passage of time, their innovations have been accepted because they constitute "a style that brings the music closer to the contemporary dancers, moving within a modern framework of tones more relevant in the musical context of their sociocultural environment" (Loyola 2000, 10–15). They are emblematic of the evolution of Cuban dance music: they innovate and enrich, always honoring *la clave*, and never abandoning *el son*.

In 1973, Irakere was founded under the leadership of pianist Chucho Valdés and contributed elements that opened new horizons for popular dance music. They incorporated Afro-Cuban religious instruments (batá drums, chequeré, agogó, etc.) until then used only in ceremonies, or on occasion in a few cabaret shows or academic demonstrations. Among the contributions of Irakere to popular dance music (which have been expanded in timba), Cuban musicologist Helio Orovio names the jazz piano of Chucho Valdés, the harmonic-unorthodox guitar of Carlos Emilio, the jazz-reggae guitar of Carlos del Puerto, the conga rumbera of Jorge Alfonso, the trap drum playing of Enrique Plá, and the jazzy attack of saxophones and trumpets so characteristic of the group and members like Arturo Sandoval and Paquito D'Rivera. Irakere changed the horn format to two trumpets and two saxophones, the pattern followed by many timba orchestras. Los Van Van and Irakere developed the format and playing style of dance-band horn sections, borrowing concepts from U.S. funk and soul bands like Parliament and Earth, Wind and Fire.

Los Van Van and Irakere enjoyed great popularity throughout the 1970s and 1980s during the height of the New York salsa movement. Despite the U.S. embargo against Cuba, the stance of old-guard Cuban musicians (Padura 1997; interview, 2003), and the government's position (Perna 2005) against "refashioning or co opting" of vintage Cuban music, there was contact between salseros from New York and Latin America (in Cuba called "salsa from the outside") and Cuban popular musicians on the island. For example, in the late 1970s and early 1980s, there were visits made to Cuba by the Fania All-Stars, Típica 73, Dimensión Latina, and Óscar D'León. Also, Nuyorican bandleader Willie Colón and the Panamanian Rubén Blades—both popular U.S. artists—were played on Cuban radio.

Cuban band leaders, like Juan Formell and Adalberto Álvarez, made format and recording adjustments based on influences from New York salsa (Formell 2002).[3] According to Cuban musician and historian Leonardo Acosta, young musicians accepted the adjustments and additions; they exchanged ideas and experiences with the salseros of the Caribbean and New York. In fact, Formell recognizes that the leveling of the various tracks that make up his recordings originates from the style used by the salseros from New York, who situate the drums almost as prominently as the solo voice, a strategy that provokes the dancer. At the same time, he denies that the trombones of his orchestra have anything to do with Willie Colón (famous for his trombone sound) or any other salsero. Rather, he says he added them to compensate for a deficiency in the middle range that was inherent to the charanga format (Formell 2002).

Adalberto always stayed informed about the latest developments in New York and Caribbean salsa; in his words, it was his "obsession," and he determined to use elements of that style to avoid making music that was too local. He always conceived his musical production to please dancers throughout the Caribbean and the world, and he considered it crucial artistically to compose with the sound of the other salsa in mind. The fact that many salseros were winning popularity and using his compositions also convinced him to enter that market with his own orchestra, appropriating elements from its best exponents (Padura 1997).

Percussionist Yoel Driggs "The Showman," former member of Los Van Van and current musical director of Puro Sabor, told me that he owes a great deal of his own artistic personality and charisma to his experience playing with the great Venezuelan salsero Óscar D'león on his legendary trip to Cuba in 1983 (interview, 2003). This was a "turning point" that reawakened young people's interest in Cuban popular music, now with a fresh new sound (Leymarie 2002, 173). Clearly the timberos with their subaltern voice and unique flavor owe something to the New York and Latin American salsa of the 1970s and 1980s as well.

All of the styles discussed so far were created and practiced most widely and intensely by Cubans of color. They incorporated elements from other styles within the black diaspora.[4] For example, Orquesta Aragón traveled the world and became Cuba's number one band of the mid-twentieth century spreading the chachachá, a rhythm developed primarily in dialogue with black dancers in Cuba. Though Cubans of all colors danced chachachá, it was undeniably a black creation. Afro-Cuban or Latin jazz is heard everywhere and at the Cuban Jazz Festival. Like the styles of the past, timba is undergoing a similar process. It is heavily criticized as "uncouth," "indelicate," and so on (Casanella 1999), yet it is increasingly recognized as a valid genre rather than just a vulgar fad (Perna 2005). In 1999, Chucho Valdés told me "no pasa nada," nothing is happening with timba (personal communication, October 1999). Nevertheless, at that time and even now, timba is heard everywhere in Cuba, and there have been government-commissioned "national anthems" in timba style—for example, "Aquí estamos, los cubanos" (Here we are, the Cubans) on Cuban television. Chucho's Irakere (reincarnated in the 1990s sometimes as a dance band after a long embrace of mostly jazz) has recorded timba numbers, and in 2003 he honored timbero Paulito F.G. by performing with him at Paulito's record-release concert at the Karl Marx Theater in Havana.

Diasporic Connections

Many authors have discussed the existence of certain African Diaspora components that are found across a wide array of music and performance practices (Carpentier 1946; Chernoff 1979; Merriam 1960; Ortiz 1965; Bilby 1985; Rivera 2003; Sloat 2002). It comes as no surprise that these sociomusical concepts are present in timba because it was created by Afro-Cubans in dialogue mostly with other African musics: "la musique moderne" of the Democratic Republic of Congo; jazz, funk, and hip-hop from the United States; Brazilian samba; Jamaican reggae; and so on. Argeliers León, the dean of Cuban musicology, writes, "People appropriate those elements that have some similarity or proximity with what they already have, they search for a kind of link by analogy" (1984). Jazz, hip-hop, reggae, and samba are all subaltern forms (in some moments of their history or in some aspect of their present projection), forms that, like timba, are bold, and dreaded by some. It is partly an untamed, "maroon" identity that links timba with other diaspora music forms.

Like Trinidadian *soca*, for example, timba can be evasively political, using double entendre and coded language to veil social commentary. It is also an important vehicle for masses of people to find ecstasy through dance (Moonsammy 2009). Like *Congolese rumba* or *soukous*, timba draws on a history of musical syncretization and oral traditions in the form of old and new folk wisdom (Stewart 2000). It speaks for "the common man," incorporates influences from religious music, carnival traditions, and folklore, and employs modern instruments (synthesizers, drum machines, etc.) and Western harmony. Like Jamaican dancehall, timba gives free rein to ways of expression considered vulgar and improper since the expressions touch on race, class, gender, and national identity (Cooper 2004; Stolzoff 2000; Hope 2006). Opposition to dominant ideology and determination to "tell it like it is, no matter what" are part of timba and part of the scene—an attitude demonstrated through gesture, dance, and dress, as well as lyrics.

A few concepts set out by ethnomusicologist Peter Manuel (1995) are useful to understanding timba. Collective participation is a characteristic applicable to timba events in which musicians and audience/dancers are mutually dependent, locked in a complementary relationship that makes the performance "happen." If a band's sound is uninspiring then no one dances. If there is no dance, *there is no musical event*, even if the musicians continue to play. As in many

African and Caribbean contexts music, song, and dance form a complex whole.

One of the most important characteristics of timba is call-and-response. In timba's musical structure improvised *inspiraciones* from a lead singer alternate and interact textually with a refrain that is repeated by a chorus. Cuban philologist Liliana Casanella has noted a kind of linguistic dialogue between singers and the public (see below). I argue here that there is a dialogue, a performative group conversation, taking place in the dance spaces under consideration. Collective participation, call-and-response, and total atmosphere combine to establish behaviors, which are then used strategically to create a specific identity. These behaviors are not only performed during the musical event, but beyond in everyday life. In this way, the performances—behaviors, interactions—in the dance spaces actively *produce*, just as much as they reflect, the contours and choreography of social relations in Cuba today.

Timba is part of a process of transculturation in which the presence of Latin American culture in the international market is increasing and has resulted in more references to Latino culture through Spanish melodies, lyrics, choreography and dancers in music videos, and so forth (see songs by African American Puff Daddy, Nuyorican Fat Joe, Haitian American Wycleff Jean, and Jamaican Beanie Man among others). The reggaetón craze, which has swept many parts of the world including the United States and Spanish Caribbean, is part of this tendency too and is criticized by many for being excessively "pop" or commercial (see Rivera, Marshall, and Pacini-Hernández 2009). Like the forms mentioned, timba runs the risk (perhaps inevitable) of losing some of its power through commercialization and its resultant creative stagnation.

Timba: A Way of Making Music

The instrumentation of timba bands and the particular ways of executing specific instruments in timba reveal increased timbric resources and enriched expressive and technical arsenals for arrangers, allowing infinite possibilities for the music in general. It is important to note that there is not a fixed or obligatory musical format that is aligned with or designated for timba. In fact, *changüí* groups or *charangas* (for example, the famous Orquesta Aragón) at times play in timba style, using traditional instrumentation for their respective formats.[5] This suggests the lasting effect timba may have on Cuban popular dance music in general.

Throughout Havana, small groups entertain at bars and restaurants performing traditional *son* that is integrated with clear inflections of timba in their arrangements. For example, at a local bar called Siete Mares (the seven seas), a quintet with bongó, flute, guitar, violin, and a singer played traditional Cuban music for most of the evening, including songs by Benny Moré, Pablo Milanés, Elena Bourke, and others. They would regularly infuse these compositions with timba-style breakdowns, thereby using the same acoustic instrumentation in a different way.

Following Charles Kiel's analysis of the African American blues (1966) and Deborah Pacini-Hernández's discussion of Dominican bachata (1995), I examine timba in terms of four main stylistic elements: structure, timbre and texture, content, and context. In addition, I trace the history and describe the performance of timba dance.

Structure

In timba the traditional organization and interpretation of *son* composition sections, that is, "introduction, exposition and *montuno*," are altered. Challenging conventional configuration, arrangers often displace the introduction and begin with a rap or a short tease of an *estribillo* or chorus, which is reintroduced or stated fully later in the *montuno* of the song. At times, the presence of *estribillos* throughout compositions, right from the start, separated by song verses or spoken sections by soloists, makes the entire piece sound like one extended *montuno*. At times, songs are voiced as full ensemble singing until the montuno begins, at which time a soloist then dialogues with the chorus. Sometimes the role of soloist is passed among the main singers of the orchestra right from the song's opening.

Most often, there are four sections in timba: (1) *la salsa*, which is of moderate tempo and performed by a soloist; (2) *el montuno*, which is a refrain that is introduced in call-and-response pattern as the tempo markedly increases; (3) then *los pedales*, which features a hip-hop/R&B-like backbeat and strong movement in the bass guitar as the tempo recedes and the soloist talks rhythmically, introducing another (more dynamic) refrain. During these first three sections most people dance *casino*. The next section is (4) *el despelote* (the breakdown), where a rapping chorus answers the soloist, and both dancers and musicians go into a frenzy, inspired now by the percussive slapping and plucking of the bass guitar (à la Bootsy Collins of funk bass guitar fame in the 1960s and 1970s in the United States). During this section, people dance *reparto*

(the neighborhood) and *tembleque* (the quake), which are discussed below under timba dance. The band then returns to *el montuno, los pedales*, and so on, at will to add new refrains and change the intensity of
the performance (La Charanga Forever, personal communication, 1999).
The image of a train pulling out from the station (*la salsa*), riding
steadily on a plateau (*el montuno*), pushing harder at a slower pace to
climb a hill, then pausing at its peak (*los pedales*), and rushing down (*el
despelote*) gives a rough idea of how energy is manipulated over the
course of a song. Each of the added chorus refrains can also be called *so-
bremontuno*, as in above and beyond the first. Compositions often end
with a cooling-down section that acts as a coda or ending, returning to
the mellower salsa style used in the opening.

Such structural changes in form have opened the way for free combinations of instruments and uninhibited ways of playing. These take
Cuban *son* and *rumba* as points of departure for experimentation, and
feature patterns from other music styles in the Caribbean, (Black) North
America, Brazil, and so on. Orchestras like those of El Médico de la
Salsa and Paulito F.G. incorporate the electric guitar noticeably, at
times in rock-style solos, while the group Dan Den of Juan Carlos Alfonso distinguished itself by adding a set of bells that originated from
the rural outskirts of Havana. Changes in instrumentation correspond
to jazz and rock sources (e.g., the drums, the keyboard, the electric guitar played rock style à la Carlos Santana), Afro-Cuban folk music (batá
drums, agogó bells, etc.), and borrowings from earlier formats within
Cuban popular music forms (such as the *orquesta típica* and the Cuban
jazz band with emphasis on trombone and saxophone).

Timbre and Texture

Musician Orderquis Revé, brother of the late great orchestra leader and
dancer of the 1950s Elio Revé, says that "without changüí there is no
son, and without son there is no salsa" (*sin changüí no hay son, sin son
no hay salsa*) (Orderquis Revé, interview, 2002). In addition, master percussionist and singer Luis Abreu Hernández of Los Papines says that
without rumba, without *clave* and *tumbadora* (conga drums), timba
could not exist (Luis Abreu Hernández, interview, 2003). Describing
timba in general, music researcher Danilo Orozco emphasizes the pre-
dominance of the *clave* or rhythmic pattern from rumba-guaguancó, at
times substituted by the *clave* of son or other related rhythmic patterns
that appear at various points within the same composition. Generally

there is a tendency to vary and to fragment phrases, lyrics, and choruses, which he illustrates by the use of the bass guitar, which no longer marks the stable tumbao pattern that is closely associated with Cuban *son*, but instead attacks in a disjointed way that is still graceful in its propulsion of the music and the dancers. The classical harmonic and rhythmic tumbao of the *son*[6] has been left behind, replaced now by musical phrases that are more related to *reggae* and *funk* in terms of their harmonic progressions and their rhythmic attack, but which nevertheless remain very Cuban and danceable with steps derived from *son*.

Cuban popular dance music specialists Liliana Casanella and Neris González also refer to the extreme fragmentation of the classical tumbao, the reoccurring counteraccentuations, and the juxtaposition of elements and textures with hard and tense sounds. More specifically, they cite the rhythmic and percussive use of horns and the melodic execution of disjointed phrases, performed often in the sharpest, most strident registers, which gives timba its aggressive sound. With regard to actual percussion instruments, the authors underline the segmented polyrhythm of the different timbric or qualitative sound layers, as well as the break from the timbric-expressive functions of previous eras. Now, groups incorporate trap drums, congas, bongó, and timbales with bass drum (*bombo*)—all improvising freely—along with güiro, maracas, clave, chequeré, and bell. The piano part in this new tumbao is called *guajeo* (Leymarie 2002, 254); it uses a percussive attack that is enriched by jazz harmonies. The simple enumeration of so many elements gives an idea of the infinite combinations and effects that are possible rhythmically.

Variation in the patterns of all the instruments mentioned causes a perceived acceleration, which can be real or only suggested. In addition, we have a formula to make dancers delirious when we consider the rhythmic role of the horn section leading to climactic moments inside compositions, working in the polyphony of incredible counterpoint and polyrhythm called *mambos* or *champolas*. For example, the horn section of NG La Banda is affectionately known as "los metales del terror" or metals of terror. So important is the work of the horn section inside the timba format that this naming of the horn section itself has become common—take, for example, "los metales de la salsa" of Issac Delgado, "Los chamacos" (the boys) of El Médico, "La zorra y el cuervo" (the fox and the raven) of Aramis Galindo, "Los metales de la élite" (the horns of the elite) of Paulito F.G., or "Los metales del cariño" (The horns of tenderness) of Manolito Simonet y su Trabuco—that respond to exhortations such as "¡Dále mambo!" (Give it mambo/flavor/energy) or

"¡Champola pa' tí!" (Take this horn lick). This tendency in timba is closely related to its roots in jazz.

In his composition "El secreto de la liga de mi son con rumba" (The secret of the link of my *son* with rumba) César Pedroso warns, "Don't get confused, the secret I bring is the blend of son with rumba." Certainly! Rumba has been recognized as an important source inside Cuban music, incorporated by Cuban composers of great renown such as Amadeo Roldán, Arsenio Rodríguez, Benny Moré, Pablo Milanés, and others. It has also been utilized for community projects-performances to promote solidarity among Cubans and to stimulate tourism (e.g., Rumba Saturday, El Callejón de Hamel; see Daniel 1995). Still, rumba continues to be a marginal music whose penetration in the Cuban mainstream represents a transculturation with consequences for both the recipient mainstream culture and the marginal donor culture. The mainstream is disturbed as it assimilates and/or rejects the new sounds, the jive talk, and the appearances/self-representations that enter its domain. The marginal donor culture tastes the ethics of the market, feels the bitterness of rejection and repression, and, as a result, sometimes changes its own song.

Timba vocal style, in turn, is more emphatic than the singing of past eras, as a result of the direct influence of rap with whole sections spoken in hip-hop style rather than sung in the way of the traditional Cuban *sonero*. Timba song style also has characteristics from *rumba* and black American R&B, especially in the phrasing and adornments that bend and play in between written notes. Casanella and González cite Mario "Mayito" Rivera, former singer of Los Van Van, as an example par excellence of this first tendency—phrasing and adornment (as was Óscar Valdés with Irakere in the previous generation). Singers Michel Maza (who set the vocal style still used by new members of La Charanga Habanera) and Ricardo "Amaray" Macías from Manolito y su Trabuco are good examples of the second tendency—to use vocal riffs patterned after Luther Vandross, Keith Sweat, and other African American R&B and gospel stars.

Content

There are several general categories into which timba song texts fall. As in other styles of diasporic popular music, timba songs deal with so-called Western style and heterosexual relationships. Issac Delgado—an excellent *salsero* whose music exists at the frontier of timba and international salsa with influences from Puerto Rico, New York, and Colombia—sings in "Mi romántica."

Ella es muy linda por fuera pero más bella por dentro
Donde están los sentimientos más sinceros del amor
Donde se resume la vida en un segundo
Donde se abre una flor, donde ha crecido el mundo . . .
(Chorus)
La niña más linda, la niña más bonita, la niña que yo quería
¡Quién lo diría?

She is very pretty, and even more beautiful within
Where the sincerest feelings of love are
Where life is summed up in a second
Where flowers bloom and the world grows
(Chorus)
The prettiest girl, the most beautiful, the one I always wanted
Who would have thought?

Songs of betrayal address situations in which a woman deserts her man in favor of a rich foreigner, often depicted as Italian. Playfully, Manolín, El Médico de la Salsa plans to torment a lover who has scorned him this way by making constant collect phone calls.

Te di mi amor del alma
Te brindó amor sincero
Pero más pudo el interés
Por todo ese dinero.
Y sé que me dejaste
Y sé que me fallaste
Adiós, qué te vaya bien
Good-bye, my love, *te quiero*

(Chorus)
Te voy a hacer
Una llamada telefónica
A pagar allá

I gave you love from my soul
I gave you sincere love

But greed was stronger because of all that money
I know you left me
I know you failed me
Adios, farewell
Goodbye, my love, I love you

(Chorus)
I'm going to call you
By telephone
Collect!!!

There are boasting songs, which parallel hip-hop, dancehall reggae,[7] and soca[8] in their references to the singer's skill as a musician and a lover. In these two veins respectively El Médico toasts:

Somos lo que hay
Lo que se vende como pan caliente
Lo que prefiere y pide la gente
Lo que se agota en el mercado
Lo que se escucha en todos lados
Somos lo máximo

We are it
What sells like hot bread
What people prefer and request
What sells out in the stores
What's listened to all about
We are the most

and La Charanga Habanera (1996) boasts:

Yo soy cabillero
Tengo mi medida
Fundo la cabilla que tú necesitas

I'm an ironworker
I've got my size
I do the pipe work that you need

As time has gone on, more and more songs have contained references to Afro-Cuban religious practices and have used pieces of ritual chants or made percussive references to ritual rhythms or *toques*. According to Adalberto Álvarez, the early 1990s "coincided with a time when religious spirituality found a space within the institutional life of the country" (de la Hoz 1997). In October 1991 Communist Party membership was opened up to revolutionary Christians and other religious believers (Braun 1999, 80). After this, "Catholics, Protestants, and Jews return[ed] to their churches and synagogues openly, and Santería practitioners no longer [hid] their rituals" (Behar 2007, 274). In 1992 the Cuban Constitution was changed to reflect that the state is now "secular" rather than "atheist" (274). In jest, but accurately, people say that religion was "depenalized" around the same time as the dollar. As a result, "to sing of the orishas became fashionable in popular music, for good and bad," says Álvarez. On one hand, "one of our cultural roots was being recovered, and, on the other, many imitators appeared on the scene with a pseudo folklore that bothers me" (de la Hoz 1997).

El Tosco and his NG La Banda often sang of *los santos* or the *orisha*. In "Santa Palabra" (holy word), they actually incorporated ritual gestures associated with a Lucumí (Yoruba) cleansing ceremony called *ebbó*, in which negative energy is removed and then thrown backward over one's shoulders.

> *Hay muchas personas que esconden los santos*
> *Por el día y por la noche llanto*
> *Para abrir el camino Echu Beleke busca un Eleguá*
> *Pues sin este santo todo va pa' tras . . .*
> (Chorus)
> *Despójate, quítate lo malo*
> *Échalo pa' tras, límpiate mi hermano*

> Many people hide the saints
> Crying day and night
> In order to open the road, Echu Beleke, find an Eleguá
> Without that saint nothing goes right
> (Chorus)
> Strip away, get rid of the bad
> Throw it backward, clean yourself, my brother

César Pedroso, who is a *babalawo* (diviner and ritual specialist) in addition to being a composer and pianist, has used batá drums in timba compositions. Another group, La Charanga Habanera, makes a clear reference to *los santos* when the *timbal* performs a rhythmic sequence in the song "El Bony" that is traditionally played on batá drums for Ochun in ritual settings. The very popular singer and timbera Haila Monpié was initiated and wore white, as is custom, during stage performances, and regularly sings to the orishas on her recordings. (She was a former member of the popular group Bamboleo, founded by pianist Lázaro Valdés in 1995 and known for its complex jazz-influenced arrangements as well as the shocking crew cut hairstyle of its two excellent female vocalists, Haila Monpié and Vania Borges.) Many say that when times get tough, religion becomes more important, and perhaps this is a factor in the development of timba song texts.

Timba has evolved during a time of intense social change as one way in which Cubans have responded to socioeconomic stress—musically. Timba is festive and irreverent. As stated earlier, it developed at the start of the 1990s, coinciding with the Soviet bloc collapse and the so-called special period in Cuba when rationing and resource management increased. The image it portrays is rough and sometimes contrary to authority. For this reason it has been compared to hip-hop, particularly *gangsta rap* (Acosta 1999). Compare the following song lyrics, which were performed by Chispa y sus Cómplices, at La Casa de la Música in April 2003. They talk caustically and directly about the continuing slippage of the Cuban peso in relation to the U.S. dollar.

> *¡A veinticinco!*
> *¡A veintiséis!*
> *¿Cómo se ha puesto el fula?*
> *¡Duro pero duro de matar!*

> At twenty-five!
> Then at twenty-six [pesos to one dollar]!
> What's happened to the greenback?
> It's playing hard to get!

Like rappers, timberos defend their music (lyrics and image) as a reflection of reality, what takes place daily in the street (Acosta 1999). After years of playing traditional Cuban music for tourists at foreign resorts, La Charanga Habanera had been relaunched in 1992 under the direction of David Calzado, with a raucous new style that helped to define the timba movement. By 1997, La Charanga was infamous and even banned by the state for its "vulgar" lyrics and risqué stage show. In a song entitled "No estamos locos" (We're not crazy), they sing, "Pero, ¿qué loco de qué? si lo que canto es lo que es" (Why am I crazy, if what I sing is what is?).

Controversial texts are common in timba. González and Casanella (2001) assert that timba expresses definite sociological messages through both its lyrics and its sound. In terms of lyrics and song structure, the estribillo, by its repetitive and catchy nature, is a favored vehicle that employs double entendre with the function of social criticism to salute los barrios, personages, and tourist places of Havana or to share an anecdote or *dicharacho* (slang term) from everyday life. In an interview with Emir García Meralla for the magazine *Cuban Salsa*, singer Issac Delgado says that "an estribillo makes or breaks a tune, there is no in between," and El Médico adds that "estribillos speak and summarize popular wisdom . . . one is obliged to add a touch of *guapería*, of street talk, so that you can feel the authenticity of *Afro-Cubanness*" (emphasis added; see chapter 3 on Afro Cuba).

This last comment comes from the entertainer known as the "King of the estribillos." El Médico is the one responsible for commandeering day-to-day speech of the people and placing it into many timba refrains: for example, take "Hay que estar arriba de la bola" (You've got to be on the ball), "Prepárate pa' lo que viene" (Get ready for what's next), "Pelo suelto y carretera" (Hair down, open road), "Te maté con el detalle" (I killed you with the detail, outwitted you), among many more (Casanella 1998). All of these phrases have an undeniable Afro-Cuban swing, which marks the origin and one primary audience of the style. According to Paulito F.G., "the estribillo is the synthesis of the message that one wants to express . . . [and] the secret lies in the treatment of the estribillo inside the literary body of the song" (Tabares 1997, 26). For some, like Juan Carlos Alfonso, director of Dan Den, too much emphasis on the chorus is also a danger: "People are abusing the chorus a great deal, the majority of the lyrics do not say anything" (Armenteros 1997).

Casanella, a philologist, discusses the linguistic exchanges between musicians and the public, in which phrases from colloquial slang are taken by musicians and used to popularize compositions (because this is the language of many of their fans), and vice versa. In the latter case, musicians invent a phrase or take it from a small circle of use (which makes it unknown to most), popularize it and spread it, inserting it into popular speech momentarily or even permanently. For example, take "Tunturuntun" by Adalberto Álvarez, which during 1999 and 2000 was on everyone's lips and meant "Get outta here," or "No es fácil" (It ain't easy), which was coined in the 1980s by Juan Formell and to this day is commonly used.

On many occasions, song texts are also related to timba choreography. The steps and accompanying gestures match the lyrics, for example, in "Masca la cachimba" (Chew the pipe) of NG La Banda, "El baile del toca toca" (Do the touch dance) by Adalberto Álvarez, or "Te pone la cabeza mala" (It drives you crazy) of Los Van Van. "Arriba de la bola" (On the ball) by El Médico had its own dance and coded meaning. Penned during the special period, many say that "to be on the ball" meant that one had to hustle or survive by any means necessary. About the dance that accompanied the song, Cuban dance historian Balbuena writes, "It is characterized by the execution of very sensual, sometimes exotic movements. It is done with arms in the air, bent, hands open, pretending to manipulate a ball or something round [perhaps a globe]. At the same time the hips, waist, and torso are rotated" (2003, 89). Like the texts themselves, the choreographies are submitted to the creative reinterpretation of the public, and thus la cachimba (the pipe) or la bola (the ball) semiotically and choreographically take on meanings beyond the intention of their authors. A song called "De La Habana" (About Havana) by Paulito F.G. (discussed later) in which he talks about so-called especulación seems a clear example.

In a kind of intertextuality, timba compositions make reference to works from diverse musical traditions, both Cuban and foreign. This practice serves to dynamize the improvisations of the soloists and (when the reference is only musical) specific passages of songs, recontextualizing borrowed licks that momentarily evoke the experience and meanings of other musical works. "¿Qué pasa con ella?" (What's wrong with her?), on the famous 1997 album Te Pone La Cabeza Mala by Juan Formell y Los Van Van, is a good example. When the montuno begins, after the opening argument of the song, most of the improvisations by the lead singer are bits and pieces from other Los Van Van hits within its then thirty-year career. In this case, the fragments are used to invoke the humor or quality of a particular song and underline the group's staying power over such a long time. "When the singer improvises on the main theme of a song, he or she creates new utterances and also rearticulates and culls phrases from other songs of various traditions. The singer opens up a sonorous space of freedom, improvisation, and innovation, clinging simultaneously to tradition and reaffirming collective memory" (Aparicio 1998, 84). Overall, timba shares its approach to content with international salsa and many other popular music styles of the African Diaspora.

Context

Timba's association with Afro-Cuban culture and with shifts in the Cuban economy as well as Cuban social life plays an important role in perceptions of it as rebellious music. The genre was closely linked to the promotion of tourism in Cuba and was aided by legislation that sought to engage Cuba, at least partly, in the world capitalist economy. For example, take Paulito F.G.'s song "De La Habana" with its famous refrain *¿Dónde están los especuladores?* (Where are the speculators?) from 1997 (perhaps the height of the timba boom); it was irresistible dance music with a striking message. In contemporary slang, *especulador* (literally speculator) means a "show off" eager to accumulate, enjoy, and flaunt wealth, a polemical identity in a socialist nation. The word echoes and puns on the older use of speculator referring to those who, at the start of the Revolution, were too slow in embracing necessary sacrifices (surrendering businesses, properties, etc.). Whereas leaders exhort musicians to "think about their society and its values and to write pieces that reflect such [socialist] values," works that depart from this mission or seem to question it become problematic (Moore 2006, 24). In the words of Latin American literary scholar and cultural critic José Quiroga, "This is where the vanguard of expression collides with the vanguard that wants to preserve tradition" (2005, 147).

> The liberating force is music, but the beat of the music is never allowed to stray from the beat of the state. Music and the state seem to dance around each other, and with each other: music involves musicians and dancers, and these demand venues, and the venues produce a collective expression that may or may not fall into line with what government policies seek to promote. (2005, 147)

It seems that some, especially the ones that criticize timba, imagine that timba has nothing to do with authentic Cuban music, that of yesteryear, or other contemporary forms of good (or better) taste. We have seen that what is considered proper music is a highly contested and shifting terrain. Acosta calls timba "the most important phenomenon of the 1990s and the first [Cuban] music of international popularity and importance since the 1950s" (Acosta 1998). He corroborates what other writers say, noting the fierce passages from horn sections, elaborate arrangements, rhythmic patterns from rumba and Santería, hip-hop style vocals in a context of call-and-response, disorienting tempo changes, the spontaneous nature of timba music and dance, the use of street language with a festive and irreverent character, lyrics considered vulgar, violent, sexist, and "ghetto." But even more interesting, he asserts that timba is heir to a long musicosocial tradition in which Afro-Cuban forms debut only to face very strong opposition, which is nourished by racial prejudice and the desire that Cuba (and therefore the music that represents Cuba) not be considered black.

Timba Dance

For some, timba's customary meter and tempo changes (both increasing and decreasing) make timba difficult to dance. Aggressive sound, as performed by top bands like La Charanga Habanera, Manolito y su Trabuco, and others, is characterized musically by driving staccato piano patterns, virtuoso cascades of notes and percussive blasts from the horn sections, funked-out bass lines, and rapped lyrics that affect dance movement (Acosta 1999, 12). Orozco says that timba relies on tension and that it is hard or aggressive at times; he describes the dance, timba's corporal expression, as "disconnected" or "disjointed." For Orozco, these movements impede couple dancing in closed partner dance position and favor open-pair or group dancing. In the process Cuban *rueda de casino* (casino wheel) dance has been lost. He concludes that timba represents "a transgression and subversion of musical, dance, and sociocommunicative values."

According to Casanella and González, timba dance is a constellation of abrupt movements, dislocated and aggressive, with strong sexual innuendo in which the traditional custom of the couple dance is practically lost (agreeing with Orozco). However, others contend that timba rescued the "casino wheel" dance after a long period of decline, because timba inspired new interest in contemporary Cuban popular music (Balbuena 2003; Nieves Armas Rigal, interview, 2003). Timba enticed people back onto the dance floor.

In my personal and fieldwork experience, a few styles of dance are used with timba music. Some performers dance traditional Cuban *son*, emphasizing the "and" count of beats two and four with their shoulders and feet. Most folks dance *casino*. Cuban dance historian Bárbara Balbuena has done an excellent social history of *casino* dance, which she calls the most recent development in the progression of Cuban *bailes de salón* (ballroom dances), starting with *danzón*. She notes that *casino* was part of Cuba's folkloric dance curriculum where she studied during the 1970s. She traces the basic step that developed from the characteristic formations and open partner positions of various "country dances" from Spain, England, and France; then she incorporates the continuous spinning of dancers embraced in closed partner position from the waltz, which would become the main pattern for Cuban (and Latin) popular dance thereafter (2003, 29). This *paso básico* entails alternating the feet in four musical beats—advancing or retreating in space, or dancing in place. In the first three beats/counts, the foot is fully on the ground, and on the fourth, it only taps the floor, permitting the pattern to alternate on each foot and begin again. Cuban *son* gave *casino* a special emphasis on rhythm, dancing just so (*con sabor*), *with and also purposefully against* the *clave* of the music. *Son, chachachá,* and finally timba would be danced this way also.

According to Balbuena, *casino* developed into its current form over three epochs. During the first epoch of the 1950s, influences such as stellar musical production, vibrant and plentiful dance spaces, and foreign influences—especially rock-and-roll (black) dance—established *casino* as a major form of expression and entertainment among Cubans. She notes that the taste for acrobatic elements and turns, and the common back-and-forth movement "Pa' tí, pa' mí" (for you and for me), are derived from U.S. rock-and-roll dance (2003, 40). Television, introduced in 1950 to Cuba, also popularized the dance.

In the second epoch, from 1960 through 1980, casino became even more wildly popular. It was promoted by state organizations like the Consejo Nacional de Cultura (under whose auspices Conjunto Danza Moderna researched, developed, and instituted the form in dance curricula of ISA and all technique training of national dance companies), and it grew through innovation by individuals and groups—among them cabildo-descended *comparsas* like Los Guaracheros de Regla (Balbuena 2003, 61).[9] New innovations like "Díle que no" (Tell her no) were added and have become part of standard *casino* dance vocabulary. In the third stage, from 1981 to the present, inspired by the resurgence of Cuban music, both on the island and abroad, *casino* gained new popularity after waning in the 1970s. The energy of the timba musical movement and the fiery compositions of NG La Banda, El Médico, Paulito F.G., and others translated into dance.

In the current era, *casino* has maintained its basic form while adding new elements. Male dancers continue to lead the dance (except when women dance together, one of them leading the other), deciding on the turns and figures executed, while women show their skill by allowing themselves to be led without losing the beat or getting out of step (Balbuena 2003, 72). But whereas before, the majority of the time people danced in closed partner position and let go only to *guarachar* (improvize, groove) briefly and return immediately (72), dancing nowadays is much more open. It can be danced in closed partner position, in separated partnered couples, in a circle, or in rows. Rafael (an informant we will meet again) had this to say.

> I'm at my best when I dance casino! It's my favorite and I've created my own style. I like to add steps from different kinds of dance into casino—mambo, chachachá, rumba, guanguancó, folklore, hip-hop. It's my way of expressing myself. It's a question of spirit. (interview, 2003)

The other dances that can be added to *casino* include the *reparto* (the neighborhood), a kind of vibrating "robot" dance, and the *tembleque* or *pingüe*, a hip-rolling dance similar to the *whinin* performed by Jamaican "dancehall queens" or Congolese "dancing girls." The complex of dances, gestures, and physical attitudes surrounding timba reaffirm the genre's quality of unpredictability; it revitalizes one of the roots of Cuban popular dance (*la rueda*/the wheel dance) and at the same time approaches dance styles from Africa and its diaspora (such as reggae and soukous) because they emphasize community dance (in groups and in couples) and deemphasize or eliminate closed partner position dancing. According to Rafael:

> *Repartero* is the name for someone who dances to salsa music all by themself without a partner. [dancing now] You have to pop and drop and move different because you're dancing alone. It's a way of heating yourself up.

The dances that accompany timba music seem to be combinations of the steps and gestures that made up the dances for several rhythms of the past—pachanga, bembón, collude, pilón, and so on. History, fashion, and popular dance repeat themselves. According to Nieves Armas Rigal, coauthor of *Bailes populares tradicionales cubanas*, the dances called the *despelote* and the *tembleque* (also a coconut-flavored pudding) performed today within timba are no less than the derived product of the above-mentioned dances, that besides summarizing and extending the Cuban popular dance tradition through movement and gesture also emphasize the African roots that nourished it (Nieves Armas Rigal, interview, 2003). This jibes with anthropologist and dancer Pearl Primus's assertion that "the spirit . . . responsible for the dynamic [African] dances of yesterday is merely underground . . . sometimes it will spring forth in a seemingly new form" (De Frantz 2002, 121). About this, César "Pupy" Pedroso says, "Our idiosyncrasy as Cubans is very African. We are descendants of the Africans [and] all these dances that have come and gone, what we call timba today, the despelote—all of it is nothing more than African dance" (César "Pupy" Pedroso, interview, 2003).[10] Hip-hop *crumpin'* (featured in the documentary film *Rize* by David LaChapelle) and the *dutty whine* craze in dancehall reggae exemplify a similar spirit of eroticism, aggression, and "African revival" in different genres of popular music/dance from the Black Atlantic.

In 2000 during carnival festivities in Matanzas, a city known as an important center of Afro-Cuban culture, I observed a salsa/timba band perform an *oro cantado* to the principal Yoruba orishas (mixing Yoruba and Spanish, this means "tradition sung," an ordered series of songs and chants in acknowledgment and praise of the various Yoruba deities still venerated in Cuba). During this performance, the soloist asked that children or initiates of each orisha join him on stage to dance the steps traditionally associated with them, performed now however to the timba beat. The dancers always began with traditional, Afro-Cuban religious movements, and as the music intensified their style changed, evolving quickly into timba, with its own strong African energy. This illustrates well the sacred-profane, ancient-modern continuum spanned by Cuban popular music, this time incarnated as timba.

Like other forms of popular dance music, the movements represent "the fundamental connection between the pleasures of the sound and their social realization in the libidinal movement of bodies, styles, and sensual forms" (Chambers 1986, 135). The dance, then, is "a social encounter, which can be [in] a dancehall, a club, or a party, where bodies are permitted to respond to physical rhythms that elsewhere would not be tolerated; the moment when romanticism brushes against reality, and a transitory step out of the everyday can be enjoyed" (Chambers 1986, 135). Timba dance implies "a going out of one's self, the creation of alternative space, a state of mind that may function as therapeutic or political liberation" (Aparicio 1998, 103).

Beyond mimicking the lyrics as described earlier, dance also responds to broader political events and their local consequences. This is readily seen in rueda steps that signal Cuba's sudden isolation during the special period with motion and distance between partners (Leymarie 2002, 254). The maroon is present in dance too, as timba dance draws upon "the rumba, drumming, and the merengue [that] were prohibited in the colonial [and postcolonial] societies of the Caribbean" including Cuba (Aparicio 1998, 103).

Maroon Musicians: "The Wild Deer Is No House Pet"

Two periods or attitudes can be perceived in the timba production of the 1990s: one spontaneous, visceral, impassioned, of music in frank dialogue with the Cuban experience, the other in which the music is commodified for the international record market. Copying the best of the timba produced in the first period led to the homogenization of the music, a dizzying number of new bands (mostly fragments broken off from established projects), and audience burnout. Some artists abandoned the timba sound for the smoother, more reserved sound associated with the international salsa of New York and Latin America. Of these two moments, the first best exemplifies the maroon spirit due to its sincerity and power. Most anthemic timba songs date from this golden era that lasted between approximately 1993 (a year marked by the opening of El Palacio de la Salsa and the legalization of the U.S. dollar) and 2001 (when El Médico defected to Miami).

NG La Banda was born in 1988 for the purpose of breaking obsolete molds and breaking new ground in the field of popular dance music. Through the creativity of its director, José Luis Cortés, and the talented daredevil musicians that accompanied him, the group unified the classical and the popular, traditional and contemporary, at the service of the dancer. NG is known for the virtuosity of its arrangements and the confidence with which they move (very often in one piece) between musical reference points, citing son, funk, and Caribbean musics, including soca, merengue, and reggae, and exhibiting a clear command of the language of jazz. According to Casanella and González, within timba and within José Luis Cortés "flow[s] the deepest inheritance of Cuban son, the footprint of funk, Caribbean music, flamenco and rumba, specific reference to hip-hop/rap and the clearest jazz influence, as well as a solid formation and systematic understanding of the codes of classical music." They conclude that the work of the orchestra is a "real fusion of songo, rumba, afro and jam session in [the] function of dance."

During the early 1990s the orchestra enjoyed tremendous popularity, daring to call itself "la banda que manda" (the band that rules), and with good reason. Many of NG's successes of that period marked true revolutions in how Cuban dance bands would make music. For example, their hits "La Bruja" (The Witch) and "La Expresividad" (Expresiveness) by Cortés show the complexity of composition and arrangement (especially in the first piece), the hard sound that would earn for their music (and that of the timba movement they initiated) the denomination of "heavy salsa" or the "heavy metal de la salsa." From the start, strong use of the colloquial extremes of Cuban slang earned them harsh criticism from the academic world and various defenders of "good taste," among them religious zealots. The very personality of director Cortés is offensive to many, although his talent and mastery as an artist cannot be denied. People say that he is a "pesao," a clown, a monkey, a thug: "I can't stand him . . . but he is good." A great deal of what is said of NG, its music, and the personality of its director echoes the criticism that has faced popular dance music and all types of expression that have been generated clearly from "el pueblo," in Cuba and many other countries as well.

In the past and in another artistic genre, Cuban poet Nicolás Guillén was criticized for his work *Motivos de son* based on black rhythms. Intellectuals like Ramon Vasconcelos asked why he spent his vast creativity on such a thing, and to them Guillén attributed a tendency to think with "imported heads," despising their own culture and seeking to be European (Guillén 2002, 16–18). According to writer and literary critic Carolyn Cooper, the same thing happens today in Jamaica where dancehall reggae is criticized for its frequent, lewd sexual references, descriptions of violence, promotion of deplorable values, and use of the lingua franca of the country, patois—for some, backward and embarrassing. Not to mention the case of hip-hop which many accuse of being little more than noise.

For this reason also, in her book *Black Noise*, Tricia Rose affirms that the hip-hop genre was born from the margins of U.S. American society, the poor black and Latin districts of New York. It utilized forms of expression through sound and wordplay that shocked many because they did not understand and did not want to understand (Rose 1998). It is well documented that what is happening at present with timba has happened in Cuba with previous manifestations of popular dance music, specifically *danzón, guaracha,* and *son* (see Acosta 1998, Carpentier 1946, González and Casanella 2001, Feijoó 1986, León 1985, Moore 1997). Similar perceptions of El Tosco and timba as untamed and unwelcome should be no surprise, and connections between timba and other musical forms from the African Diaspora make sense as well.

In an article entitled "José Luis Cortés: Between el Barrio and Beethoven" by Jaime Sarusky (1999), the topic of people's perceptions of this timba musician comes up.

> JS: Would you say that it is NG or your own personality that has been criticized?

> JLC: Musically it would be difficult to criticize NG. Like so many things, it has a great deal to do with hidden racism, with our different economic situation, with envy harbored by many right now.

Subsequently, in answer to another question, Cortés explains how some see him "as a flashy, eccentric, self absorbed person" because NG never had musical competition and was very successful artistically and economically. "[People would always say] 'These guys come out of nowhere, succeed in the street and in the theater, do jazz, do rock, do classical music, go to the best places in Europe, the United States, and then this black guy shows up with a tank top jersey on' and they wanted to see me with a briefcase and suit, but that is not my image. I am a black man from the neighborhood, *el barrio.* I was born in El Condado and this is still very deeply rooted within me."

Here he asserts the validity of his own will; the fact that he should not necessarily follow the dictates of a society that is dominated by folks who are unlike him in many ways.

> JS: Let's return to your image, since just as you wear a tank top jersey you also know how to wear a suit.

> JLC: I have a few.

> JS: But it is not only having them but knowing how to use them.

> JLC: I am responding metaphorically to your question.

JS: Well then, as a musician, as an artist that must project himself to the public, do you project that image to a certain sector of the public with which you especially want to communicate?

JLC: I think that I would enjoy playing with the symphony orchestra dressed in jeans and a T-shirt with my cap turned to the back, and I'd like to perform in the neighborhood in a suit and tie, because it is what you respect more.

The first shall be last and the last first. In this interview we note a confidence/defiance based on Cortés's tremendous capacity as an artist and his decision to be himself despite the expectations and desires of others, a characteristic that links him to the maroon, who is also respected and hated. Cortés shows his refusal to be dominated or trapped, in this case by the questions of his interviewer, and his capacity to confound with his intelligence and, metaphorically, to escape. All familiar with him know that he dresses with great charisma and a unique flavor—whether or not you believe his red suits, wide-brim hats, and alligator skin boots are really elegant. It is fascinating that he would dress casually for the people of high society (for him aliens) and formally for the people of the neighborhood, his "pueblo yoruba" (Yoruba people) as he often calls them. He enjoys breaking rules and "crashing" closed social spaces, bringing with him styles and behaviors that are alien to specific contexts. We know that his music is multidimensional and aims to reach diverse audiences with different tastes; nevertheless he establishes a special focus for his creativity, and it is el barrio, the marginal world, to which he orients himself and pays highest respect. He exalts "the school of the street," placing it on par with the academy, recognizing the value of popular knowledge and creativity (Roy 2002, 180).

Seeking antecedents of timba and its image, and indicating contradictory perceptions, it is interesting to consider that the personal and artistic projections of José Luis Cortés are similar in various ways to those of Cuban *sonero* Benny Moré—who although he has no exact comparison is an important marker in the history of Cuban (and Caribbean) music and society for the boundaries of race and class that he crossed. Both artists, under discriminatory and adverse conditions (although different), were determined to show their ability, to shine their inner light out into the world and, once their greatness was recognized (though not without criticism), show an irreverent attitude in their self-presentation—speech, dress, gestures, and so forth. What is irreverence but self-affirmation against the grain of accepted societal rules? Those who have fought a great deal to succeed, at times offending with the intrusion of their presence (like Benny creating a jazz band of blacks and mulatos that he called his "tribe," when normally these bands were composed of white musicians), when their time comes to shine they express the pain and frustration they have experienced as eccentricity (for example, take African American jazz guru Miles Davis).

"After reaching the height of popularity, Benny wanted to continue living as he had before becoming a legend. That was the origin of all the clashes with those who tried to change him. It is nearly impossible to impose unnatural rules on a man accustomed to living free, and so Miguel Matamoros said of Benny '*Muchachos*, leave Benny alone, the deer is no house pet'" (Faget 1999). This episode recalls Cortés's affirmations that he was just "a black man from the neighborhood" and that fame would not change him. Although the two musicians are considered *escapao* or *fugao* (colloquial words that express great skill in a specific activity, in this case music, and at the same time evoke the maroon, literally meaning "escaped" or "fled"), they do not enjoy equal popular acceptance, perhaps for several reasons.

Undoubtedly Benny Moré is one of the most important musicians of Latin America and one of the most representative figures of Cuban culture. In the words of Leonardo Acosta, he was a "figure of synthesis"[11] of Cuban music, the creator of an opus that is timeless. Keeping in mind this fact, and also that Cortés has marked Cuban music history, it is the element of time that helps Benny to be more easily digested. The truth is that both have been considered "niggers that don't know their place" (Faget 1999, 30). The historical (i.e., absent) maroon is preferred over the present-day rebel for the danger that the latter represents. Again, Carolyn Cooper (in her book *Sound Clash* about dancehall reggae in Jamaica) argues that the work of new artists who critique life on the island is often despised or ignored, while Bob Marley is held up as the only true and timeless voice of reggae music, partly in order to silence the new artists.

An anecdote I heard told about José Luis Cortés recounts an instance of his "provocative nose thumbing" at polite society and the powers that be (Roy 2002, 199). In a television program interview, he was asked just why he represents Cuban music in such a vulgar, offensive fashion; and instead of responding he changed the subject, offering to play a piece of classical music for flute supposedly known by all "cultured" people. The host assured him that she was familiar with the work. Cortés proceeded to play a masterpiece of colors and arpeggios and afterward asked if the famous piece was well performed. The interviewer said yes, and at that, Cortés declared that what he had just played was no famous composition at all, but rather his own virtuoso improvisation, which embarrassed the host and surely many who shared her perspective. The maroon escaped; but not before landing a painful blow. ¡Qué peligro! What danger! As in the words of Cuban scholar Antonio Benítez-Rojo about the marginalized Caribbean identity in general, Cortés is "a consummate performer with recourse to the most daring improvisations to keep from being trapped" (1996, 24).

Timba was born as a maroon music in the face of challenges posed by a radically changing Cuban society in crisis throughout the decade of the 1990s. It has been necessary for certain Cubans—blacks and mulatos especially—to reaffirm their identity, presence, and importance in their own terms inside the culture and social structure of Cuba. In terms of maroon aesthetics, timba employs the strategies of "raiding" (borrowing elements from diverse musical sources) and "improvisation" (creating new musical language and styles for emergent social circumstances, according to old performance principles). Like maroons of the colonial period, *timberos* are in relationship with national/colonial governments and/or international markets, negotiating power and opportunity from a marginalized position.

The penetration of marginal Afro-Cuban culture into mainstream Cuban culture in the form of aggressive sounds, marginal themes, vulgar coded lyrics, and eccentric or "ghetto" self-representations is but an affirmation of identity that intends not to destroy Cuban society but rather to find a just position within it, as has always been the case in the fight of blacks and mulatos in Cuba (Fernández 1994). So it is that timba and the reaction of Cubans toward it (and similar movements) are quite significant, complex and impassioned. Timba will have many repercussions, not only musically, but also within the history of Cuba and its Revolution.

How can we pin down the relationship between the music and the constellation of important extramusical social phenomena that influence it? African heritage impregnates all of Cuban culture and is one of the matrices that sustain popular music—knowledge that has been maintained, transmitted, and transformed across generations since the period of slavery (Roy 2002, 11). The next chapter describes the social environment that gave birth to timba; it examines the performance of individuals and communities who construct identity to the timba beat. It focuses sharply on the black experience in Cuba as a backdrop for further discussion of timba's development. By exploring the notion of Afro Cuba we better understand timba and its meaning as maroon music in the context of Cuban culture and dance music.

CHAPTER 3
Afro Cuba

> The African contribution to Cuban culture, whose genesis was in the sugar mill, possessed a strong dose of rebellion against the oppressive atmosphere. All culture that the Afro-Cuban projects is defensive [self-defense].
>
> —MIGUEL BARNET (1981, 249)

This chapter considers the notion of "Afro Cuba" and the cultural processes that created and continue to shape it. By exploring various perspectives within the relevant literature, and through the personal experiences of Afro-Cuban people, I show how characteristics such as a West African cosmovision, extreme creativity (especially in the areas of music and dance), low social status, and patriotism developed among Afro-Cubans according to their historical experience in Cuba. In part one, I survey sites that are important in the formation of Afro-Cuban culture throughout Cuban history. I make the case that in contemporary Cuba the public dance has taken on many of the functions of cabildos, selected political organizations, Afro-Cuban societies and clubs, and periodicals. Dance spaces are extensions of old organizational traditions and avenues for the continued development of Afro-Cuban culture and discourse. Timba, as discussed in chapter 2, voices the concerns of Afro-Cubans in the immediate context of the 1990s, and it echoes the aspirations of Afro-Cubans throughout Cuban history. Just as these organizations and publications were important Afro-Cuban spaces, so are the public dances where timba is played—singing and dancing identity from the particular social position of Afro-Cubans.

Part two discusses the relationship of blacks to the Revolution under Fidel Castro. Information from interviews conducted with white and black Cubans is framed in terms of Mark Sawyer's "inclusionary discrimination" and "race cycles theory" to give a picture of the social circumstances under which timba developed as an Afro-Cuban cultural expression. Part three examines the text of a song by Mario "Mayito" Rivera that speaks to the past, present, and future of Afro Cuba.

47

2. Con Martí/With Martí, 2003.

Africans came to Cuba starting perhaps as early as Columbus's first journey and were an important cultural factor on the island by the seventeenth century, even before the massive slave importations that would make Cuba *the* world superpower of sugar for a long time (Barnet 1981, 183). For this reason, the plight of black Cuba does not concern Afro-Cubans alone. Cuba and Afro Cuba have been part of each other from the start. Mandingo, Mina, Ashanti, Madagascar, and many other ethnic groups arrived in Cuba; however, Yoruba, Fon/Arará, Congo, and Carabalí/Abakuá cultures[1] remain most clearly discernible due to sheer numbers, time of arrival, and particular characteristics of the varied groups. For example, related Yoruba peoples arrived in large numbers from the 1820s to the end of slavery in 1886 and brought with them a religious system that was compatible in many ways (with its saintlike orishas) with the slave master's Catholicism. The Yoruba (and other African) traditions in the island have served as an important element of cohesion, strength, identification, and pride, and have also become a theoretical and philosophical base for the colored Cuban population in their resistance against slavery and their later struggle against racism (Martínez 2007, 42). From diverse origins, the various elements of Cuba's black population evolved together toward a cohesive Afro-Cuban tradition that permeated not only the artistic and intellectual spheres but also the social and religious spheres of Cuban life (Moore 1988, 102). Africans came together first on the slave ships, and successively in the barracoons, *bateyes*, and *cabildos* of plantation society, and later they and their descendants shared the *solares* of Cuba (Barnet 1981, 243).

In each of these contexts distinct African ethnicities and identities mixed with poor Hispanic and even Asian elements to create *lo afrocubano*.[2] According to Cuban writer/poet Pedro Sarduy, the term *Afro-Cuban* is used in a way similar to the term *black* in the U.S. context. In Spanish it is inclusive of both *negro* (black) and *mulato* (mulatto or brown), and it contrasts with *Euro-* or *Hispano-Cuban*. *Afro-Cuban* is an *academic* term, first used in 1847 by Antonio de Veitia, later popularized in the writings of Cuban ethnologist Fernando Ortiz. It refers to dark blacks and a whole range of color mixture between *negro* and *blanco* (white). Some refuse to use the term *Afro-Cuban* "because in actuality the entire Cuban population and Cuban culture are indeed Afro-Hispanic" (Martínez 2007, 11). Also, the terms *negro* and *mulato* in Spanish have often been diluted into general categories like "race of color" or "colored class," thus avoiding the narrowness of words like *negro, moreno,* and *pardo.*

Afro-Cuban is synonymous, then, with *colored* in the sense that this term was used in the United States to refer to African-descended people of various skin shades. "These constructions . . . underline the common experience of subordination and discrimination suffered by all Afro-Cubans" (de la Fuente 2001, 31). Cuban poet Nancy Morejón (2003) emphasizes that "the Afro-Cuban essence" exists. As a term, however, *afrocubano* is almost never used by nonacademic Cubans (white or black), although it is not offensive. The terms *negro, moreno, niche,* or *chardo* have basically the same meaning—Afro-Cuban or black—and are heard much more often as self-identification among Cubans of color.

Shades of Race in Cuba

As in many other places in the world, there are many comely, dark chocolate to blue-black Africans in Cuba. *Negro fino* (refined), *negro bonito* (good-looking), and *negro serio* (serious) are a few positive designations that acknowledge their clear African heritage and honor with respect the contributions of black Cubans like General Antonio Maceo, political leader Juan Gualberto Gómez, and militant political organizer Evaristo Estenoz to Cuban history. When *negro fosforescente* (coal black), *negro bembón* (big-lipped black), *negro fula* (brother up to no good), *negro verde* (angry), *mono* (monkey), or *negro pasmao* (broke black man) are used, negativity is being expressed in terms of undesirable, "ugly" African features, stereotypically black (mis)behavior, and social and economic underdevelopment.

There are also Cuban categories that fall in between and augment the main ones. For example, very dark-skinned people with fine facial features (slim noses, pursed lips) and good (read "straight") hair are called *moros,* after the Moors who are present in Cuba's Spanish heritage. Some contend that Spain learned its color-based (rather than blood-based as in the Anglophone world) racial ideology from the Arabs (Moore 2007, 103–6). Sometimes in order to flatter someone, utilizing the subtle language of race, you might refer to them as *moro* when more accurately they should be described as negro. For example, one evening a gentleman approached me to sell several pairs of eyeglasses in very

3. Mora/Moorish girl, 2003.

poor condition; in order to butter me up for this hard sell, he immediately began calling me *moro*.

On another occasion I was being summoned by someone and did not realize they were talking to me because they kept calling me, "Hey you, mulato!" *Mulato* or *mulata* is a vague term that refers to a mixture between black and white, giving the offspring the best of both worlds: passion and soul, *pelo bueno* (good hair), and fine features. Light-skinned mulatos are called *mulato claro* (light), *mulato blanconazo* (big white mulato), or *adelantao* (advanced/evolved), while the darker-skinned can be called *mulato oscuro* or *mulato con trova* (with soul, a little more of Africa). In the black/white continuum, the mulato and mulata are not simply median but are said to be *la combinación perfecta*, with a mystique of sensuality and beauty that is evoked to represent Cuba itself. Cuba is known by many *por sus habanos y sus mulatas* (for its cigars and its women). There are ladies in La Habana drinking Mulata brand rum as they speak of this or that *tremendo mulato* (hunk). Again, the main character in one of Cuba's most significant works of literature from the nineteenth century, Cirilo Villaverde's *Cecilia Valdés*, is a beautiful mulata.

4. ¿Cuál?/Which?, 2003.

Mulatas and mulatos are said to be good for sex. This is part of a logic that portrays and embodies black male sexuality through the image of the black beast that is incapable of love and tenderness, but is a crude rapist of white women. A similar image was attached to black and mulato women, both supposedly wanting only vicious sex (Martínez 2007, 90). Literary scholar Vera Kutzinski notes how the sexual and racial stereotype of the mulata has "intricate and contradictory ties to the ideological construction of that imagined community called Cuba." For her, Cuba encodes its identity in the iconic figure of the mulata—that of the Virgin of Charity who is Cuba's patron saint—not to mention in the countless images of mulatas that have been circulated in the island's literature and popular culture roughly for the past two centuries.

In fact, by the early twentieth century, terms such as *cubanidad* and *cubanía* (which designate different versions of, or approaches to cubanness) were, for all intents and purposes, synonymous to mestizaje. Most saliently contradictory about such discursive entanglements is the symbolic privileging of a socially underprivileged group defined by its mixed race or phenotype, its gender, and its imputed licentious sexuality. In the case of the mulata, high symbolic or cultural visibility contrasts sharply with social invisibility . . . there is no place for the mulata in the culture and the society that so consistently represents itself through her. (Kutzinski 1993, 7)

In the United States the term *mulatto* is not frequently used, because all African Americans are considered black no matter the relative lightness or darkness of their skin. In Cuba, however, it is necessary to scratch through several layers of identity before all can agree that negros, moros, and mulatos are "all black."

Jabao is another category: a kind of median, like the mulato, however stripped of the idyllic qualities of sensuality and beauty. Jabaos usually have light skin with kinky hair and clear African facial features (wide noses, thick lips, etc.). Some have reddish or even blond hair and are said to be *la candela* (fire), extremely mischievous and picaresque. It is said that *los jabaos no tienen raza* (jabaos have no race) and that they do not mix well (genetically) with other races. *Los jabaos son malos* (jabaos are bad) is another often-heard phrase.

In the barrios of Havana you will inevitably find someone who responds immediately to the nickname *chino* or *china*. The Chinese, who started entering Cuba in 1847 as indentured servants to augment slave labor, established long-lasting communities and left their genetic legacy. During the slavery era Chinese men reproduced with free black women and mulatas because steps were taken to keep the Chinese laborers and the enslaved separate (Pérez de la Riva 2000, 79). Besides working in sugar production, the Chinese worked in urban areas as rapid transporters, in construction and cigar rolling, on the docks and railroads, and in coal mines (Pérez de la Riva 2000, 81–82). Anyone with slightly slanted eyes is likely to be called *chino*, identified with this early mixture or that which took place as Chinese continued to migrate as businesspeople (e.g., so-called *californianos* arriving via the Golden State). Chinese people arrived in Cuba throughout the 1920s and 1930s as ambassadors and students.

White folks in Cuba would not really be considered white by U.S. racial standards. They are slightly dark, tawny, marked by the influence of the Moors on their Spanish ancestors' side and by over 500 years of sharing the island of Cuba with descendants of Africa and the more recently arrived Chinese. They are not considered white alongside U.S., French, or German whites, for example. In Cuba people with certain physical traits "close enough, although sometimes not very close, to the original Iberians that colonized the island at the end of the fifteenth

5. Desia mi abuelo/My grandfather used to say, 2003.

6. Quien no tiene de congo, 2003. Literally the phrase means, "Who doesn't have *congo* [African] blood, has *carabalí* [African] blood." All Cubans share African genetic and cultural heritage according to this view.

century" are considered white (Martínez 2007, 8). This phenotype is preferable when it comes to attractiveness and social acceptability, although it also implies the clumsiness and lack of grace/rhythm attributed to whites in the United States. True influence is marked by access to white partners, as they are considered best for love and marriage. This is linked to a social system that assigns social positions by color and endeavors to keep darker peoples subordinate and marginalized. This mentality has been passed down almost completely intact to the present generation, through contemporary accommodations, circumstances, and distinctions.

It is clear that Africa has permeated Cuban culture in everything, from the exquisite shades of skin, the multiple rhythms of speech, and nourishment from dance and music, cuisine, and worship practices. However, Cuban society rejects elements that are too African, that reveal the legacy of slavery (e.g., blacks' weaker economic position or shorter history of formal education), or awaken fears of violent protest. It seems that positive evaluations of "black" are anomalies that disrupt the normal perception of black as bad, antisocial, or inferior. Dynamic, talented blacks are sometimes referred to as *blancos echados a perder* (white folks gone to waste). Blacks, especially women, are said to be best suited for labor rather than love. *Negrito* is a common derogatory diminutive; however, at the same time *negro* or *negra* is also a term of endearment regardless of a loved one's color.

Indeed, the person that resembles the Black Cuban most is the White Cuban. Both share the same ethnicity—the same habits, customs, religion, approach to life, taste for food, rhythm and musicality, and in many cases the same ancestors. Whites in the European sense, and blacks in the African connotation, are both in the minority in Cuba after the long and historical miscegenation that has taken place over centuries (Martínez 2007, 11).

Most people on the island would agree that, in the words of Cuba's national poet Nicolás Guillén, Cubans are "todos mezclados" (all mixed up). This mixedness is an important part of Cuban identity and what is called racial democracy. Used in different versions in Cuba, Brazil, and throughout Latin America, this view contends that race is no issue because diverse elements have fused through *mestizaje* into a cosmic race.[3] This stance at once moves to include (at least rhetorically) all members of the nation regardless of color and, at the same time, denies any space or reason for the struggle for equality based on race, in response to racism. Racial democracy proclaims the problem of racism solved, even though to do so it must ignore vast disparities in quality of life and access to opportunity between the colors/races. In Cuba, this way of thinking is associated with Cuba Libre: the struggle for a sovereign Cuban nation, linked to Martí's notion that "being Cuban is more than being black, more than being white." According to Cuba Libre, a tight level of racial cohesion is necessary to create and sustain the nation. Endeavoring to engage issues of race head-on, rather than through discourse about the nation or social class, has been interpreted as racist (Helg 1995; de la Fuente 2001). Since the abolition of slavery (1886), resurfacing at various points in Cuban history, there has been an anxiety about black enclaves that might/could threaten the cause of Cuban national unity in the face of both Spanish colonialism and, after 1898, U.S. economic and political imperialism. This "black peril" has always been used to thwart blacks' claims for equal citizenship.

Actually, darker-skinned Cubans never wanted to govern the white people, nor at any time were they interested in monopolizing power in Cuba. They want their final emancipation, and freedom from being categorized on the basis of the color of their skin and the features of their phenotype. They want their rightful and true place in Cuba, full recognition as a collective self, and bold futures and aspirations like any other human. They want to be completely equal in all aspects of life to the rest of their compatriots and to share the political, economic, and social power that has been exclusively in the hands of the lighter-skinned population (Martínez 2007, 124).

Fidel Castro called Cuba an African-Latin country, "the blood of Africa" running deep in its veins. In fact, "few nations can boast the advances made in Cuba since the Cuban Revolution in breaking down institutionalized racism." Even so, however, "it would be shortsighted to think that racism has been eliminated" (Sarduy and Stubbs 1993, 7). African American political activist Assata Shakur echoes this opinion in Cuba, noting both shortcomings and gains regarding the race question that signal contradictions in people's consciousness and society in general: "Some people think light skin is good, that if you marry a light person you're advancing the race. There still needs to be de-eurocentrizing of the schools, though Cuba is further along . . . than most places in the world" (Shakur in Parenti 2003, 430).

Unlike Carlos Moore, who sees Cuba's revolutionary government under Fidel Castro as but an extension of paternalistic, white supremacist rule on the island (Moore 1988, 354), Sarduy and Stubbs (1993) and Shakur (Parenti 2003) emphasize that progress has been made toward

7. Café con Leche, 2003.

racial equality.[4] Still, some argue, "the day-to-day experiences and expectations of white Cubans have nothing to do with those of darker-
skinned peoples. There are wide and systematic inequalities of status
and power between the two groups and this biased power relationship
exists outside and beyond social classes" (Martínez 2007, 19).

Part One: Barracoons, Cabildos, and Societies

Africans who were enslaved to cultivate cane sugar were housed in the
barracón (barracoon, slave quarters), and there an incipient Afro-Cuban
culture developed. The barracoon was "a grand jail house, multiplied
throughout the sugar plantation zone, where the slaves lived like pris-
oners" (Barnet 1981, 195). The enslaved were considered property,
forced to labor to create wealth for Spanish colonial masters. This housing style, with two rows of stalls/rooms facing each other, no ventila-
tion, and one main entrance that was locked at night, reflected their de-
graded state. Still, the enslaved would practice African religion and
herbal medicine, play games, and make music to exalt themselves and
stay grounded. "The game of Mayombe was linked to religion . . . you
played Mayombe with drums. You put a nganga or big pot in the middle
of the patio. . . . The blacks asked about their health, and their brothers'
and sisters' health, and asked for harmony among them" (Barnet and
Montejo 1994, 26).

Africans possessed "saving myths and a philosophy that gave them
a security the whites lacked" (Barnet and Montejo 1994, 249). Members
of various African ethnic groups lived side by side and intermixed. In
the midst of the hard work and suffering, they developed a sense of collective identity. The same can be said of the *solar*, which developed
later—an urban freedmen's barracoon, if you will—where poor families
lived in close quarters and Afro-Cuban cultural practices like rumba
flourished. The presence of Asians and whites in these marginal spaces
meant they, too, participated culturally just as they mixed genetically.

Cabildos

Another important space that contributed to the Afro Cuba we know
today is the *cabildo*, which was established in urban areas in contrast to
the rural barracoons (Fernández 1994, 7; Bastide 1971, 9). The cabildo

tradition came to Cuba from Seville and was aimed at organizing social classes on the basis of mutual aid and religion (Moreno 1999; Ortiz 1992, 6). In Cuba they specifically functioned to organize, receive, orient, and regulate Africans who were brought to the island according to various ethnic groups or "nations." Distinct ethnic groups formed separate *cabildos*. Ortiz refers to Cuban historian Hortensia Pichardo's definition of the *cabildo* as a "reunion of blacks directly from Africa (*bozales*) in houses established for the celebration of [Catholic] feast days, on which they play drums and other instruments from their country" (Ortiz 1992, 1). Dance events were among the greatest attractions for the members and an important reason for cabildos' longevity (even up until the time of Ortiz's writing on the subject in the 1920s). However, dance and music were second priorities to mutual aid or self-help among cabildo members. As benefits earned through dues and proper conduct, cabildos cared for sick members, paid burial expenses, and bought the freedom of elder slaves (Ortiz 1992, 6–7).

Cabildos were usually headed by the oldest male member who was called the king (*rey*) or captain (*capataz, capitán*) of the organization. There was a queen of the cabildo, as well as other posts like flag bearer (*abanderado*) and the king's second in command, the "*mayor de plaza*" (Ortiz 1992, 2). Despite the high levels of organization that Ortiz documents, he cites Pichardo again saying that any meeting of inept, disorganized people can be called a *cabildo de congos*. Thus Ortiz shows that cabildos were subject to racism and the prevalent notion of black inferiority as a natural condition. In the Cuban republic of the early twentieth century, middle-class blacks that desired to create intellectual, "modern" organizations also ridiculed older associations as antiquated and too African. Most cabildos had their own buildings (especially during the eighteenth century) in addition to being incorporated as *cofradías* (associations) with parochial churches. They were connected to, yet separate from, dominant state and religious authority.

Cabildos were used to control blacks, both slave and free. Part of their aim was to "thwart the unity of the slaves and keep alive rivalries among the different tribes and ethnic groups" (Fernández 1994, 7; Moore 1997, 16). They also made sure that Cuba's Africanity was expressed in prescribed ways and at specified times and places. *Cabildos* were carefully regulated and subjected to the authority of established powers with the right to approve or disapprove their rules, to review their accounts, and even to dissolve them. This facilitated political control over the ethnic group more effectively than if the individual mem-

bers, especially the free ones, were dispersed and uncontrolled, associating among themselves in noninstitutionalized social gatherings
(Moreno 1999, 7). One official statement from 1835 makes this clear:
"The cabildos and dances of the blacks can only be celebrated on signaled festival days and at the *margins of the city*, from 10 am to noon
and from 3 pm until prayer time, under penalty of four ducados for cabildo organizers, double for the second violation, and relief from duties
for a third infraction" (Moore 1997, 10; emphasis added). If music/dance
was not the soul, it was surely the heart of the cabildo organizations
(Ortiz 1992, 9). The heart could not beat freely, as it were; neither was
it totally controlled.

Cabildos were also used for mutual aid and cultural continuity.
They helped preserve African religious practices and music, which are
extremely important carriers of African culture in Cuba (Bastide 1971,
9). Cabildos allowed perhaps the most important manifestations of
reaffirmation and reproduction of black collective ethnicity. These institutions were the principal loci, and sometimes the only ones, in
which a type of "associationism" not tolerated by the authorities in
other contexts could develop (Moreno 1999, 3). Africans were provided
a semblance of family structure, slavery having nearly shattered the nu-
clear and extended family in the Caribbean. African traditions were able
to survive due to continued practice. Cabildos were institutions of social control, which also facilitated African cultural continuity as
Yoruba, Ewe, Bantu, Wolof, and other Africans and their descendants—
along with Spanish and Asian elements—became Afro-Cubans. Located
at the bottom of the social order, the cabildos gave the only opportunity
(or at least one of the few) for blacks in the Spanish world to organize,
whether in Seville or Havana. In Cuba, the cabildos "became indis-
putably the meltingpot that enabled the cosmogonies, languages, musics, songs, and dances related to those systems of worship to preserve
their life and significance" (Roy 2002, 13).

Starting in 1764, cabildo processions would converge on the colonial
palace on January 6, Día de Reyes (Day of the Three Kings), to perform
for officials and their families with drums, dance, and song. This practice continued until 1885 (Ortiz 1992, 11). During these festivities,
"Africa, with her children, clothing, music, languages and chants,
dances and ceremonies, religions and political institutions, was trans-
ported to Cuba, principally to Havana" (25). The conditions of slavery
eased up on celebratory occasions like Día de Reyes or patron saint
days, for example, the Virgin of Regla on September 8 or Saint Barbara

on December 4. Ortiz affirms that there is "an intimate relationship between the cabildos, the Día de Reyes celebration, and modern comparsas that still roam the streets of Havana" (38).

The participation of cabildos in these celebrations allowed Africans, displaced in Cuba or born there, to adapt and extend processional purification rites from various parts of West Africa and West Central Africa (Ortiz 1992, 44). In this way, cabildos and their processions maintained sacred knowledge and embodied wisdom (Daniel 2005). Many of the seemingly outlandish costumes that highlighted the festivities represented the priestly casts of various African religious systems. According to Ortiz, for example, the so-called *culona*, a masked dancer with a wide grass skirt that hides what seem to be exaggeratedly large buttocks, is associated with an African word *kulona* or *lonna*, which means *sabio* or wise one. Classic characters in postemancipation carnival *comparsas*, like *la culona*, *el alacrán* (scorpion), and *la víbora* (snake), are directly descended from figures in cabildo processions (Roy 2002, 36). These were medicine men and diviners (or representations of them), not always simple jesters. The magicoreligious systems that cabildos and their processions helped to preserve continue to shape people's life experience in Cuba. Nancy Morejón affirms being shaped by these forms of cultural expression and resistance, even though she was from an atheistic family in the 1960s revolutionary era (Behar 1998, 131).

Cabildos provide a valuable perspective on the maroon mentality that I have brought up before, but now they are seminal to discussion of Afro Cuba. Runaway slaves preserved African life and culture by absconding to the hills, and both spiritually and physically establishing for themselves a home base away from the centers of power in Cuban society. Urban slaves in the context of the cabildo, however, used the maroon mentality in a different way, by "hiding in plain sight" (Sublette 2004). They absconded internally, responding to asymmetrical power relations in a symbolic way; within the paradigm of colonial control, represented by royal decrees and Christian religion, they reiterated remembered performances (Moreno 1999).

Carnival processions were periodically prohibited, either as punishment for slave revolts or during wars of independence. Combatants took advantage of masquerades to obtain arms and spread news. Carnival processions were definitively prohibited during the 1884 Feast of the Epiphany (Roy 2002, 35). In the aftermath of slavery, the principal players within carnivals were precisely the former slaves and their descendants, the mulatos, and poor whites who lived side by side on the outskirts of Havana, making commentary on current events, either directly or through double meaning (36). Many times "drums were hidden away, and rituals continued covertly, even attracting whites and orientals" (Leymarie 2002, 12).

Many musical works, such as Benny Moré's song "Los compone-dores," derive from old cabildo tunes (Leymarie 2002, 12) and many of the musical and philosophical elements that function in timba were preserved largely through cabildos and their processions. Using the same performative language (the procession, call-and-response form, and so on), timba establishes alternative, oppositional black cultural space. This space and the discourse therein are neither totally separate from nor antagonistic toward "white" Cuba. In this way, they promote integration and well-being for the community and the nation.

Historian Tomás Fernández Robaina emphasizes that "it was not only art and mystic wisdom that Cubans inherited from the Africans and their descendants" (Fernández 1994, 8). Love of liberty, human dignity, and rebelliousness in the face of injustice are their legacy too. The closing of the cabildos by the Spanish after abolition (1886) meant that other organizations or institutions would function as the main spaces for Afro-Cuban cultural expression. In 1887 the colonial government forced cabildos to submit to fellowship legislation that transformed them into mutual aid societies open to all people of color (regardless of African ethnic origin), under the aegis of a Catholic Saint (Roy 2002, 13).

El Directorio Central de la Raza de Color (Central Directory of the Colored Race)

El Directorio Central de la Raza de Color (Central Directory of the Colored Race) was one of the most important black organizations at end of the nineteenth century and the start of the twentieth (Fernández 1994, 23) and as such reflected important issues and struggles of the times from the perspective of Afro-Cubans in that era. Founded in 1887 by Juan Gualberto Gómez, its goal was to organize and coordinate unified action among Cuba's many cabildos and mutual aid societies of color (Fernández 1994, 24) and to challenge Spanish authority (Helg 1995, 35). Through the Central Directory, Afro-Cubans could counter the ethnic and class divisions that cabildos fostered, without disturbing their positive functions of mutual aid and cultural continuity.

El Directorio also looked to clarify the position of Afro-Cubans and their claims to equality vis-à-vis Cuban society. Their constant claim was that blacks were not a danger to the country: "No, we are not inciting race war by demanding equal social conditions among the inhabitants of this country. On the contrary [the ones who are fomenting the fear of a race war] are those who refuse to give blacks equal rights, and who take our claims for aggression. . . . there is no race question, what is at hand is only the fight for justice, progress, and equality" (Fernández 1994, 32). To this end, they sued white and Chinese individuals for discrimination. Not intimidated when provincial courts ruled against equality, they exhausted all legal possibilities and brought their cases to the Spanish Supreme Court in Madrid. There they often won and directly contributed to the promulgation of new nondiscriminatory legislation. They also took action to ensure that new laws were carried out at the local level (Helg 1995, 35–36).

From its founding until 1894, El Directorio won legal victories granting equal access to public places and schools, the right to travel in first-class carriages, and the right to be called *don* or *doña* in official documents. So strong was the Directory's organizational network and record of service that revolutionary activist and national poet José Martí chose its head, Juan Gualberto Gómez (from abroad), as the coordinator of the independence movement in Cuba (Martínez 2007, 91, 100–101).

In that spirit, two publications, *La Fraternidad* and *La Igualdad*, also inspired and directed by Juan Gualberto Gómez, demanded equal rights for Cubans of color. They linked their struggle to Cuban independence in the years leading up to the war, and they called for union between blacks and mulatos within the community of color (Fernández 1994, 29). Comparative analysis of Cuban and North American racial systems led to the argument that Afro-Cubans stood to lose a lot if the island became annexed to the United States or fell too much under its influence. The position of the publications was that "Yankee authorities would protect whites more than blacks, [and] blacks and mulatos wouldn't be allowed to board trains, pray in the same temples, etc." (Fernández 1994, 32).

El Directorio was short-lived despite its serious attempts to unite all of the black mutual aid societies and orient them toward a politics of social development that would uplift blacks in colonial Cuba (Fernández 1994, 25). It ceased to function with the start of the War of Independence in 1895 and was replaced by El Comité de Veteranos y de Sociedades de la Raza de Color (Committee of Veterans and Societies of Color), which was also short-lived. The incipient nation's concern with achieving independence and the need for a unified, raceless front, followed by the prohibition of political organizing based on race, undid these journals and organizations.

El Partido Independiente de Color

In 1908, the Agrupación (later called Partido) Independiente de Color (PIC) was founded under the leadership of Evaristo Estenoz who said, "Free men deserve two things: to be loved and respected . . . and if the first cannot be achieved spontaneously, the second must be imposed" (Fernández 1994, 52–53). Up to that point political parties in the new republic had only used the black vote to gain political advantage but had done little to help Afro-Cubans. Blacks were represented in small numbers, and by politicians who were considered figureheads. The demands of PIC included, among other things, free education for all from six to fourteen years of age; free university education; an egalitarian republic without distinction of colors or class separation; and free immigration for all races, as long as they were willing to work for the well-being of Cuba. *Previsión* was the publication of PIC, and their party platform in some ways presaged the reforms of the 1933 revolution and the 1959 revolution under Fidel Castro.

The Morua Law was passed in 1910, which outlawed political organizations along racial lines. This precipitated armed protest within Cuba's eastern provinces by the PIC in 1912. The protest was violently repressed by government troops sent by President José Miguel Gómez, resulting in the slaughter of around 4,000 Afro-Cubans, many of whom were not protesters (Portuondo Linares 2002). The event is referred to as La Guerrita (the Little War). It shows that there was no perfect union among Cubans of different colors. On the contrary, "Cuba was profoundly divided along racial lines, and white Cubans continued to look at their compatriots of color as the other and the enemy . . . to be paralyzed and placed on the margins of society, and permanently kept in a subordinate position" (Martínez 2007, 121). Any attempt by Afro-Cubans to establish their own political, economic, and social agenda, in order to achieve full recognition and equality, constituted a mortal threat. With the demise of black political organizations and according to their new realities, Afro-Cubans developed new ways and new methods of struggle to achieve their goals (Martínez 2007, 129).

Sociedades de color

After 1890, *cabildos de nación* were progressively replaced by *sociedades de color* (social clubs or societies for persons of color). These black organizations, which were established by middle-class, professional Afro-Cubans, became numerous throughout the island, adapting a type of mutual aid society from Spain that attended to their needs of separate entertainment, community assistance, and integration in the wider society (Helg 1995, 30). After political organizing along color lines was prohibited in 1910, they professed a strictly nonpolitical and nonreligious focus. They were intended for mutual aid, cultural development, and what we call today "networking." Some *sociedades de color* also founded small elementary schools for the children of their members (Helg 1995, 30). As important centers in the Afro-Cuban community and in the context of a political system with full manhood suffrage after 1902 (women gaining the vote after 1934), *sociedades de color* came to wield significant political influence.

Especially after the introduction of North American "whites-only" social clubs in Havana, which lasted until the triumph of the Revolution in 1959, *sociedades de color* became the most important groups for Afro-Cubans apart from religious group practice (which was largely clandestine). While whites attended a social club called Casino de la Playa, blacks had the Unión Fraternal, Club Magnetti, and Club Atenas. In addition to mutual aid the societies also organized dances. Like the barracoons and *cabildos*, this was a space apart, removed from the mainstream, where strong Afro-Cuban culture continued to develop. Soon after the Revolution triumphed in 1959, these societies were disbanded because, at last, all of Cuba was for all Cubans. The clubs were considered unnecessary, and once again, a space for Afro-Cuban discourse was shut down, which forced a shift in how and where the discourse would continue.

"Ideales de una Raza"

During the time of the sociedades, which were officially nonpolitical, black Cuban thinkers wrote about race relations and politics. Between 1928 and 1931, a Sunday column called "Ideales de una raza" (Ideals of a Race) by Gustavo Urrutia espoused and analyzed the sociocultural concerns of Afro-Cubans. It opened up a forum for dialogue between both black and white intellectuals in a printed call-and-response format. "Ideales" was not the only publication dedicated to such concerns; however, its placement as a column within a very widely distributed periodical called the *Diario de la Marina*, rather than as an independently published column, gave it a large, diverse readership (Helg 1995, 126). A section within the periodical, ironically called "Armonías" (Harmonies), discussed the racial system in the United States and, like many earlier papers, emphasized how much better the Cuban situation was, despite its problems. "Ideales" printed translations of the works of African American scholars like W. E. B. DuBois and provided weekly bibliographies of nonwhite authors in Cuba. These kinds of publications were important in the process of making all Cubans aware of the social concerns and the intellectual and artistic achievements of blacks not only in Cuba but also abroad.

For white Cubans who would deny or ignore these accomplishments, the essays, reviews, and interviews that appeared in "Ideales" emphasized blacks as undeniable parts of the soul of Cuba. Such columns and publications were also a great source for blacks and mulatos who doubted the greatness of their racial heritage, who lacked perspective on their local condition, or who were interested in following debates on the struggle for equality at home and abroad. They were also principal showcases for Afro Cubanism/Afro Antilleanism and its various manifestations in literature, music, and the visual arts (Kutzinski 1993, 148).

Afro-Cuban Arts

In Cuba, African influence on the arts has been acknowledged most in music and dance (Ortiz 1993, 12). Robin Moore, for example, notes how by the mid-nineteenth century a number of Afro-Cuban slave genres emerged or gained prominence: "*tajona* and *yambú* dances, the *baile de maní*, and other precursors of the present-day traditional rumba; sacred song and dance associated with *Santería*, and related ceremony; and the *tango-congo* and *abakuá* music and dance performed by street revelers in Día de Reyes or Kings' Day celebrations" (Moore 1997, 17). Syncretic Afrohispanic genres developed that were popular among working-class Cubans of all races: *caidita, cachumba*, the *cangrejito*, the *con-*

tradanza, and *danzón* (Moore 1997, 17). *Son, mambo, chachachá, pilón, coyude, tembleque,* and other dances, which are discussed later, are more recent extensions of this dance phenomenon. The iconic entertainer Rita Montaner expressed the black and white, African-Hispanic blend: "That huge, little woman whose golden skin symbolizes the two races that crackle in her heart and leave her lips in one fiery breath" (Guillén 2002, 249).

Nicolás Guillén paid homage to the African roots of Cuban music by writing poetry based on the rhythms of *son*. Writing about Cuban poetry, he asserts that the first truly Cuban verses came from black voices (Guillén 2002, 96). According to him, early Cuban poetry was lackluster because it copied Spanish bards, focused too narrowly on the concerns of white *guajiros*, or was based precariously on indigenous cultural sources that had long since been decimated (Guillén 2002, 96).

> Another kind of popular, anonymous poetry begins to show signs of life with a pure authenticity: it begins with the song, starting point of the poetic. Song loaded with rough salt, burning knavery, in which the man in the street releases his innermost feelings . . . the clear voice of el negro . . . (Guillén 2002, 97)

The Afro-Antillean or negrista poetry, much of which was, ironically, written by white authors, showed that black cultural expressions could give voice to Cubanness beyond color, "ni negro, ni blanco."

> Not the guajiro . . . whose social dimensions were too limited, nor [the] Indian whose existence was a fantasy, could project a truly national poetry; only *el negro* in the flesh, beaten by the whip; the black fused with white . . . Afrohispanic drama, all the inerasable *mulatez* of Cuba. (Guillén 2002, 100)

Despite the physical separation of slavery, Afro Cuba has made a permanent contribution to Cuban society and culture through verse.

Afro-Cubans in the Labor Movement and the Communist Party

The National Federation of Sugar Workers was founded in 1938, under the leadership of Jesús Menéndez, a black Cuban whose father had been part of the Liberation army in the last war for independence. He was a charismatic, knowledgeable leader until assassinated by an army official in 1948. It should be no surprise that a union of sugar workers, led by a black Cuban, should defend black interests like the rights of immigrant workers from Haiti and Jamaica in eastern Cuba. Lázaro Peña, a national trade union leader, and Aracelio Iglesias, of the ports and harbor union (stevedores), were Afro-Cuban labor leaders who were politically connected to the Communist Party, though they had a strong appeal of their own.

Many Afro-Cubans in the working class and among the unemployed saw the ideas of Marxism and the practice of the Cuban Communist Party as a way to channel their struggle for equality and collective advancement. In fact, the Cuban Communist Party was the only national political entity that included equality and the eradication of racial discrimination on its agenda. Secretary-general Blas Roca was the only nonwhite party leader in Cuba before the triumph of the Revolution. Within the Party, other Afro-Cubans like Aracelio Iglesias, Severo Aguirre, Salvador García Agüero, and Nicolás Guillén held national responsibilities (Martínez 2007, 144). From the 1920s on, individually and collectively, Afro-Cubans used active participation in the labor movement and leftist political parties to advance their struggle for equality.

Part Two: Afro Cuba and Revolution

The mystical *güijes* that sang freedom songs and the *cimarrones* who escaped slavery to establish settlements called *palenques* presaged the attitude and actions of blacks and mulatos when the first War of Independence began in 1868 (Sarduy and Stubbs 1993, 61; Fernández 1994, 14). Afro-Cubans have been central in all of the island's revolutionary struggles because of their subordinate position as slaves or peons and their passion for freedom (de la Fuente 2001; Ferrer 1999; Helg 1995; Martínez 2007). They served valiantly, for example, in the Liberation Army that over a thirty-year period fought three wars—the Ten Years' War (1868–78), La Guerra Chiquita or Little War (1879–80), and the final War of Independence (1895–98). This army was unique in the Atlantic world because it was integrated; black soldiers like Antonio Maceo and Quintín Banderas ascended through the ranks and even commanded white soldiers. Some historians estimate that at least 60 percent of the Liberation Army was composed of men of color and that by the end of the thirty-year period as many as 40 percent of commissioned officers were of color (Ferrer 1999, 3). With each incarnation of Cuban revolution, conditions have improved for blacks, but not as much as they should or could have.

Afro-Cubans were disenfranchised under U.S. rule after the defeat of the Spanish in 1898, and they were massacred in 1912 for organizing and protesting their disenfranchisement. In the aftermath of the 1912 massacre, black political efforts were merged with those of all the Cuban working class in labor organizations; there was no separate black party or black voice. After the 1959 Revolution, the emphasis on Marxism and racial democracy limited Afro-Cuban struggles, continued their "linked fate," and worked, along with state repression, to prevent black mobilization (Sawyer 2006, 16). Moore suggests that the very term *Afro-Cuban* (i.e., Cuban blacks as a separate and distinct population segment) was officially discouraged (1988, 102). Martínez cites what has been called the "Enemy Theory," "Siege Mentality," or "Surrounding Syndrome" as a mechanism to put Afro-Cuban concerns on hold.[5]

Today, inequality remains in contemporary Cuba, as blacks are lowest and whites highest in the social hierarchy, and the gap widens between them with regard to health, wealth, and standard of living (de la Fuente 2001; Sarduy and Stubbs 1993; Sawyer 2006). For these reasons, many Afro-Cubans complain or express ambivalence about the Revolution. On the other hand, they identify as its *co-owners* because black soldiers fought valiantly and decisively in all revolutionary battles, and they are *grateful* because, as the poorest Cubans, they have benefited from education, labor, and housing reforms that were implemented by the Revolution. (This dual identification counters the view of blacks as only passive recipients of freedom, citizenship, and education, who should be grateful and not complain.) They also cleave to the Revolution because the alternative leadership option in Cuban Miami is considered racist and reactionary (Sawyer 2006). Many Afro-Cubans claim to be open to a different way of life—possibly—but not necessarily a capitalist way because neither a capitalist nor a communist/socialist paradigm has sufficiently transformed their plight so far.

A system of color-based inequality has survived in Cuba from Columbus's arrival through to the present day. Positive steps taken by the revolutionary government have had widespread effects for Cubans of all colors, not only blacks. Landless peasants have received parcels of land and soft credits to assist them in agricultural production. Electricity and telephone rates were significantly lowered, and rent payments were cut in half by law. Workers demanding higher salaries received them. Racial discrimination was legally or officially outlawed. However, the revolutionary government has allowed little or no official space for a distinct Afro-Cuban agenda. The black and mulato population as a whole has been submerged in the category of poor people needing poverty alleviation and little else.[6] This is what makes the spaces that are inhabited by timba music so important. Like *palenques, cabildos, sociedades de color,* and the other social organizations of the past, they are focal points for the creation of Afro-Cuban discourse and expression.

Sarduy writes, "The abolition of slavery and independence from Spain, the 1930s labor uprising, the 1950s insurrection and the 1960s revolutionary euphoria were key moments in contemporary Cuban history when levels of unity and social cohesion were achieved that could bridge the divides [between races]. The return to a more routine social order almost inevitably entailed their resurfacing, in newly defined forms" (1993, 7). Following this line of thought, political scientist Mark Sawyer proposes the "race cycles theory" and the concept of "inclusionary discrimination" to explain the back-and-forth movement as well as contradictions in Cuban race relations. He argues that racial politics in Cuba "have followed patterns of opening and retrenchment that have been driven by the need of the state to mobilize blacks to support state projects and to protect the state from hostile forces" (2006, xxi). Sawyer relates the effect of state policy on racial politics and highlights the agency of subordinated individuals and communities to transform racial politics. The race cycles perspective has five central points.

> First, racial politics is driven by mechanisms such as state crisis, regime change, racial ideology, transnational politics, and endogenous shocks to the system, or critical events. Second, mechanisms like state crisis, transnational politics, and critical events lead to transformations in racial politics. These transformations are followed by the process of state consolidation, which relies on racial ideology to limit and ultimately halt any gains made as a result of the mechanism. Third, because of conflicting state priorities, each mechanism provides opportunities for gains for subordinate racial groups, but it also places limitations on the magnitude and duration of these gains. The mechanisms that drive the change trend toward an equilibrium position of stagnation in the racial situation. Fourth, gains in racial politics are directly related, in positive fashion, to the magnitude of the state crisis, but the duration of

the gains is inversely related to the degree of the crisis. Finally, following a significant shock and subsequent consolidation, a new equilibrium is created that is different from the previous one. As a consequence, racial ideology and policies are altered. (Sawyer 2006, 4)

From the view of longtime examiners of Cuban affairs Cuban Pedro Sarduy and U.S. American Jean Stubbs, "there are two sides to every crisis: one bodes extreme difficulty while the other holds the promise of new possibilities" (Sarduy and Stubbs 1993, 11). While the 1996 Declaration of Havana endorsed UNESCO's "Slave Routes of the Americas" cultural heritage tour, and in 1998 the race issue was raised at length by the National Union of Writers and Artists (UNEAC), there was also a demonizing of Afro-Cuban religions in the Cuban popular media. This accompanied a general bolstering of Hispanocuban historical and cultural hegemony, with Afro-Cubans excluded from meaningful roles in Cuban television and other media while Afro-Cuban folklore was commercialized for the tourist market (Sarduy and Stubbs 2000, 7). In their book *Afro-Cuban Voices* we hear from black families who, on one hand, see their educational and occupational mobility as a product of revolutionary change and, on the other hand, reflect on what they perceive as dire, unsolved racial problems.

My own fieldwork provides a similar conclusion. Gissell, a college student of mixed black and white parentage whom I interviewed, says she loves Cuba but also wants to leave, mostly because of its underdevelopment and racism. She speaks of how extraordinary it was for her father, a successful white man, to marry her black mother. The more common thing would have been to have a child with her without acknowledging the child or the relationship officially, or simply to live together without formal matrimony. She remembers the things people used to say to her parents: "*Ay hombre,* how could you marry *her?!,*" "Excuse me, but are you the mother or the nanny of this little [very light skinned] girl?" Their love was in line with Cuban theories of *mestizaje,* race mixing, and Cuba Libre; yet it still flew in the face of commonly held beliefs. Legal declarations cannot erase belief systems, nor can they deeply affect interpersonal (as opposed to professional or civic) relationships. Furthermore, the existence of racism in interpersonal interactions like these raises strong questions about its existence in the machinery of government. After all, *individuals act* within institutions. They may act out their personal beliefs, albeit unconsciously or against the expressed goals of the system of which they are agents.

Another fieldwork example suggests unequal access to wealth and restricted access to certain social spaces. One afternoon I was walking through Playa, a posh neighborhood in Havana, and entered a cafe at the corner of Seventh and Thirtieth streets. It seemed like another world, different from the Cuba I had seen up until that moment, although everyone was Cuban. Many people were talking on cell phones and drinking bottled water with their meals of pizza, hot dogs, or fried chicken. As far as I had seen previously, any Cuban buying bottled water must be insane or rich; and I knew that not many of my friends could afford these high-priced items. Everyone there to dine or *consumir* (purchase, consume) was white. A black woman janitor looked at me, at first with surprise, then gladness to see me. There was a pause and she smiled as I bought and sipped a bottle of water. Here the ideal of racial democracy was marked/marred by a distinct reality for black Cubans. Rather than formally segregated, black Cubans are structurally denied access to sources of wealth that would give them entrée. The end result is still marginalization.[7] This scene recalls historian Louis Pérez, Jr.'s writing about U.S. influence in the island during the first half of the twentieth century (Pérez 1999). Status and identification with North American values were claimed and displayed through consumption of American products. Then too it was mappable by color.

In his novel, *Príapos,* about Cuba in the 1990s, Daniel Chavarría describes an Afro-Cuban man who, "like many potential beneficiaries of the Revolution, never did understand it; but was not its enemy." Without being a criminal, this character "refuses to 'work for the government' as the enemies of the Revolution would say, or 'submit himself to the process' as official government language put it" (2005, 56). This ambivalent connection reflects the "inclusionary discrimination" experienced by Afro-Cubans: limited access to the nation's resources, persistent inequality and prejudice, despite official policies that guarantee the rights of all Cubans.

One recognizes pathways that were opened to blacks through the Revolution, and appreciates its noble goals and continued work to improve Cuban and world society. Many black Cubans certainly benefited from programs of the revolutionary government that aimed at the poor and promoted cultural revival. They felt proud of Cuba's involvement in African liberation wars in the early 1960s (Congo) and in the mid-1970s (Angola), when Castro defined Cuba not only as Latin American but also as a Latin African nation (Sarduy and Stubbs 1993, 6). At the same time, however, the pinch of reality has been a nagging pain, signaling continued systems of racial inequality. The economic crisis that has gripped Cuba from 1990 to the time of this writing has, among other effects, made the position of blacks in Cuba all the more precarious and ironic. Afro-Cuban culture (music, art, history, bodies) attracts foreign visitors that support the national economy, while Cuban blacks remain marginalized from political power and access to wealth.

The breakdown of Cuba's integration into the eastern European bloc and the tightening of the thirty-year-old U.S. blockade put the island under siege in such a way that black Cubans likened Cuba to a modern-day *palenque*—maroon or runaway slave settlement. Many blacks' response to the "special period" of austerity in the new situation was that blacks were used to it; theirs had always been a special period, and now the special period was for all (Sarduy and Stubbs 1993, 4; emphasis in original).

Amaury's Story

A black friend of mine, Amaury, came to visit and ask for a loan. I gave it to him, and afterward we sat down to talk for a long while about many things. I mentioned to him how strange it was to see "white" Cubans (especially women) who in their speech, dress, and their "swing" seemed quite tinged with black, but who at the same time are quite racist and denigrating toward things black. It was always a shock to observe. He assured me that I wasn't crazy, and that this happened all the time. He told stories that exemplify common conceptions of blackness in Cuba.

1. His mother felt justified in an argument with a neighbor because "she was definitely lighter skinned" than the neighbor.
2. That same day a blond woman said to her black girlfriend in jest, "I'm gonna slap the black off you, and I'll be doing you a favor!" When it was suggested that she was racist she could not believe it.
3. On a radio show Amaury sang a tune that imagines "What if God were black?" and a white man responded, "Yes, as fucked up as the world is, God *must* be black!"
4. A glass falls and shatters between two friends. If the black person is responsible people might say, "Look at his color and forgive him" (*Mírale el color y perdónalo*).

5. During this time Pedro Calvo, a former lead singer from Los Van Van, sang "Esa rubia no quiere un negro palmao" (that blond woman doesn't want a broke black man) underlining the low social perception of blacks and the value of wealth/consumption as redemption from that second-class status.

Amaury felt that blacks learn from a young age that they have no worth (*no tienen valor*). Like some scholars, Amaury noted how, in school, Antonio Maceo is presented as a mighty soldier with a machete, but his superior intelligence and charisma are downplayed (Martínez 2007, 152). He said that Cuban blacks underestimate *themselves* and therefore underachieve. In the words of Cuban historian Fernando Martínez Heredia, "That great indignity [slavery] cast a shadow over nonwhite Cubans," which did not motivate them to redress their situation or seek rights but rather served as a vehicle for low self-esteem and shame (Portuondo Linares 2002, xv). Amaury was a self-described delinquent before he met Nehanda, a black American exile in Havana, who helped him to believe that black is beautiful.

I talked with a man from Sudan, Arcangelo, who considers Cuban blacks fools because "they do not fight for their rights, they don't express themselves, and do not value their own beauty and culture." We both laughed a little at how black Cubans argue about "who's lighter." This man highly respects U.S. American blacks because they have demanded their rights.

Nancy Morejón, too, feels that African Americans have confronted and challenged some stereotypes that still exist in Cuba with little or no contestation or alternative image (Sarduy and Stubbs 2000, 165). According to Morejón, there are few alternatives to the slave, the sports star, the musician, or the brute type she calls "the black ogre" in terms of television or other iconic representations of blackness. "The black is seen as stupid, as someone who talks bad, who sweats and shouts and gyrates, and behaves in a socially inferior way" (Sarduy and Stubbs 2000, 167). She gives praise to the work accomplished by the Revolution and notes that blacks have made progress: "Never as much as now has there been such a visibly strong black and mulato presence in middle positions [of government leadership] that are sometimes more important than those at the top, because they are closer to reality" (Sarduy and Stubbs 2000, 168). However, she says, these strides are undermined and hidden by negative stereotypes. For example, "a great ballet dancer, a black Cuban ballet dancer who is acclaimed abroad, sees his image reduced because the image representing him is Boncó, the comic black on television" (Sarduy and Stubbs 2000, 168). This exemplifies Sawyer's "inclusionary discrimination": inclusionary because the dancer was trained in schools to which blacks had very limited access before the Revolution, discriminatory because the popular imagination (here the television) still insists on black barbarism and inferiority.

For Morejón, music is the clearest expression of *cubanidad*; however, to enter this discussion is dangerous, for this view leads into the stereotype of "the bad black, the vulgar black that talks and acts bad" (Sarduy and Stubbs 2000, 167). She finds the connection in the adjective *chabacano* (vulgar) or the noun *chabacanería* (vulgarity) used often to evoke the black ogre or Boncó in regard to music and dance. "All Cuban blacks and mulatos get accused of [*chabacanería*] one way or another," but this speech is almost never leveled at someone whose skin isn't dark. Morejón is against the chabacanería that exists but also sees behind the word a "rejection of the black." She agrees with my friend Amaury that black Cubans accept these images and limit themselves: "It's only a vision, and there's a passivity: that is, I take that image, which is the image they give me of myself, and I accept it." Behind the stereotypes there is "a noise, a terrible colonial rumbling, of values that are supposedly against those we have fought for" (Sarduy and Stubbs 2000, 167–68).

Ortiz also writes about the particular relationship of Afro Cuba to music in Cuba.

> We understand Afro-Cuban music to mean that which the Cuban people received from the blacks from Africa, adopted with some modifications, and recreated in Cuba under the influence of the African musical traditions of various origins. . . . Cubans have exported more dreams and delights with our music, more sweetness and power, than with sugar. Afro-Cuban music is fire, deliciousness; it is syrup, *sandunga*, and relief; like sonorous rum quaffed through the ears, uniting and equalizing people through its trade, dynamizing life itself . . . There is no doubt that the music most characteristic of Cuba, that which has given [it] resonance the world over is that music founded with African roots in this tropical melting pot, a product of black and white transculturation. (Ortiz 1993, 13–14)

Unlike sugar, which was transplanted to the Caribbean and brought pain, Cuban music is *criollo*, homegrown, intended to provide relief and spread joy.

Part Three: El Poeta de la Rumba

If Africans did not reach Cuba earlier by their own navigational devices as some scholars suggest, then at least within a few years of the European encounter with the Americas they were present (Van Sertima 1976, 1–18). Soon afterward Africans became the object of a specialized, large-scale international trade system. This continued until the last slave ship arrived in Cuba in 1873 (Barnet 1981, 268). The discourse of Afro Cuba also began with the first blacks who arrived on the island, and it has been extended and shaped through the lives and work of Maceo, Martí, Juan Gualberto Gómez, Rafael Serra, Lino D'ou, Evaristo Estenoz, Gustavo Urrutia, Walterio Carbonell, Juan René Betancourt, Carlos Moore, Pedro Serviat, Nicolás Guillén, Nancy Morejón, and countless others including musicians like Chano Pozo.

A song by vocalist Mario "Mayito" Rivera, *el poeta de la rumba*, continues the discourse on Afro Cuba with rhythm and energy. In his song, he alludes to the history of pain and to the shame felt by some blacks about their color, their Self. His song is no lament, however, but rather an affirmation and a challenge. At the start he locates his message in the discourse of Afro Cuba with the drum rhythm of rumba guaguancó, then by exclaiming a fragment of Fernando Ortiz's motto "ciencia, paciencia, y conciencia" (science, patience, and conscience).

> ¡Conciencia!
> Yo tengo la piel oscura
> Así de negra es de pura
> Tan dulce como el azúcar
> De tanta caña cortada
> Sabroso como el café
> Que tomas cada mañana

> I have dark skin
> As black as it is pure
> Sweet as sugar
> From so much cane cut
> Delicious like the coffee
> You drink every morning

Here Mayito further situates his *canto* (song) in the discourse of Cuban history as well as Afro Cuba by setting up a counterpoint similar to that used by Ortiz as a metaphor for Cuba. Whereas Ortiz discusses Afro-Cuban and Hispano-Cuban (black and white, among other counterpoints) through the labor and social relations involved in the production of sugar and tobacco, Rivera offers sugar and coffee, both associated with black labor. His song takes a historically grounded approach from an Afro-Cuban perspective.

> *Mi piel tiene larga historia*
> *Que si yo te contaría*
> *Quizás así entenderías*
> *El porqué de mi sabor*
> *Mi piel conoce el dolor*
> *Amiga de la tristeza*
> *Pero mi mayor riqueza*
> *Es ser dueño del tambor*

> My skin has a long history
> If I told you
> You might understand my flavor
> My skin knows pain
> Friend to sadness
> But my greatest wealth
> Is that I own the drum

He sings of a history unknown to many. He sings of the ironic beauty of a flavorful culture born largely through pain. He claims the drum—Africa, blackness—as his greatest treasure. He is addressing all of Cuba: Amaury and all the Afro-Cubans who undervalue themselves and those who enjoy white privilege and power and would denigrate blacks as inferior. The last phrase, "My skin knows pain . . ." he sings twice, the second time ending in an impassioned cry. Then his *soneo* (improvisation of verses) alternates with the following estribillos:

> *(1)*
> *Negrito bailador, bendito sea tu color*
> *Tú eres dueño del tambor*

Black dancer, God bless your color
You own the drum!!

(2)
Negrito, moreno, chocolate

(3)
Oye como viene el negrito, oye como viene el moreno
Look, the black man is coming on!

The first chorus cites the propensity of blacks (*negritos*) to dance. The tone, however, despite using the diminutive *negrito* does not diminish the practice of dance or portray it as a quaint stereotype. On the contrary, it proclaims the power and honor of being master of the drum—a central cultural legacy from Africa maintained and developed by Afro-Cubans. "God bless your color," it says. Subtly employing the language of race, the second chorus moves from an ambivalent *negrito*, to a polite *moreno*, to unquestionably sweet *chocolate*. This transition traces an evolution of consciousness (*¡conciencia!*) that Afro-Cuban leaders and thinkers like Macco, Juan Gualberto Gómez, Evaristo Estenoz, Rafael Serra, Carlos Moore, Gloria Rolando, and Nancy Morejón would probably endorse.

Along the way Mayito exhorts over and over again, "levántate" (rise up), "son las horas" (it's about time). At one point he asks, "Why do you get so mad when they call you Big-Lips?" We feel the cycle of suffering and struggle, action and reaction, which leads always to an improved but by no means ideal racial situation in Cuba. The condition of blacks has gotten better, and their contribution to Cuban culture is increasingly acknowledged and evoked for various ends. However, negative realities still exist even as fading shadows, receding against the light of the Cuban struggle for social justice. The final refrain proclaims that the black man, the Afro-Cuban community, is coming on, making progress. Mayito's last words, *aquí to' el mundo está mezclao* (every one here [in Cuba] is mixed), bind Afro Cuba to the nation at large, invoking national unity in a way that invokes racial democracy, Cuba Libre, and Guillén's "Cuban color." He is clearly interested in nation building, not separatism. The key difference though is that he acknowledges the unique experiences and perspectives of Afro Cuba.

Conclusion

Afro-Cuban heritage is an entire body of knowledge, experience, and values that is transmitted orally and through customary practice, stretching from the colonial era to the present day (Roy 2002, 15). This is the sense in which Morejón's "Afro-Cuban essence" really does exist. It exemplifies a maroon aesthetic because it represents *embodied knowledge passed down from generation to generation* since colonial times. In the process a distinct Afro-Cuban culture has developed, which has been gifted with a popular imagination that is capable of substituting elements and adjusting philosophical values to new social situations with great improvisational virtuosity (Barnet 1981, 265). This purposeful transmission of culture under hostile conditions, elaborated by the techniques of raiding and improvisation, has sustained the black population of Cuba and enriched the nation as a whole. I call it Afro Cuba. It is made of history that is both beautiful and ugly.

Since the beginning, the aim of Afro-Cubans has been to gain recognized positions and to act as full members within the society. To survive along the way, they took refuge in cabildos, fraternal societies, celebrations, and expressions of worship that encouraged unity and struggle against their oppressors. At times, Afro-Cubans expressed themselves through newspaper publications or through left-wing political organizations. As these spaces were closed, new ones developed where the discourse of Afro Cuba is still carried on. Timba, the music of Cuba now, is black music, maroon music: *mestizaje musical, música mulata,* musical mixture, stories to tell, open spaces filled with Afro-Cuban voices. Timba, as a contemporary development of Afro-Cuban music, uses the maroon aesthetic to express Afro Cuba, to articulate Afro-Cuban social concerns, which are, it must be emphasized, more about nation building than separatist claims for blackness.

CHAPTER 4
Doing Identity

Man is a self-performing animal . . . in performing he reveals himself to himself.

   —VICTOR TURNER (1986, 81)

¡Tremenda especulación!

   —PAULITO F.G.

Recently in Cuba a social stereotype or character has surfaced; it is referred to as the *especulador*, a seeming reincarnation of *los negros curros* discussed by Fernando Ortiz, who were a unique, flamboyant nineteenth-century type from among the free class of blacks in Havana. They were similar in some ways to the dandy of Renaissance Harlem referenced by Zora Neale Hurston, and also similar to modern-day "sapeurs" from the Congo noted by several African and Africanist scholars (Gandoulou 1989; Gondola 1999; Pype 2007). The character is typically male and identifiable by the (real or affected) ability to enjoy the luxuries of expensive clothing, food, and entertainment (which the majority of Cubans only dream of) and also by the willingness to flaunt this privilege. In fact, the verb form—*especular*—means "to show off" or "to high-side" in Cuban vernacular Spanish. The especulador is closely linked to the lyrical content of contemporary Cuban dance music called timba, as well as to the ways musicians and audiences perceive and "perform" for each other.

    I argue that there is a call-and-response of self-performance that parallels the musical call-and-response, acknowledged as essential to much African-based music by prominent ethnomusicologists (Alén 1999; Chernoff 1979; Manuel 1995). In this performative call-and-response, musicians and their audiences engage each other with language, dance, gestures, and attitudes that respond to the realities of Cuban life today. Social stereotypes or characters like the "especulador," which are based on ways of dressing, speaking, gesturing, and a kind of popular philoso-

8. ¡Tremenda especulación! (Paulito F.G.), 2003.

phy about how to confront reality, are the results of this kind of call-and-response dialogue. The stereotypes are connected to music and its performance, yet they extend beyond. People use certain understandings of race, class, gender, and nation in relation to music to "tamper" with their identities (Jackson 2001).

The figure of the especulador that is expressed in timba is important because it dramatizes the marginalization of Afro-Cubans in contemporary Cuba. Like the free and outlandish *negros curros* of the colonial Cuban port cities, especuladores are the product of transculturation and diaspora; they are tied to specific social spaces and periods of history, and express themselves through individual performance (Ortiz 1995, 1). Through what anthropologist John Jackson Jr. calls "constellations of behaviors" *especuladores* use "practices to shore up their identity" (2001, 185, 187). The practices or actions they choose reveal a lot about the issues of race, class, and gender in Cuban society. Ortiz predicted los negros curros would "live again," and it seems they have returned in the form of the especulador (1995, 3).

This chapter uses the anthropology of performance to examine human behavior in the dance spaces of contemporary Cuba. I discuss the especulador as a pivotal character that is assumable by anyone, no matter their color, yet at once specifically tied to notions of blackness. As part of

this performance, people choose from and employ an array of understandings and representations of race, class, gender, and national identity.
Above in chapter 2, I outlined some key elements of popular music
throughout the African Diaspora that help to explain why the especulador has appeared in Cuban dance spaces to the timba beat. Here, I comment on the social atmosphere in Cuba from the early 1990s to the present, a period during which timba evolved as one of the most dynamic
innovations in Cuban music (Acosta 1999, 10). I weave my discussion of
the especulador around two poles "wealth" and "revelry," each of which
holds a key to his significance as a cultural type or way of being.

The especulador contests some dominant modes while reaffirming
others. For example, he disrupts the association of blacks with poverty
by displaying wealth, and simultaneously reinscribes the common perception of blacks as gaudy or tasteless. At the same time, the especulador invokes folk wisdom through the persona of the "negro curro."
"Curros," who lived in Havana as they had in urban Seville and Lisbon,
were tied to the colonial slave system as workers and interpreters between subjugated Africans and European masters. They used European
styles and took pride in their familiarity with European culture in general. At the same time, they too carried the maroon spirit. Their opposition, however, was not usually physical. Rather it was stylistic and
performative: an internal renegade stance expressed outwardly through
adornment and a pronounced African way of being.

Curros were using both European and African styles to express their
unique identity in colonial Cuba. Their braids displayed a common
African hairstyling technique, perhaps affected also by a desire to imitate or satirize Spanish masters. Clothing styles that were popular in
Seville, Naples, or Lisbon were worn according to aesthetic principles
from Africa (Ortiz 1995b, 39–41). (To make this point Ortiz discusses
the importance of colored fabric, especially head wraps, in various con-
tinental African and Black Atlantic contexts.) The speech of the curros
mixed the grandiloquence of Spanish bards and colonial governors with
the ironic, defiant, verses of *la hampa afrocubana,* the Afro-Cuban un-
derworld. According to Ortiz, through these elaborate outfits, outlandish speech patterns, hairstyles, and so forth the negros curros as-
serted their different status vis-à-vis other Cubans of color and the
dominant white culture, because they were free and because they were
"closer" to Spain and colonial culture by virtue of their often trans-
national origins and metropolitanism. Curros used hybrid styles "to distinguish themselves as free blacks, to chart out and control their own

public space, and resist conventional identity assignments" (Brown 2003, 16). Ortiz approved of using the curro "character" or "type" in contemporary carnival settings, happily stripped of the criminal associations of the real curros of the past.

Bands like La Charanga Habanera and NG La Banda simulate latter-day curros, singing about *wanikiki* (money) and women and driving convertible cars; their performative images are taken from the especulador model. Before analyzing the especulador further, however, allow me to discuss the social circumstances in Cuba that conjured him into being.[1]

Life in Contemporary Cuba, 1990–2000

Ask anybody in Cuba old enough to know and they will probably tell you that the 1980s were heaven. Cuba was a paradise relatively free of tourists, serious crime, and disease and where everything—food, medicine, education, and even some luxury items like televisions and cars—was available. The fall of the Berlin Wall in the autumn of 1989 and the breakup of the Soviet bloc in summer 1991 were, for Cubans, the entrance into a tunnel, a prolonged *apagón* (blackout). Sixty percent of Cuban factories closed down or produced at bare minimum capacity. Electricity generation plummeted, as did the food supply. By Latin American standards, no one was malnourished or starving in Havana, but the daily intake of vitamins and protein fell drastically. After the fall of the Soviet bloc, Cuba could no longer count on a network of trade, credit, and aid with the Soviet Union and Eastern Europe. One joke said, "The revolution has only three problems . . . breakfast, lunch, and dinner" (Cluster and Hernández 2006, 255). However, this crisis reached beyond physical hunger to affect the Cuban outlook on life.

The end of the Cold War also posed new threats to Cuban national security. The Soviet Union had provided a partial shield against U.S. power and influence. In 1992, President George H. W. Bush signed the Toricelli Bill, which effectively tightened the U.S. embargo against Cuba. The key aim of that legislation was to cut off Cuba's trade with U.S. subsidiaries in third countries. The law also tried to block the shipping of merchandise of all kinds to Cuba, stating that any vessel to touch a Cuban port would not be allowed to enter U.S. territory for six months. Finally, the Toricelli legislation gave the U.S. executive the possibility of using communications, information, and ideological influence against Cuba (García Luis 2001, 279). Four years later, Presi-

dent Clinton reluctantly endorsed the Helms-Burton Bill. He was co-
erced to sign it after the Cuban air force shot down two U.S.-owned
planes over international waters (Pérez-Stable 1999, 202–3). The Helms-
Burton Act set forth a detailed program for the recolonization of the island under U.S. trusteeship and demanded compensation for the U.S.
property nationalized in 1959 and 1960. It also demanded compensation
for Cubans (largely Batista supporters) who later became U.S. citizens
and whose property was expropriated after January 1, 1959 (García Luis
2001, 279). The result of these political policy shifts has been a crisis
that is as much political, moral, and physical as it is economic.

The *período especial* or "special period" is the name given to the current time of austerity, but here I describe from 1990 to the present (Sarduy in Bettelheim 2001, 166). It means rationing of resources as if the island were at war. The collapse of the Soviet market, coupled with Cuba's
lack of capital, credit, and energy, which was exacerbated by the U.S.
trade embargo, shook the economy and the collective spirit of the country. Gissell, whom we met in an earlier chapter, is a young woman musician (clarinetist, choral singer, and pianist) and musicologist. She is a
mulata, daughter of a white father and a black mother, both of whom are
medical doctors. She recalls the start of the special period in 1990.

> I remember being around twelve years old and everything was fine. I did
> not want for anything; my parents took me often for ice cream and shop-
> ping. The family had a car, a gift from the State in return for outstanding
> medical service by my parents in Angola (1978) as part of Cuba's project of
> intervention in anti-imperialist wars abroad. There were enough eggs to
> waste, throwing them about for fun or to disgrace those who were leaving
> the island, "abandoning" the Revolution. Paper could be thrown away.
> There was no stifling, ever-present "need" [*necesidad*]. And then one day
> Fidel came on TV and said "Things are going to begin to get scarce now,
> but don't panic . . . be patient." And the very next day there was nothing in
> the stores, and soon after there was chaos, chaos, chaos. There was no gas,
> the car broke down and there was no way to fix it. Everything was scarce.
> It was a very sudden and jarring change. (personal communication 2003)

Gissell's memories are instructive: this was a major rupture, a
shock, and a crisis. In Havana's ever-evolving slang, the eggs she used to
take for granted became known as *americanos* because no one knows
when they are coming or how many there will be. There were no more
Bulgarian canned vegetables, Russian canned meat, German sausages,

or Hungarian wines and sweets (Cluster and Hernández 2006, 256). To cope with the shortage of fuel, cars like the one her parents owned were largely replaced by nearly one million Chinese bicycles, which were distributed through workplaces and flooded the streets of Havana in the mid-1990s (Kapcia 2005, 182). Because buses were few and far between, many habaneros traveled as many as five to fifteen miles to and from work every morning and afternoon. My godmother in Marianao quit work because she didn't earn enough to afford the shoes and clothing she "spent" traveling to and from her job (porque gastaba demasiado en zapatos y ropa yendo pa'l trabajo).

In the new situation, food was scarce and luxury goods were out of the question for most. The fact that Carnival, so important to Cuban culture, was canceled altogether from 1991 to 1996 indicates how difficult things got (Sarduy in Bettelheim 2001, 166). Many had to go without even the respite of television entertainment due to shortages of electric power. The exceedingly popular Coppelia ice cream parlor stayed open, but going for ice cream became an all-day affair, with lines sometimes four hours long. This example of Cuban humor, known as choteo, is common.

> A man walks up to the Coppelia ice cream shop and gets excited. "Coño, there's no line!" And the guard says to him "Not so fast, it's that there's no ice cream . . . Can you imagine a Saturday with no line at Coppelia!?"

Cubans use this kind of dark, ironic humor to mock the very serious lack of resources. In order to create revenue and survive, Cuba has been forced to rethink its economic strategy. For example, unable now to trade sugar with the former Soviet nations in exchange for technology and oil, Cuba has placed new emphasis on health tourism and its pharmaceutical industry, which has been only marginally successful (Feinsilver 1989, 1994; lecture by Cuban economist Pedro Monreal 1999). Economic ties to other Latin American nations like Brazil, Argentina, and especially Venezuela were strengthened during that decade. These and other changes influenced popular music.

Economic Collapse and Recovery Measures

In the decade of the 1980s, an important part of the monetary income of the entire population came from its relationship with the state. Ninety-five percent of employment was state sponsored, and there was a salary system in place that ensured a relatively low level of income inequality (Ferriol Muruaga 1998, 94). At the start of the special period in 1990 the functioning economic model of the national economy was centralized planning and the use of state rather than private capital. By 1985, the government had already made adjustments that allowed some autonomous entrepreneurial activity, for example, opening artisan and farmers markets. Such changes began to negatively impact the social and economic spheres; however, it was not until later that Cuba was forced to more fully incorporate capitalist market strategies, which were undoubtedly at odds with the nation's socialist vision.

There were various responses to the 75 percent decrease in importations from the Soviet bloc. From 1990 to 1993, Cuba's new strategy for economic survival included a package of state-propelled, nonmarket austerity measures, such as reducing electricity consumption and oil deliveries, further rationing food products and consumer goods, and cutting back on bureaucratic personnel (Pérez-Stable 1999, 176). On a social level, the government took measures to stabilize the waning economy: maintaining jobs and pay steady with only gradual adjustments, implementing a stepped-up food-rationing program, price hikes for luxury items (like cigarettes and alcohol), conserving social programs, especially health and education (with less access to medicine, but more doctors to compensate), as well as discussion and consultation with the public about these steps. Schools, hospitals, clinics, and other essential social services all kept functioning, albeit with less resources. Structural changes included opening the island's economy to foreign investment, joint-venture business, and tourism (González 1998; Daniel 2010).

In 1993, the government took steps to address the profound economic crisis by implementing some market reforms—creating a mechanism for the intake and circulation of divisas, liberalizing agricultural cooperatives, and legalizing self-employment in a limited number of activities (Pérez-Stable 1999, 176). On the macroeconomic level, the most drastic change was the legalization of the U.S. dollar. The so-called dollarization of the Cuban economy created an awkward situation in which most people—employees of the state—earn in pesos while many goods are available for purchase only in dollars (Formento 2002).[2] Writers Cluster and Hernández give the example of a white Cuban woman who, after feeling the sting of the special period and even engaging in the black market, finds work by acquiring clothing and shoes to sell in dollar stores, also known as *el shopping* (Cluster and Hernández 2006,

259). Some in Havana opened home restaurants called *paladares*, as part of the reinstated *cuenta propia* (entrepreneur) sector. Fifty or a hundred dollars sent or brought each month by relatives and friends living abroad began to signify a way to survive, especially for many families without other income in dollars (Cluster and Hernández 2006, 262). Soon the total of these remittances equaled 800 million dollars throughout the island (but concentrated mostly in Havana). Some habaneros were able to find refuge in the foreign business sector.

Habaneros of color, however, were largely shut out from this percolating economic world, because they lacked homes to open restaurants and lacked capital to start other kinds of enterprises (for example, a small audio CD pirating business that requires computers, discs, and so forth). The feeling was common in this population sector that old patterns of racial discrimination had reared their head (Cluster and Hernández 2006, 259; Sawyer 2006). Hence, as a dollar economy thrived, Havana also included many of those who had been left out of the recovery: those working in health and education (like El Médico de la Salsa who left that field) and those who lacked remittances and lived in the traditionally blacker districts of Habana Vieja, Centro Habana, and Cerro.

Though corner *bodegas* (grocery stores) continued to distribute minimum rations of staple foods like rice and beans, the dollar stores became the main source for other basics like cooking oil, pasta, canned goods, dairy products, and soap. Throughout Cuba, but especially in Havana, efforts to generate hard currency, through employment in the foreign sector or remittances, accentuated differences between Cubans who have access to dollars and those who do not. With regard to monetary income, what contrasts the present situation with that of the 1980s most is that income associated directly with "illegitimate" work has become more important. This fact has made its mark and transformed previously accepted social values, such as the role of work, the benefit of working for state-run businesses, and the importance of education (Cluster and Hernández 2006, 95).

After being almost totally closed off throughout the 1960s and 1970s, and blossoming some in the late 1980s, Cuba's leadership decided to fully embrace tourism in the 1990s—welcoming visitors interested in the island's diverse terrain and unique wildlife, those in need of health care and surgical procedures unavailable or too expensive elsewhere, those who were hungry for revolutionary lore, or those in search of Afro-Cuban culture (Hagedorn 2001; Daniel 2010; Vaughan and Aldama 2012). By 1990 about 340,000 tourists had visited Cuba, and these numbers increased 82 percent by 1994 to 619,000. Figures for 1995 reached nearly three-quarters of a million tourists, and by 1999 1.6 million people visited (Scarpaci, Segre, and Coyula 2002, 291). Primarily European and Canadian investors engaged in partnerships with the state to build hotels and increase Cuba's popularity and viability as a vacation destination (299–300).

Today tourism is Cuba's number one industry, called the *zafra nueva* (new harvest) because it has displaced sugar as the largest moneymaker. "One of the most controversial projects in Havana in the mid-1990s was the construction of a new five-star hotel . . . the $70 million Meliá Cohiba," which symbolized the push to attract tourist revenue (Scarpaci, Segre, and Coyula 2002, 301). Hotels like Meliá Cohiba, Hotel Riviera, and others, along with nightclubs, are important spaces to attract visitors by presenting music. Like in Renaissance Harlem where jazz flourished in the United States, competition for patrons in Havana provided many opportunities for musicians to ply their trade. El Palacio de la Salsa opened up in Hotel Riviera in 1993. In the same year La Casa de la Música opened its doors. Both were closely associated with José Luis Cortés (director of NG La Banda), timba, and entertaining foreign visitors. Cuban musicians are now allowed to tour in the United States and negotiate recording contracts with international companies to make money, a portion of which is retained by the state as tax. This was unheard of before the special period (Acosta 1999). The number of bands that performed abroad from 1996 to 2000 is comparable to the 1950s, when Cuban music experienced a previous boom (Roy 2002, 192).

As the Turquino Bar of the Habana Libre, the disco in the Comodoro, and the emblematic Tropicana became exclusive spaces for visitors with dollars, alongside La Casa de la Música and Palacio de la Salsa, Cubans without dollars (who were overwhelmingly Afro-Cuban) experienced what some began to call "apartheid tourism" (Cluster and Hernández 2006, 259). The Malecón or Havana's seawall around the port bay, always a center of activity, literally filled at night with people who came to socialize. They came with guitars, homemade rum, and portable radios because they could go nowhere else.

In Cuba, there exists what might be termed an inverted social pyramid in which so-called prestigious professions, such as doctor, teacher, or lawyer, have lost their prestige and earning power in relation to other activities. Activities associated with tourism and the emerging dollar-economy have become more valued (Cluster and Hernández 2006, 95). The inequalities and tensions of the market economy create opportunities for so-called simple economic activities (e.g., selling cigarettes, homemade popsicles, or cigars) to be exceedingly lucrative (Cluster and Hernández 2006, 26). As happened in the former Soviet nations, since the state could not supply people's needs, everyday people struggled to provide for themselves, developing in the process a huge repertoire of strategies for obtaining consumer goods and services.

These strategies, called the "second" or "informal" economy, span a wide range from the quasi-legal to the definitely illegal (Verdery 1996, 27). Thus, inasmuch as there came to be little correspondence between "legitimate" work and income, Cuba risked creating or resurrecting previously suppressed social ills as the citizenry tried to make ends meet. Although this second society never took definite shape as it did in Poland, for example, where dissidents were inspired to live "as if" in a free country, the crisis of the domestic economy, the collapse of communism, and the erosion of the Fidel-patria-revolution saw the people adopt solutions like leaving the country or doing whatever was necessary to put food on the table (Pérez-Stable 1999, 200).

In addition to meeting basic needs, many Cubans (especially young Afro-Cubans) are eager to experience the lifestyles and material comforts to which they are exposed through foreign visitors (mostly from Spain, Italy, Canada, and Mexico) and by Cuban musicians who travel abroad and return as windows on or bridges to the outside world. Cuba's embrace of tourism and the dollar, without providing Cubans full access to either, has created tension within the society. The tension is even worse for Afro-Cubans, who, historically, have experienced marginalization and lack to a greater extent than other Cubans. Today, the verb *trapichear* means to work in the informal economy (Fernández 1997, 54). This comes from *trapiche*, or sugarcane-crushing machinery, evoking the long history of Afro-Cuban slave labor in sugar (see Fraginals 1978; Ortiz 1995a). It is suggestive language because Afro-Cubans are excluded from legitimate economic opportunities and make do instead through the black market.

Often people had no alternative but to purchase on the mushrooming black market. Only there could one find beans or vegetables brought privately from the countryside, as well as powdered milk, cheese, yogurt, and other commodities stolen from the dollar stores in tourist hotels or those maintained for diplomats (*diplotiendas*). The black-market value of the Cuban peso dropped to 150 per dollar in the early 1990s. While Havana saw a tolerated and relatively well-off informal sector, there were also greater levels of discontent and atomization (Kapcia 2005, 182). Skyrocketing inflation, scarcity of food and other life essentials, and a limited sense of individual agency in improving the situation translated into a vicious cycle that was altogether demoralizing (Scarpaci, Segre, and Coyula 2002, 146).

This new attitude is precisely what is most disturbing (and criticized) about *Dirty Havana Trilogy*, the controversial novel by Pedro Juan Gutiérrez. The protagonist, Pedro Juan, and those surrounding him live in a constant struggle to *resolver*, to survive. They seem caught in a malaise of hopelessness that leads to depression and depravity, expressed through loveless sex and shady business. Pedro Juan raises pigs on the rooftop to eat and sell, manages a bootleg rum hustle, and on occasion exchanges sex for gifts from foreign visitors. Through Gutiérrez's work, we enter a Havana landscape where, "as the already weaker sense of community disintegrate[s] in the face of an individual search for survival; the greater the informal sector and ordinary Cubans' access to it, the weaker 'community' [becomes]" (Kapcia 2005, 183; for scholarly perspectives on the special period see also Hernández-Reguant 2009).

These are the folks who took to the streets by the hundreds on August 5, 1994, in the first tumultuous demonstration of popular discontent in Havana in twenty-five years. In response to this unrest the government announced the opening of new farmers markets where small farmers, cooperatives, and state farms could bring fruits, vegetables, and pork from the countryside to sell at prices regulated by supply and demand. These *agromercados* remained expensive in relation to average monthly income but were much cheaper, more accessible, and less morally compromising than the black market (Cluster and Hernández 2006, 260).

As capitalist practices are reintegrated within a socialist framework, the neat duality of two systems in opposition to each other is destabilized. Furthermore, the second economy, which provisions a large part of consumer needs, is parasitic upon the state economy and inseparable from it. Rather than simple opposition, the relationship between the state and the informal economy is symbiotic. As part of the turn toward an international commercial market, the term *timba* was coined to differentiate contemporary Cuban dance music, also called *salsa cubana* or *new salsa*, from the salsa of Puerto Rico, New York, and Latin America, in hopes of increasing its commercial success.

In 1997 the Dream Team Cuba-Timba Cubana was invented by Juan Formell to counter the Buena Vista phenomenon and cash in on renewed international interest in Cuban music with the new sound of Cuba's younger generation (Roy 2002, 181). The group included highly visible bandleaders Adalberto Álvarez, José Luis Cortés, Paulito F.G., Issac Delgado, and El Médico along with other all-star musicians that emerged from each of these groups. According to producer Joaquin Betancourt, who participated in the project as an arranger, Dream Team Cuba failed in the end because it lacked unity. Each member wanted to impose his own style and did little to really collaborate with other artists (interview, 2003). The idea of *the individual over the group*—as displayed by these all-star timberos—is key to the especulador.

Locally, for the most part only Cubans involved in the informal economy could afford to attend the new spaces like El Palacio de la Salsa or La Casa de la Música where timba was engaging international visitors. People's behavior around music—in dance spaces, fiestas, discos, and clubs—often expresses that which for one reason or another cannot be said or sung. It comes out instead *bailando y estando*, dancing and being. For anthropologist John Jackson Jr., interpretations of people's everyday behaviors are useful because what people do locates them within their society in terms of race, class, and gender (2001). This is precisely why it makes sense to think about the especulador. The especulador comes to life through consumption and the ways in which this consumption is signaled to others, invoking at once the maroon and the curro of the past.

The especulador, though usually not mentioned by name, is implied in most timba. Paulito F.G. and other timberos contend that during the most difficult moments of the special period people found solace and escape through their music. People used the music "to forget the shortages, the cutoff electricity, the bad transportation, to find refuge" (Paulito F.G., interview, 2003). I argue that the character of the especulador, like timba, distills several reactions to the economic and subsequent moral and philosophical tensions that have been experienced since the early 1990s. Through behaviors associated with the especulador, people propose identities for themselves. By examining the especulador's connection to wealth and revelry we can understand something about the current Cuban experience, the goals and desires of Cuban youth (especially Afro-Cubans), and how musical and social structure, as well as musical and nonmusical performance, interact.

Definitions of Especular and Especulador

One who is smug and artificial (*autosuficiente y artificial*)

People with "possibilities," ways and means (*gente de posibilidades*)

Folks who like to wear a lot of gold

Pamplinero/pamplinera, or foolish people

One who shows off beyond his real means

One who has never had and wants to show off what little he's got now

A guy who wastes a lot to impress others

More fantasy than reality (*más fantasía que realidad*)

Someone who wants to show what he has to the society, and in a vulgar way

Many Cubans identify the especulador with negative characteristics like falseness, foolishness, or vanity based on external trappings like gold displayed to gain social capital. Everyone has stories about silly people who put on airs of superiority as they wear expensive foreign clothes. Maibelys Carión, a dancer, laughed as she told me about a man who loudly ordered "Beer for everybody, on me!" when really his friend would pay. Musician Pedro Fajardo felt that "to speculate" (*especular*) is to think oneself a god or "endiosarse" (interview, 2003). In contrast to these evaluations, another informant, Rafael, had a different opinion about especulación. He was an intelligent, streetwise man of about forty years who had lived many lives. For him, *especular* (the act of being an especulador) is the way each person expresses his or her Self (*su propio yo*). Here the especulador bears no stigma. Rafael's grandfather had always told him, "According to how [you] dress will be [your] social position" (see fig. 5 in chapter 3).

Their experiences as dark-skinned Afro-Cuban men impressed on them the importance of representing outwardly (performing), through signs like crisp white clothing and clean two-tone shoes, their perceptions of themselves and their hopes for social recognition and success. Because biology (their phenotypic blackness) and geography (their social and physical location among the lower/working class) were set, action was their only way of "tampering" with their identity. If they failed to "do" their identity, identity would certainly, constantly be done to them in the form of race/class exclusion, even in Cuba Libre (de la Fuente 2001; Helg 1995; Sawyer 2006). This "specific conflation of identity and behavior is a potentially useful way of hewing anti-essentialist social identities" (Jackson 2001, 5).

Rafael, his grandfather, and many more black men and women in Cuba construct their own identities through action/performance, in spite of and against negative expectations and stereotypes, which also shape their lives (see chapter 3). As we shall see through the especulador (and later through the public dance), what people do—the clothing they

choose, the dance they dance, the socializing they activate and participate in—determines how they are read and treated by others, and to
some extent how people behave determines who they are. In the
process, sometimes elements of the social scene are thrown out, like
stereotypes; at other times, they are inverted or reworked; and sometimes they are reinforced.

Some people's ideas about the especulador make clear reference to
the Afro-Cuban experience of marginalization as Cuba's have-nots. One
well-known timba hit by La Charanga Habanera exhorts an anonymous
(Afro) Cuban woman to find a sugar daddy so she can have what she had
to have (*Pa' que tengas lo que tenías que tener*). The song, with its ex-
aggerated repetition of the verb "to have" (*tener*), puns on a poem by
Nicolás Guillén, "Tengo" (I have) (Guillén 2002b, 62). In this poem,
Guillén speaks as if for Afro-Cuban people grateful to the Revolution, "I
have what I had to have" (*tengo lo que tenía que tener*, i.e., education,
equality, opportunity, etc.).

The song by La Charanga is interesting because it poses *tener* in the
subjunctive mood: something yet to be achieved (or had), not quite reality. Thus it signals continued inequality, struggle, and the need for action on the part of Afro-Cubans in the context of contemporary Cuba,
referring even to the literary discourse on Afro Cuba by one of its most
important voices. In the song, a male voice commands/suggests that a
woman engage another male to achieve economic stability. This signals
the subordinate position of women in Cuba as well. The other man,
with his motorcycle and his *wanikiki* (money), as the song states, fits
the description of the especulador. Thus the especulador embodies the
marginalized positions of Afro-Cubans and (especially Afro-Cuban)
women.

The expression *especulador* came into common parlance in 1992 or
1993, around the time that the U.S. dollar was legalized, opening new
economic and social "posibilidades" (possibilities) in Cuba (Rafael
Calderón de Armas, interview, 2003). The performance of the especulador is interesting to consider in terms of wealth, which points to relevant economic causes, and revelry, which focuses on situations where
the especulador acts.

Wealth

The especulador wears gold chains and rings, Tommy Hilfiger fashions,
Nike sneakers, and Versace shades. He may drive a nice car with a fan

and a Sony radio. He is quick to flaunt his privilege, his access to these things and experiences that many only dream of. This lifestyle is possible for popular musicians or sports stars that, as stated above, travel abroad, negotiate lucrative contracts for themselves, and are national heroes, treasures, and so on. But what about people who earn between twelve and fifteen dollars monthly at government jobs? In order to portray this image they must necessarily explore alternative avenues to material gain.

The especulador performs desire and the creativity necessary to satisfy it. My madrina told me that El Médico's chart-topping refrain *Hay que estar arriba de la bola* (You've got to be on the ball) struck a chord because he was talking about surviving—by one's wits, by hook or crook, the reality of many Cubans at that time. The following are examples of what he may have meant, taken from my field notes.

> **Smugglin' Meat:** Today for the second time a police officer arrived from Las Tunas in eastern Cuba heavy with beef to sell here in Havana. He came wearing his uniform so no one would stop him with his load—a large suitcase full of frozen carne. While the meat was cut up, he talked about how folks were getting caught in the act with huge boxes of coffee, tanks of honey, etc. It was striking how he separated himself from "them," when he was doing "it" too!

> **Yogur (Yogurt):** Today I was awakened by the shuffling of *chancletas* up the stairs and into the kitchen. When I looked out I saw the family quickly packing the refrigerator with dozens of plastic packs of a milky substance. There was a feeling of urgency, but they were smiling, giddy with some delicious secret. I asked what was happening and they explained that they had gotten access to this yogurt (pronounced yo-gool in Cuban Spanish) at a very low price. They had borrowed a little money from me and purchased as much as they could in hopes of reselling it for a profit. This is what is called *luchando*—hustling by means that are technically illegal, but mostly devoid of a malicious, "criminal" intent.

On the flip side of negocio, there is another reaction to the longing for luxury on the part of Cubans. Presenting false images of affluence or "bluffing" is another characteristic of the especulador. Often those who look the part of the wealthy jet-setter are actually penniless. This kind of fantasizing invites another comparison with hip-hop artists. Take, for example, the rappers who appear in their first music video wearing platinum watches and diamond necklaces, driving Mercedes Benzes and bragging about it all as if it were theirs. Most of them have rented the cars and gotten fake jewelry for the purpose of the video shoot. They have no real wealth, only the status conferred by perceived wealth. In contemporary Cuba, wealth—even this imaginary or symbolic wealth—brings status and a modicum of relief from the tension of desire. It manifests itself through a kind of (ritual) performance in which the desired object is imitated and thus made "real." For example, there is a popular joke about especuladores who nurse one beer all night long at dance spaces like La Casa de la Música in order to present the image of financial means and hide actual lack thereof. *Hasta las familias especulan*—families speculate too—as photographs for weddings and quinceñeras, very important in Cuban culture, are staged using borrowed garments, rented cars, and so forth to give the impression of wealth and abundance.

The especulador definitely echoes the *negros curros* that were the subject of Ortiz's research in the 1920s. Ortiz writes that their self-presentation or performance—the ostentatious clothing, big jewelry, fancy hairstyles, and grandiloquent jive talk—aimed to express their difference from and superiority over the average, enslaved, noncosmopolitan Afro-Cuban person in their community. The curros used pants that fit loosely through the leg, coming to a point at the ankles, and shirts with ruffled sleeves and collars. They also used colorful bandanas around their neck, waist, in pockets, in hand, as well as wrapped around large straw hats (Ortiz 1995b, 49). Pointed-toe, backless shoes called *chancletas* were part of the curro style too. Ortiz emphasizes that they used the Spanish (Andalusian) fashions according to African aesthetic principles, which is an example of transculturation and opposition (à la Burton 1997) in a society that was anticolor and anti-Africa (Ortiz 1995b, 41).

Costume and accoutrement details highlight the importance of appearance over reality and smack also of today's especulador. As far as jewelry, the curros were known for large hoop earrings of gold, which were often fake. The curros wore braided hair like blacks in many parts of the world, but in the context of Cuban society of the time they used the style in a scandalous, exhibitionist way (Ortiz 1995b, 55). Braids have come back again in Cuba. In terms of language, the curros had a unique way of speaking, at once high or elitist sounding in the manner of Spanish poets but incorporating also a special jive all their own, unintelligible to many. They spoke with "a unique inflection in their voice, an overblown speech, a particular language, at once physical and nonsensical" (83). Their way of speaking was accompanied by emphatic, expressive gestures, which were intended to communicate their status as curros. Ortiz also notes that there was an "insolent and challenging" aspect in the curros' speech. "Everything about the curro was public and exhibitionist." The curro moved by "individual initiative and aims" (5–6). The curros were cosmopolitan, reflecting influences from Spain, Africa, and the New World in their unique way of being. Many of the synonyms for *curro* during that time describe today's especulador.

> *mojo:* a person who in actions and dress takes liberties; luxurious, decked out
> *currutaco:* very affected in one's rigorous use of fashion
> *taco:* sharp dresser, affected in one's dress

Both the curros and the especuladores are exhibitionists. At one of the high-energy points in his song "De La Habana" (About Havana) in which he addresses los especuladores, Paulito sings: *¡Levanten la mano pa' que te vean!* Put your hands in the air so that you can be seen! Through their ostentation the *negros curros* at once expressed their condition as freemen, a certain proximity to dominant white culture, and specifically their ties to Andalusia. *Curro* also means "from Andalusia," and most of them came to Havana from there, specifically the city of Seville, economic and naval capital of the Spanish empire. Both the *negro curro* and the *especulador* need proper recognition (*necesitan no ser confundidos por nadie*) and are strongly tied to La Habana, Cuba's metropolitan center (Ortiz 1995b, 14, 51–52).

The performative nature or strategy of these characters was so strong that a verb and related adjective form manifested: *acurrar, acurrado* (Ortiz 1995b, 54), just as in the case of the especulador. Victor Turner's thoughts about performing the self politically apply to both characters: "Self is presented through the performance of roles, and through declaring to a given public that one has undergone a transformation of state and status, been saved or damned, elevated or released" (Turner 1986, 81). The notions of freedom and oppositionality (even despite complicity) link curros and especuladores to the maroon.

The performance of marginal male identity that the especulador exemplifies finds parallels in other parts of the African Diaspora. The *sapeurs* and *sportifs* of the two Congos, *freaky hype types* of Jamaica (Hope 2006, 34–35), Harlem *zoot suiters* (Hurston 1985), and *hyphy boys* in Oakland, California, are similar characters. In each case, appearance (clothing, accessories), performance (speech, gestures, actions), and music (instrumental, voice, dance) are key in achieving some kind of transformation: they "envelop and develop the body, draw the cultural contours of the social group, and bring out a plurality of egotistical identities," remaining always, however, "a response, a way for this 'sacrificed' youth to adjust to changing realities over which they have virtually no control" (Gondola 1999, 48). All of these characters are associated with and shaped by specific sounds (music styles/subcultures) in particular spaces (*inna di dancehall*, public dances, dollar-only clubs, and so on)

In the "cousin especulador" phenomenon of the Congolese *sapeur*, young men use fashion (*sape*) to tamper with their identity or to "blur social lines and make class values and social status illegible" (Gondola 1999, 31). Sapeurs emerged in the early years of the nineteenth-century colonial era and became visible during the war years of the 1910s. They were linked to the dawn of barlike dancehalls in Brazzaville and Kinshasa. According to Gondola, the sapeur is "an illusionist . . . concealing social failure and transforming it into apparent victory" through the use of fashion and performance. Like the especulador, the sapeur is "artificial" (Gondola 1999, 26, 31). He discovers himself as a being and a social actor through the identity that appearances obtain for him. Interestingly, Gondola notes that beyond actual clothes, "a spoken (*even sung or danced*) clothing [performance] makes the sapeur the actor and conjuror" of his assumed identity (Gondola 1999, 25; emphasis added).

For sapeurs themselves, "Sape is a value. It means rediscovering something that's ours. Sape reflects us . . . It makes us" (Gondola 1999, 32). These perspectives mirror views about the especulador in Havana—considered "*artificial*" and "*fantasioso*" but also a genuine way of expressing one's *self*. Fantasy and artificiality are strategies to construct and transform identities. Both the especulador and the sapeur are "hybrid models of manhood that originated in the hedonistic culture of *l'ambiance* [*la farándula* or nightlife] located in the bar and expressed by . . . music" (Pype 2007, 265).

Also in the Congo, *sportifs* (fighting boys) "use their body to become someone" in a different way (Pype 2007, 251). Rather than fashion, sportifs use physical fitness and intimidating body language to transform themselves socially. By training in martial arts and competing in tournament-like daytime matches and nighttime brawls that often end in serious injury or even death, sportifs barter "bodily strength for social prestige" (Pype 2007, 258). They are linked to music because important musicians hire them as bodyguards. Their way of posturing and walking has been caricatured in Congolese popular dance.

Similarly, in Oakland, California, so-called hyphy boys use erratic behavior and aggressive body language to give the impression of craziness. They have converted the clothing of poor ghetto youth into a fashion statement that is respected by those who use it and feared by those outside of the style (like the elderly or bourgeois). They wear oversized white T-shirts, jeans, and dreadlocks in their hair. They are associated with hip-hop musicians from the San Francisco Bay Area like E 40, Mr. Fabulous, Eazy A Ski, and others. Hyphy boys are known to perform a dance—called "goin' dumb" or "gettin' hyphy"—in which they shake their dreadlocks, jump, twist, and contort their visage into what they call the "thizz face." By donning the oversize white T-shirt, the dreads, and so forth, young black men in Oakland disappear into this hyphy identity, celebrating their marginality within the city and evading individual responsibility for any rumpus they might kick up there.

Across the diaspora we see people using "technologies of the self," including dress/fashion, dance, gesture, athletic training, speech, violence, and even magic, to tamper with identity (Pype 2007, 260–61). One troubling fact of these characters and strategies is that they seem to value economic strength above all else. This echoes W. E. B. DuBois's warning to African Americans in the aftermath of slavery and Reconstruction not to follow mainstream U.S. culture in its thirst for wealth at the sacrifice of goodness (DuBois 1994, 47–55). The performative strategies used by marginalized peoples to access wealth and status and adjust their identities in relation to European-controlled resources and values evoke again the maroon aesthetic and the concept of "opposition," that is, resistance from within a system, using tools and logic borrowed from the system (Burton 1997, 6). The strategies chosen mark the marginal position of these people in society and also their boundedness within it. Each character is tied to specific spaces, each with his own social dynamics.

By the mid-1990s, the Cuban economy had stabilized somewhat. In the summer of 1995, Castro noted, "All openings have entailed risks. If we have to carry out more reforms, we will do so. For the time being they are unnecessary" (Pérez-Stable 1999, 177). The government was adamant that Cuban socialist values would not be sacrificed in the name of economic reform. Although in 1995 the government authorized additional activities for self-employment, it continued to dampen private initiatives by sporadically confiscating "illegal gains," harassing "profiteers," and imposing stiff taxes payable in hard currency (Pérez-Stable 1999, 177). Reflecting on the atmosphere of the time, Paulito F.G. suggests that the timba movement lost state support and, in fact, incurred some hostility because of the wealth and love of wealth/especulación that were being generated by it. Tension developed because the creation of wealth helped support the Revolution, but at the same time it upset the ideal of economic equality.

> There was a time during the special period when we [los timberos] were an important economic help for the Revolution, but later this changed—precisely because of the great demand we had created—this became something that was frowned upon in a society like this one. (Paulito F.G., interview, 2003)

Timba focused world attention on Cuban music while also highlighting uncomfortable social realities in Cuba (see chapters 2 and 3). As he explained this, Paulito's cell phone rang—a sign of difference in 2003 (though no longer), like the curros' loud chancletas or flaming pañuelos in the colonial era.

Identity is formed and reconfigured "by acting on the body through the specific mechanisms of identification and recognition produced in the intimate interaction of performer and crowd" (Gilroy 1993, 90). Many young people in Cuba, but particularly Afro-Cubans, aspire to at least identification with and some qualities of the especulador. Many of these qualities are defined and communicated through music and its performance and temporarily mask the especlador's often frustrating socioeconomic realities.

Revelry

In his smash hit song "De La Habana," timba singer Paulito F.G. describes the especulador. According to him especuladores are "la gente que te regala una sonrisa por la mañana, y después salen a formar lo suyo de madrugada, porque les gusta la salsa" (the ones who give you a smile in the morning and are gone in the wee hours of the night to do their thing, because they love salsa). As the song ends, the chorus asks "¿Dónde están los especuladores?" (Where are the speculators?), and Paulito exhorts them to wave their hands in the air, adding that Havana is the place for the most tremendous "especulación." The image in Paulito's song is one of a party-loving, self-aware individual, interested in enjoying life and being recognized. Conspicuous wealth and consumption are important parts of the image. The nightclubs, dancehalls, bars, and busy streets of Havana are ideal places to assert one's especulador status, and often individuals will go out to do just that.

As Paulito sings, the audience takes in his cool, cocky persona that is expressed by talent and also by wealth (clothes, jewelry, and so on). As they dance, many are inspired to emulate him without the means to do so. The especulador character has developed as an entity and identity that express this desire. He is both real and imagined, as those that are emulated and those who emulate (through negocio/business or bluffing) are both especuladores. This character may be a symbolic representation of how Cubans perceive themselves in the encounter with the capitalist ethic in North American and Western European tourism. It makes sense that musicians who are perhaps most in touch with these intruders should be mediators in this relationship.

Manolín, El Médico de la Salsa, one of the brightest and most charismatic stars at the height of the timba movement, is also the picture of the especulador. He was always smartly dressed, often in a dapper suit with a hat, elegant and slightly gangsterish. There was the air of a trickster about him. The fact that he was no great vocalist technically made him rely on storytelling and pithy, rhythmic phrases that express everyday life and make people dance. His background as a gynecology student who turned to music out of dissatisfaction with his life possibilities reflects the frustration of an entire generation of Afro-Cubans. Manolín came out in 1992, and by 1994, there were antigovernment riots in the streets of Los Sitios in Havana, a black neighborhood. In this way, Manolín was "a character perfectly tuned to the new social reality of the special period" (Perna 2005, 67).

> As the life of ordinary Cubans receded to 4th World levels, the stars of salsa projected a representation of success and sophistication, an image of escapism and self-empowerment, which, in the context of the decline of the economic role of the state, acquired obvious political meanings. (Perna 2005, 66)

In 1996, a doctor earned $15 per month, while Manolín earned $9,200 per month. His success seemed to represent the triumph of materialism and individualism over revolutionary moral values. According to Manolín, "people started associating money with me" (Cantor 1998). Manolín, Paulito F.G., and bands like La Charanga Habanera and Bamboleo became symbols of the new market-adjusted pop artist, articulating into a modern, cosmopolitan image the desires and aspirations of their young black barrio audiences (Perna 2005, 73). Like Manolín, the especulador speaks and performs in the language of the black barrio; in Manolín's words, with a little *guapería*, that Afro-Cuban feel.

El Médico became so popular that by the time of my interviews (roughly ten years after his start and two years after his departure from Cuba), people talked about their experiences dancing to his music in a rapturous way. Many described those times at La Tropical and the public dances as the best moments in their lives. "Todo lo que hizo pegó" (Everything he did was a hit) (radio personality Rolando Zaldívar, interview, 2003). His duels with archrival and friend Paulito F.G. are the stuff of legend.[3] The choruses would go on and on; there was always another humorous, funky phrase to inspire the massive crowd to dance. Some regretted never seeing El Médico at El Palacio de la Salsa or at La Casa de la Música, because they couldn't afford it, while others talked about the chic, exclusive crowd and people's desperation to enter those clubs. When Manolín defected in 2001 he left a mark on the musical history of the island.

The comparison of Manolín, El Médico de la Salsa, with the especulador shows how the especulador expresses a desire for a quality of life that is difficult, if not impossible, for most Cubans to achieve in contemporary Cuba. There is a joyous abandonment of socialist values in favor of financial gain, and the individual is placed above the collective. Due to the pressure that a character like the especulador exerts against the socialist structure of the country, he is politically charged. Musicians were allowed to negotiate their own contracts for foreign tours and with recording labels (Decree-Law no. 140, 13 Aug. 1993, Resolution of the Ministry of Culture no. 61, 4 Nov. 1993). Touring was encouraged and became relatively easy, while entrance fees to clubs were charged according to demand. The cover charge to see Manolín or Paulito soared to $30.

At the same time, we should not imagine that timba artists were totally free agents. Historical features, musical vitality, and business politics occasioned timba's boom (Roy 2002, 9). Timberos were enmeshed in state systems that organized labor, including music. For example, in 1989, Artex was created as a state-owned agency for managing the foreign engagements of Cuban artists, replacing older, less efficient institutions with similar functions. Musicians worked as members of various agencies (*empresas*) that Artex coordinated. Recording brought fame, but money was earned through live shows. Popularity was won through radio play, which exposed artists to censorship, as certain songs could be excluded (Perna 2005, 91).

¿Dónde están los especuladores?

I asked Paulito to explain what he meant to say in his song "De La Habana."

> PFG: To me la especulación de La Habana is a song that denotes a nostalgia that Cubans outside Cuba feel, the sense of talking about my city in a warm, tender way. . . . You know the world is full of Cubans and they're all asking 'How's Havana?' But why do I use the term especuladores? It's that everywhere I go . . . there is always some speculation as to what's happening in Havana. People speculate and make up things that aren't true.

According to him his song has nothing to do with our discussion of the especulador so far. He claims that people misinterpret his lyrics when they envision and embody the especulador as discussed in this chapter. However, even if Paulito's intention is not to invoke this character, the public's interpretation is just as important. The very word *especulador* is fraught with meaning. At the start of the Revolution, those too slow to embrace necessary sacrifices (the surrender of businesses, properties, etc.) were called *especuladores*. Thus at a time of economic transition and social tension the term *especulador* puns on itself and restages the performance of *el negro curro*. In many registers of language, ranging from speech and appearance to action, the especulador expresses Afro-Cuban experience in contemporary Cuba.

Conclusion

Drawing on the African, Caribbean, and other diaspora musical concepts of collective participation and call-and-response, timba articulates in its sound the tensions within Cuban society during the special period. In this social and musical context, the especulador has embodied the ideals of some Cubans in the form of a cultural type or performance. His image of flashy dress, bluffing, big spending, and machismo is significant in terms of Cuban responses to their current national situation. Just as musicians use already popular slang to make catchy refrains and create new slang that becomes accepted and widely used, even in nonmusical settings, ways of being—like those of the *especulador*—are developed through musical performance. By *performance*, I do not mean the simple "playing" of music. Rather, I invoke it as a life strategy in contemporary Cuba. In the words of performance theorist Margaret Drewal, performance is "a means by which people reflect on their current conditions, define and/or reinvent themselves and their social world, and either reinforce, resist, or subvert prevailing social orders" (1991, 2). Cubans (especially Afro-Cubans) seem to be defining desire, positioning themselves in relation to (systems of) wealth, and questioning the social order that denies them all of this. And while some would say "timba has nothing to do with politics" (La Charanga Forever, interview, 1999), a politicized reading of timba and the especulador deserves consideration. The Cuban social situation has spawned it, and it is undeniably charged with politics.

In the case of the especulador, musical and nonmusical performance intertwine. Musicians sing about wealth during concerts and display it to their audiences; the audiences "wear" their ideas of wealth and desire, represented by fashion, gesture, and so on. The performative dialectic between reality and illusion symbolizes the Afro-Cuban struggle for equality and opportunity yet to be wholly fulfilled. Away from musical contexts, people continue to perform these interpretations, often using the language (speech, dress, gesture, etc.) that has been developed in nightclubs in dialogue with musicians. By reading timba lyrics, considering its sound and performance elements, and analyzing the self-performance of individuals influenced by these in both musical and nonmusical contexts we learn about reactions to the social, political, and economic moment in which Cubans are living.

The sapeur, the sportif, and the hyphy boys, like the especulador, are associated primarily with men; however, each exists within wider social contexts that, of course, include women (Gondola 1999, 28; Pype 2007, 251). The *mujer chismosa* (gossip), the *jinetera* (hustler/prostitute), and the *santera* are examples from Havana, while *higglers* (entrepreneur saleswomen) and *skettels* (harlots) are similar activist, bodacious, aggressive female characters from Kingston, Jamaica (Hope 2006). Pype calls on scholars to locate these kinds of performative characters

9. Especuladores at La Casa de la Música in Centro Habana, 2003.

in relationship to others within their respective contexts. Doing so with specific attention to women is an exciting area for new research. How, for example, do women perform the especulador differently, or if at all? What other characters or performances do women inhabit or "conjure"?

To summarize my assessment of the situation: For Afro-Cubans the character of the especulador and the strategy of especulación are ways to escape perceived inferiority and unattractiveness. In the maroon analogy I have been developing, they constitute more weapons or tools with which to fashion the self, and another instance of complicit contestation. In this complicity, their emphasis on *self-determination* places the maroons/especuladores in conflict with would-be allies—for example, associating themselves with masters against fugitive slaves in the colonial era or embracing capitalist hedonism in the midst of socialist revolution. In a historical context of hostility and marginalization, what seem like unfortunate choices or stances also demonstrate the supreme importance of self-determination, above all else, within the maroon aesthetic of Afro Cuba and timba. In this way, along with sapeurs, hyphy boys, and other social types or characters from throughout the diaspora, the especulador reiterates a complex renegade stance on the part of black Cubans (especially youth).

CHAPTER 5
The Joy Train: Dance Spaces in Havana

Nowadays the transformation of our customs, easy eroticism and the grow-
ing mechanization of life have calmed the frenzy for dance in Cuba; but
still dance continues to be the main and most enthusiastic pastime of the
Cuban people, its most genuine product, its most universal export.

—FERNANDO ORTIZ

In this epigraph, published in 1951 during a moment of economic ascent
for Cuba's elite, technological advances, and the increased presence of
U.S. tourism, Fernando Ortiz recalls a past that he perceives as health-
ier because the true Cuban values were still alive, not yet compromised
to the detriment of Cuban culture (Ortiz 1951, 188). Ortiz describes a
present and near future where the importance of dance among Cubans
would decrease due to the accelerated pace and changed customs of
modern life. Whether or not he was correct in these visions, Ortiz was
right-on in affirming the central place of dance among Cubans. By that
time, Afro-Cubans were already very limited in terms of spaces in
which to express their cultural perspective. More than half a century after Ortiz's writing, dance in Cuba continues to be a great deal more than
a pastime or simple diversion, but rather a national compulsion, part of
the Cubanness of faith, hope, and love that Ortiz calls *cubanía* (in
Suárez 1996, 8).

This chapter continues to examine spaces where timba is the
medium for the performance of identities, but here I look specifically at
public dances in contrast to events at tourist-oriented spaces such as La
Casa de la Música, and at a related "intermediary dance space" called La
Tropical. Each represents a site with different characteristics, while all
named spaces share timba music as the medium for social (inter)action.
Building on previous chapters, I approach these phenomena as important environments for negotiating space in the ongoing evolution of
Afro-Cuban identity and Cubanness through performance. The free
open-air public dance, or *baile público*, is signaled as one of the most

10. Alegría/Joy, 2003.

dynamic social settings in Cuba due to the diversity of the people who are present and the power of their unified action through music and dance. I suggest again that in the absence of *cabildos, sociedades,* and so forth, public dances take on some of the functions of historical black social spaces. Thus they are important for the continued development of Cuban society and culture at large.

In his book *Gallos y toros en Cuba,* about the significance of cockfights and bullfights in Cuban identity formation, historian Pablo Riaño considers "la formación de la cubanidad" (the making of Cubanness), taking into account economic and political factors as well as the role of cultural expressions in the process (Riaño 2002, 12). Riaño's understanding of cockfights and bullfights as "everyday play and spectacle" (performance) and as "espacios de sociabilidad" (social or performance *spaces*), crucibles for social interaction, is useful in considering the significance of dance spaces in Cuba. He analyzes how the social dynamics of these spaces—*what* took place, *who* interacted, and *how*—have determined the elevation and nature of one or various national cultures (12). He introduces the idea that the struggle to determine how cockfights and bullfights fit into national culture at the turn of the twentieth century definitively affected the use of public spaces in Cuba. Always at issue are the questions, Which part of the Cuban population is affected? What are their traditions? To what do they aspire in their diversity?

Today, at the start of a new century, public spaces are still important in the process of creating Cuban identity and culture. With Riaño in mind, I focus on dance spaces that host the performance of identity for Cuba in general and for Afro Cuba especially. Because of their particular characteristics the public dances are the black cultural spaces par excellence of contemporary Cuba.

Throughout Cuba's history, instrumental music, dance, and song have been common and of great importance. The *areítos* of the native populations of Cuba (soon eradicated by the conquering Spaniards) are a precursor of the public dances of today. Fray Bartolomé de las Casas writes that "they loved their dances, to the rhythm of songs. . . . their beat, in their voices and in their steps, was a sight to see, because they brought together three or four hundred men [and women]" (Esquenazi Pérez 2001, 27–28).

Certainly the music and performance practices (both sacred and secular) brought to Cuba by enslaved Africans marked the incipient tradition of gathering to act collectively through music, song, and dance. Ortiz calls the music of the Africans brought to Cuba a music "of construction not decoration," of action not just distraction (1993b, 29). Cabildo processions on the Day of the Three Kings (January 6) served as a pressure valve for the Cuban economic-social system of slavery. They provided brief respite for the sufferers and, in doing so, reduced the threat of rebellion and improved morale, thereby preserving the plantation or economic system for its masters (336). Of course, cabildos and their activities also provided a space where African culture could develop and flourish as well as be protected and conserved. Dance spaces in Cuba, especially street processions and the open-air public dances discussed here, are part of this old tradition.

In the wake of the 1959 Revolution, *círculos sociales* (recreation centers), such as those named for Patrice Lumumba and Cristino Naranjo, opened and replaced old segregated social clubs and societies. The new centers were for all to dance together. As Dunham noted for Haiti, dance spaces offered the opportunity for diverse segments of the population, with differences of history, educational level, and skin complexion, to interact with one another in peace, in situations not regulated by laws. Nevertheless there were moments in which the dance spaces or recreational centers were not considered important in comparison to other priorities of the new revolutionary society (like literacy, housing, and national security). Many spaces were closed by the state at various times. For example, El Salón Rosado in the famous dance venue La Tropical was closed for many years between the end of the 1960s and the 1980s.

Cuba's socioeconomic crisis, beginning at the start of the 1990s, which as yet has not ended, has boosted emphasis on music and dance as economic products for trade (see chapter 4). Cabaret shows in Havana, like at the Tropicana nightclub (different from La Tropical), continue to entertain foreigners as they have for decades, as do performances by small bands and roving minstrels. In addition, recording facilities like Abdala Studios (built in 1998 with state-of-the-art technology) have been developed, along with record companies like Cubarte and Caribe Music. Ministries have been formed to better administer the production and diffusion of popular music, both traditional (son, bolero, guaracha) and contemporary (salsa/timba, hip-hop, rock, reggaetón).

In addition, new kinds of venues for music consumption were created especially for tourists: El Palacio de la Salsa, La Cecilia, and La Casa de la Música are examples. Though there has been a new focus on promoting music for the masses (especially the masses of tourists), differences in income, access to U.S. currency, and other side effects of the responses to the Cuban economic crisis have complicated the matter and made racist attitudes from yesterday resurface. Related to this, a negative effect on the perception of La Tropical and especially the free public dances held at La Piragua, Plaza Roja of 10 de Octubre, and La Plaza de la Revolución has emerged also. The perception is that opportunities for recreation and amusement for young people have decreased.

To better understand how the dance spaces reflect and influence the daily reality of Cubans, methodical observation was conducted in various dance spaces in Havana. The location of the dance space, the time of the show (day or night), the crowd with relation to the capacity of the place, a characterization of the public (age, race, Cuban/foreigner), and its interaction with other dancers and musicians as well as the orchestra are the factors that were considered routinely. The main questions that dominated the inquiry were, Who frequented which dance spaces and why? How was it that various successes in and challenges to Cuban society were expressed in the characters and behaviors that animated these dance spaces?

Following the work of Katrina Hazzard-Gordon in *Jookin'*, but not exactly, I observed two types of dance spaces in Havana: juke and commercial spaces, each with its own continuum of variations. Hazzard-Gordon's "juke continuum" refers to institutions that appear exclusively in the black community and are essentially underground, thus requiring practically no assistance from public officials in order to function (1990, x). They can be linked in form and function directly to Africa, employing group participation, call-and-response singing and musical form, and the "hot circle" as performative tools. The juke continuum in Cuba includes free open-air public dances (*bailes públicos*), *rumbas de solar*, *toques de santo*, and *pun pun* (impromptu block parties).

In my observation of Cuban spaces that belong to what Hazzard-Gordon calls "the commercial urban complex," I include nightclubs, cabarets, discotheques, and official rumba Saturdays (Hazzard-Gordon 1990, x). These events and spaces require official sanction and have no direct precursors in the African past. They reveal social hierarchy in a way that is related to, yet different from, public dances. Most often I use La Piragua (an open-air space in the Vedado neighborhood near the Malecón where free public dances are held), La Casa de la Música nightclub, and La Tropical to compare types of dance spaces; however, this chapter rests on the fact that free open-air public dances or *bailes públicos* are where timba music is dominant.

This chapter also situates La Casa de la Música where timba music was the main attraction in the form of live bands and recorded music played by deejays and where both Cuban and foreign dancers congregated for a fee. I also comment on the famous Cuban music/dance venue called La Tropical, which sits in between the public dance (*baile público*) at places like La Piragua and the dollar-only clubs like La Casa de la Música. Its price is intermediate between the free public dances and expensive dollar-only clubs. Also its history is of intermediate length, shorter than that of public dances and longer than recently developed dollarized venues. La Tropical becomes a third dance space that is a middle ground on the continuum between the public dances exemplified in La Piragua and dollar-only clubs like La Casa de la Música.

Anthropologist and dancer Katherine Dunham describes the sociological function of various kinds of group dances in Haiti (including among others Mardi Gras, Carnival, elite clubs, and peasant dances). A major function of these dances was to generate "social cohesion and solidarity" and to release the tensions of a people who were living under rigid economic, political, and social pressures (1983, 45). Dunham also notes the development of dance technique as (1) an instrument of sexual attraction; (2) gratification of exhibitionist tendencies through the performance-audience relationship; and (3) the development of artistic values and appreciation (45). These functions are true of contemporary dance spaces in Cuba. Cuban dance spaces contain vestiges of racism that persist in spite of progress, which are worked out and performed as people choose where to dance. Frustrations about living conditions in contemporary Cuba are relieved through the energy of the dance and the sociability of the dance space. Ways of being (Afro) Cuban are exhibited and negotiated.

Public Dances: La Piragua

In the United States, free public dances like those in Cuba, where first-rate acts comparable to Los Van Van or Paulito F.G. perform, occur infrequently. The North American way of life is oriented to the profit motive and not to the promotion of culture in and of itself, so it permits limited space for these types of free events. Nevertheless, when they happen, everybody takes part (imagine Sting or Earth, Wind and Fire in Central Park) with little sense of taboo or disdain from other sectors of the society (for example, the privileged or wealthy that could easily pay for the same concert). Not too many people say, "Oh no, I don't go to those things!" On the contrary, in the Cuban capital of Havana, this opinion is heard quite often.

Many Cubans say they would never attend a public dance at La Piragua (a plaza in El Vedado on the Malecón near the famous National Hotel), La Plaza de la Revolución, or especially at Plaza Roja in 10 de Octubre district. They believe they should avoid the people that go there and the problems that they create. People's opinions about timba and places where it is performed (including all three types of spaces: *bailes públicos*, dollarized clubs, and "intermediary dance spaces" like La Tropical) are tied to ideas of social stratification and black inferiority. Their statements reveal that racism persists along with a color-based hierarchy of wealth, opportunity, and status. What can be done, especially through the popular music and public dances themselves, to improve the situation? As black cultural spaces, what function do these dances serve for the benefit of Cuban society at large?

Pedro Sarduy, Cuban poet and consistent observer of Cuban society from England, writes that in the free open-air dances, the national passion for dance has few limits (2001, 171). He suggests that in the baile público something happens that nurtures the collective soul of Cuba. U.S. journalist Eugene Robinson sees them functioning as "an exercise in massively parallel computation, many minds, each solving its own bit of an otherwise unsolvable problem" through music and movement (2004, 6–7). Specific responses to the realities of daily life are improvised in a web of complex relationships with infinite possibilities—critiquing, creating, and embracing through dance. Of course, Cuban cultural theorist Antonio Benítez-Rojo has the baile público in mind when he calls the Caribbean itself a feedback machine, one that is centered on performance in the public domain (1996, 11). As part of the process of truly integrating everyone, and as an indicator of the nation's progress, dance spaces are important. Fidel Castro explained that true change couldn't come through laws but only through education and persuasion with respect to practices instilled socially over generations, especially in the case of racism (1983, 395–97). The real state of the situation is perceived through people's behavior: where and with whom they decide to spend their free time; with whom they choose to *dance*.

In contrast to the negative attitudes that were expressed by many, I have had many positive experiences at public dances. Most often they have been peaceful gatherings of people with their music. In those moments the world seemed in perfect harmony. On one occasion, while dancing at La Piragua with the orchestra Azucar Negra, I met several very decent, educated people, something I did not expect due to the bad reputation of public dances. They explained to me that they always go to the public dances because they are one of the delights of their country and a very good form of entertainment. The majority of the people in attendance were mulato or black, but I also saw white folks "getting down" with the orchestra. The mix brought to mind Guillén's phrase "Quien no tiene de congo tiene de carabalí": all Cubans have African genetic and cultural heritage. The Afro-Cuban essence confounds color. Although people danced in pairs and groups of all ages, we, the youth of between fifteen and forty years of age, predominated.

Women dressed in short shorts, low-riding hip-hugger jeans, a *bajichupa*[1] or another light type of blouse, spandex, and sometimes short dresses. The clothes were tight fitting and bright, calling attention to dancers' movements as they danced. The men wore jeans and T-shirts, representing U.S. sports teams like the New York Yankees or brand names like Adidas. They wore camouflage print pants and vests, sunglasses, ball caps, Kangol snipers, and Gilligan-style *pachanguitas*. All of these images show how much Cubans enjoy dressing in the latest fashion, showing off according to their means. Jewelry—including gold chains, both thick and slim, bracelets, and rings—was used, but not in excess in order to avoid the attention of any thieves. Some go very well dressed and others do not, but everyone dances regardless of attire. People dress very comfortably in order to endure the heat of the music and bodies in motion, and to return home on foot. The fashion of the public dance, with its provocativeness and colors, is very sensual as are the gestures of the dancers. Here again I saw an African use of European and Euro-American styles, which were reminiscent of the curros. Even with the noticeable adornment, the primary focus remained on music and dance.

The language of the dance is the language of the barrio. Phrases like *sentimiento y manana* (feeling and flavor), the terms *salvaje* (savage) and *monstruo* (friend or man), gleeful exhortations like *¡Mátame!* (Kill me!), and complaints like *¡Qué fulankere, asere!* (How terrible, man) or *estoy palmiche* (I'm broke) are used in the dance as in the neighborhood. The sayings carried a stigma of being "ghetto" (*barriotero*), vulgar, and ridiculous for some. I was reminded of the *negros curros* and their grandiloquent speech, sometimes encoding secret messages, always signifying Afro-Cuban identity.

Joy is created and identity is negotiated inside of the public dance spaces. This happens through the interaction of individuals and groups that make up the public, and also through the interaction between the public and the musical group. The main form of expression is dance. Monetary transactions, conversations, interactions between Cubans from diverse sectors of society are all galvanized by dance. Electricity fills the air as pistonlike hip movements and precise foot patterns "beat" (*machucar*) the music. Imagine the steady drop of pestles in African mortars.

The gestures of the dances are very dynamic and mark clear distinctions between men and women. Their movements are uniquely Cuban but also similar to those of dancers from Haiti, Brazil, Jamaica, the Democratic Republic of the Congo, Oakland, and other parts of the African Diaspora. Men use dance gestures taken from rumba: pulling on the legs of their pants or their crotch at certain points in the casino dance, as when male *rumba columbia* soloists displayed their virility and dance skills on the docks of Havana and Matanzas. When not dancing casino, men usually dance behind women, thrusting their pelvises slightly forward as they follow the woman's movement, echoing the *vacunao* gesture of sexual conquest from *rumba guaguancó*. Males express sensuality and machismo through dance in the force with which they care for their companions, their alertness to the approach of other men, and so on. If alone or in all-male groups, their maleness is proven by their confidence and charisma in attracting women. Gestures of protection like blocking or covering the woman while dancing are common. Similarly, there are many ways of calling a woman's attention and beckoning her to come near.

Women's movements attract attention, but women do not accept the overtures of just any man. When an unwanted suitor approaches or beckons to her, the woman's body language responds, aggressively communicating, "What are you calling me for?" and stating, "I am not interested!" Sometimes men grab women by the arm or touch them with sensual flirtatiousness, but if the lady is not amused or if her boyfriend is coming up behind her, a fight could break out. Women express strong sensuality through the dance as well. When dancing casino with men, women always follow, executing the patterns and turns that the man draws. When the woman faces away from the man she leads the dance with the movement of her hips marking the basic casino step, rocking rhythmically side to side, or rolling the hips in the *tembleque.* Men and women together exude Africa in the Caribbean.

Groups of friends form small circles within the mass, which itself creates a semicircle in relation to the stage where musicians perform.

11. End of the summer public dance, 2003.

People dance casino in closed partner dance position, executing complex turns and foot patterns, dynamic isolations of the shoulders, chest, and hips; and just as much, if not more, people dance separated. Many ask why and lament "the end of casino," which has resulted in a kind of rescue of this dance form, which was probably never really in danger. The reasons why folks dance apart include (1) the long duration of many timba songs, especially live performances that can be ten, fifteen, or twenty minutes in length—a long time to dance without tiring or wearing out one's choreographic imagination as leader of the dance; (2) the emotion of various choruses that causes a jolt of energy that is more easily expressed by a leap followed by a gyrating descent to the floor *en plie* than by a casino turn; (3) the sensuality and raw sexuality that are expressed in some songs inspire partners to dance close, free of the formality of dancing in closed partner position; and lastly (4) the great numbers of people in a limited space. If you can dance casino *en un solo ladrillo* (in one small spot), then dancing apart but *pegao* (pressed together) needs half that much space.

The function and great value of the public dance is as a space of catharsis and transformation where, at least for a time, life's drudgery can be forgotten, and one can lose his or her head and ride the train of

12. A couple dances casino, 2003.

happiness. In this way the *baile público* is related to the *areítos* of the old native population, the Yoruba *wemilere*, and creole *rumbas* in Cuba. Like those events, the *baile público* represents one of the few spaces for the cultural expression and identity formation of marginalized peoples.

A bottle of rum sells for thirty pesos (moneda nacional, Cuban money), and a half bottle sells for twenty, but when the dance gets hot and people get thirsty, the price rises to forty pesos per bottle. Snacks that are for sale are simple and do not vary much: plantain chips, pork sandwiches, roasted peanuts, cookies, gum, and suckers, as well as flavored sugar water, usually cola, orange, melon, or pineapple. When my friends and I went to dances we usually ate beforehand at home and brought our own rum or beer from some nearby bar, in order to economize. Only at the end of the night might we consider purchasing *pan con timba* or pizza from a vendor. The sale of these items in the public dance had no air of intrigue but rather one of legitimate business, maybe due to the anonymity afforded by the great mass of people who attend the public dance. There is much humanity, an endless sea of smiling faces, black and white, mulato, jabao, moro, chino . . . all of Cuba is present.

There were also some completely drunk people, but they meant no harm; they only wanted to dance in their extravagant way. One had to be careful moving through the crowd because a misstep could knock over a bottle of rum or smudge a new pair of sneakers enraging the offended party, but usually with a "permiso" (excuse me) or a "discúlpame, brother" everything was resolved. Respect and the desire to enjoy the evening and the music ruled, and at the end of the night I could walk home very content, smiling and singing. On some other occasions, there has been violence. Usually nothing too bad, but yes fights have started and have led to stabbings. These are some of the facts that reinforce negative stereotypes about the public dance.

I asked Mario "Mayito" Rivera, then singer for Los Van Van, about violence and the *baile público*, and he told me it must have to do with the heat of the Caribbean and the crowded dance spaces, but also with the very temperament of Cuban people. He said that those sorts of things happen everywhere (which is very true), and that if the public dance is maintained in Cuba, these incidents will be difficult to avoid. Others told me that problems are due to the presence of alcohol and drunkenness, and that in other eras, there were fewer problems because people enjoyed soft drinks at dances. Refresco is still present, but rum

13. Refreshments at the public dance include sandwiches, snow cones, refresco, and rum, 2003.

and beer are more popular, sold at stores or by individuals who do so illegally. I never saw the sale of drugs like marijuana or cocaine in the public dances. The police presence is limited mostly to the periphery of the dance space, and they are there to make sure the dance is not used as a place to avenge vendettas, dancers are not bothered, and vendors of food and drink are not molested.

If there is popular music at La Piragua or La Tropical, for example, the music of Paulito F.G., Manolín, or La Charanga Habanera, then mostly blacks go there to dance. This is because timba—the primary music in these spaces—is very much theirs; they carry it inside of themselves like every Cuban does, but perhaps more so (see chapters 3 and 4). Blacks also attend in large numbers because they lack money and cannot afford to enter other places (Sawyer 2006; interviews). Their presence in turn discourages other sectors of the society from attending.

For those who have nowhere else to go, the reason is because they can't afford it. The majority of these are Afro-Cuban. Director of Los Van Van Juan Formell affirms that there are many prejudices that claim that only "los aseres" and "los guaposos" (gangsters and thugs, with an implication of color) go to public dances, when in reality they are an important cultural phenomenon that should be preserved for the good of the nation (Padura 1997, 100). In fact, because *cabildos, sociedades de color,* and color-based political parties no longer exist, the public dances (*bailes públicos*) represent the largest, most consistent space where Afro-Cubans can gather.

Referencing the Carnival of Baranquilla from his native Colombia, the journalist César Pagano speaks for all the Caribbean and its popular demonstrations of music and dance when he says that in these spaces, "people commit with greater impunity the capital sins, short of murder, and surely this collective therapy, this essential sudden attack of liberty that temporarily makes rich and poor equals, reduces the causes of suicidal and homicidal violence" (1984). Nevertheless, I found a demarcation of space that revealed divisions between different sectors of society that attend the public dance. This division was noticeable also in other dance spaces that I discuss later.

Caribbean dance scholar Rex Nettleford discusses music and dance in relation to what he calls "the battle for space" in the context of the Caribbean region. His notion regards the battle for survival, progress, self-determination, integration of the nation, and social justice (1993, 86). The way space is occupied in the public dances of Havana reflects the battle for space within a specific Caribbean society. Cuba has been distinguished by its massive efforts to repair the damage of slavery and colonialism, and yet Cuban society continues to be marked today by the history of slavery, colonialism, and neocolonialism. Afro-Cubans still struggle for space within Cuban society (while, ironically, Cuba demands space among the planners of the IMF and World Bank). In the *baile público,* music and dance combine to focus "creative imagination [as an] *invaluable source of energy in the continuing battle for space"* (Nettleford 1993, 86; emphasis added).

Within the public dance, right up close to the stage, in the heart of the music where things are loud and most crowded, in what is called *el molote* (the pit) we find dancers from the marginal areas of Havana. These are the ones who at another time would be found at La Plaza de la Revolución (for free) or La Tropical (for a small fee) dancing with their favorite band, which they follow everywhere. Sometimes they come from far away (for example, from Mantilla on the outskirts of the city to Vedado, which is near the center) to dance with a good orchestra. The molote harkens back to the Day of the Three Kings celebrations in the streets of colonial Havana when processions would stop and form circles, which they filled with powerful drumming and expressive dancing

(Brown 2003, 48). These "periodic outbreaks" of African-style masquerade, dance, song, and drum rhythms are manifested today in extended dance delirium at the heart of the baile público.

Surrounding this group (behind and on the sides) are those music lovers who are thirsty for the chance to dance but unwilling to get caught up in el molote. Often they have decided to attend the dance because it is taking place very near their homes, like in the case of many of my friends from Vedado who danced at La Piragua near the Malecón. They would be much less likely to go across town (to 10 de Octubre district, for example). A young special education teacher and nursing student who was dancing near the pit said, "I might not go into el molote, but I do go to the dances. How could I not go!?" Her comments corroborate and refute common perceptions of the public dance.

Behind this group, on the periphery of the space, we find people who love the music but want nothing at all to do with el molote. Warnings like "Be very careful" and "Stay out of that molote" ring in their ears. When there is a baile público at La Piragua these folks dance on the far sidewalk or across the boulevard on the Malecón itself. There, the music is softer and they feel safer, far from all that could happen in el molote. As you get farther from the stage and el molote, the educational level and social placement of participants rise. People don't mix haphazardly; they obey some unspoken order, and the public dance becomes a kind of demographic map of Cuban society. This map reflects the history of marginalization that many scholars have documented (Scott 2005; Helg 1995; de la Fuente 2001; R. Moore 1997; C. Moore 1988; Martínez 2007). It also suggests the omnipresence and subversive power of performance.

We can always find a few adventurous tourists who insert themselves throughout the public dance space, oblivious perhaps to where they are and protected by their status as tourists, who are never to be harmed. Depending on my mood and my company, I situated myself in el molote, the middle zone, or on the periphery. (I return to the issue of positioning in chapter 6.)

People's presence at the public dance, their positioning within it, and their actual dancing express complex issues of desire, access, wealth, race and class positions, and race and class perceptions, all of which are challenges for Cuban society. These make possible the encounter, the opportunity for dialogue and the collective transformation that is necessary to make improvements in these areas. If music can be understood as a source of positive energy, power, or *aché* as many Cubans would say, then in the public dance the social order is inverted; those normally in power and at the center are now marginalized on the periphery.

Dollar-Only Clubs: La Casa de la Música

In certain ways the dollarized clubs of today evoke the segregated atmosphere of times past. In Havana of the 1950s, when white and black Cubans danced in different locales, each group had its own clubs or societies. For example, Club Náutico was for whites, and the Fraternal Union was for blacks; Club Candado was an exception because both racial groupings were able to attend. When both groups danced in the same place, a rope divided the space and physically separated them. Ironically, blacks and whites used to greet each other warmly and pass drinks over the rope, expressing the friendships and good feelings that existed between them despite the injustice and inequalities of the society (Jorge Petineaud, interview, 2003). That rope—the legacy of a terrible history—did not allow them to unite, however. Upon the triumph of the Revolution, the ropes disappeared, and a fight began against hundreds of years of learning, of hatred, misunderstanding, and separation. Suddenly, all of Cuba was for all Cubans; there were no places where blacks could not go.

Today, the parties and concerts that take place in clubs and discos with cover charges in dollars also describe Cuban social realities, but in a different way. Timba and the dollarized dance spaces have emerged as a convergence between the musical aspirations of the 1980s and the economic opportunities and necessities of the 1990s. They have exploited the fissures that were opened up by the economic and political crises; they have navigated between art music and barrio culture (chapter 2), as well as between the legal and the submerged economy (chapters 3 and 4). Timba has become not only a "subcultural manifesto" but also a "practical means to gain access to a world of sophistication and plenty" via tourist dance clubs (Perna 2005, 55). Instead of the heat and humidity of the open-air public dance (*baile público*), places like La Casa de la Música, La Cecilia, or Café Mi Habana provide air-conditioned coolness for tourists and some either privileged or fiercely strategic and enterprising Cubans.

14. La Casa de la Música in Centro Habana, 2006.

Matinee concerts take place from 4:00 p.m. to 8:00 p.m., and cost between thirty and one hundred pesos (equal to between one and five U.S.
dollars at the time of research). Night concerts cost ten to twenty-five
U.S. dollars, depending on the band. In both contexts all purchases of
food, alcohol, cigarettes, and so forth are in dollars, but prices for these
items are also higher at night. For example, Cristal beer costs one dollar
at matinees and two and a half at night. A bottle of Havana Club rum
jumps from sixteen to forty dollars, and this is where the especulador
surfaces, as there is much room for performative play with desire, dis-
parity, reality, and illusion.

Present also are folks who have worked hard on their government
job and, perhaps with a little extra hustling, have saved up to celebrate
an anniversary or a graduation. Others are enjoying money sent by relatives who live and work abroad and send money home to their families
on the island. Because everything is purchased in dollars, many of the
people are tourists and also so-called *jineteros*, the hustlers that live off
tourists. Certainly the more expensive the cover charge, the fewer average Cubans are able to afford it, so that the dancing audience is mostly
made up of middle-aged tourists and jineteros. This disturbs the close

15. Inside La Casa de la Música in Miramar, 2006.

link between musicians and the dancing *pueblo*. In addition, the dollarization of the economy has excluded Cubans from most music clubs and tied music to sex tourism and prostitution (Perna 2005, 74).

When asked about the difference between performing at El Palacio de la Salsa[2] and a public dance Paulito F.G. made this response.

> I know that my public needs me a lot. . . . my work is fundamentally based on this public, those that follow this kind of music [timba] . . . the street crowd, the majority of Cubans. Many times I've been told that I am much more dynamic and "strong" in public spaces than in cabarets [like Casa de la Música] and this is true. You have before you people who have worked very hard to be able to be there, who know all your songs, and even imitate the movements of the singer and other musicians on stage; this is the public from which I was born, the one I know best. It is an open communication, more spontaneous, a more sincere surrender. (Del Pino 1997)

The characteristics of this communication—songs about neighborhood happenings, storytelling about barrio personalities, tongue twisters and snappy lines of popular slang, choruses that describe a dance step for the masses that accompanies the song, and so on—are present in exclusive spaces but with less clarity and vigor. In the matinees at La Casa de la Música, the atmosphere is only slightly selective; the humblest elements of the city are noticeably absent, but the majority of the crowd is often Cuban. There are many tourist couples (as opposed to single men and women), which cuts down on the *jineteo* aspects of the crowd. Often Cuban women prefer not to dance with Cuban men, white women will not dance with black men, and bottom line, if you have no money to spend, "you get no play." So the party never takes off like it does at the free public dances. There are young ladies to dance with and a normal, healthy, and distinctly Cuban festive energy; however, the power of this energy depends a lot on the band, as the following anecdotes suggest.

Journal Entry, April 14, 2003, La Habana, Cuba

After a Matinee Performance by NG La Banda at La Casa de la Música

A friend from Colombia, Roberto, was with me at La Casa de la Música last night. He noted that there was a certain amount of "selectivity," that not everybody was there, especially not the most marginalized elements of Havana. Probably they were not present because they could not pay the hundred-peso cover charge (about four U.S. dollars). Inside, the show that NG did was marvelous, I'm never tired of hearing them. Yaritza kept asking me why they continue to play so many matinees (for such a relatively small cover charge); she wondered if it was because they are not considered good. But I don't think that is the reason. It has more to do with maintaining communication, the dialogue with the dancing public.

During this same concert, after the "intelligent music, for listening" and already knee-deep into the "recreational dance music" (to use the facetious terms of bandleader José Luis Cortés aka El Tosco), some talk got started between El Tosco and a *muchacha* from the audience. It did not seem to bother or distract El Tosco, however, who introduced just then a perfect chorus, responding to her comments, and everyone broke out laughing and dancing. Some bands fail to create this energy because few will pay to dance to their music; instead they enter only to meet tourists who may have no knowledge or concern about which band is playing (or even what they are singing).

Journal Entry, June 23, 2003, La Habana, Cuba

After a Matinee Performance by Yumurí y sus Hermanos at
La Casa de la Música

I danced this afternoon with Yumurí. There was a lot of jinetero business going on and very little normal interaction. There were many older, white *extranjeros* (foreigners) between forty and sixty-five years of age. There were also many young ladies between eighteen and thirty years old who were not interested in dancing with you if you did not seem to be a *pepe*, a john. There were also many young Afro-Cuban males whose focus was on dancing and teaching dance to foreign women. At this Casa de la Música it's always the same guys. No one responded to the music of Yumurí. It's not terrible, but it does not excite. You can dance, but it won't drive you wild. In fact, so much was missing from the music and the entire atmosphere of jineteo that I left early (very uncharacteristic of me).

My friend Yaritza and I went to a concert at La Casa de la Música (Centro Habana) and experienced one of Cuban life's delights: we drank cold beer, ate fried chicken, and danced furiously all night long on the joy train—*el tren de la alegría*—with Cuba's signature dance orchestra, Los Van Van. When we first arrived, we ran into *mi socio* Pedro Fajardo, violinist of the band. We chatted a while; he introduced us to Manolo (conga drums) and Boris (keyboard); and later, he invited us to join him in the VIP section where the musicians hang out before the show. We would pay him twenty dollars instead of twenty-five dollars at the door. There inside I met Mayito (singer), Hugo (trombone), Cucurucho (keyboard), Cuño (güiro), and Roberto (the roadie). Only Formell, who everyone said was ill, was not there, his son Samuel, and the two singers Robertón (Big Robert) and Jenny[3] had not yet come.

Journal Entry, April 2003, La Habana, Cuba

After a Night Performance by Los Van Van at La Casa de la Música

The concert was a great one. Los Van Van played two or three new numbers, which were excellent even though they did not excite the crowd as much as their other familiar hits. That night's version of "Soy Todo" (better known to many as "Ay Dios, ampárame"), which was sung as always by Mario "Mayito" Rivera, was extra special. When he began his *soneo*—weaving his beautiful arabesque exhortations between delicious, rhythmic responses from the chorus, someone decided to go on stage and place money at his feet, and it proved contagious. One after another, crossing their arms, "presenting" the money to their heads, or making the sign of the cross, people gave tribute as if in sacred ritual ceremony. After ten minutes and maybe thirty to fifty people, this stopped and Mayito belted out—with a fist full of bills—the question that always ends his song, *¿¡Somo' o no somo'!?* (Are we, or are we not!?). *¡Somo'!* we all shouted. And though I was ticked off because I'd left my camera at home, I still chuckled at people's jokes about what would become of that money, and just how or who had started it all off. The ritual may have become part of the show after having originated spontaneously at some public dance.

W

There is a magic that happens between the band and the dancing public in concerts at La Casa de la Música and similar places, but with different actors and with less intensity than in the free public dances at La Piragua or La Plaza de la Revolución. Cuban writer Pedro Sarduy talks about commodified "form[s] of entertainment that [have] more to do with the visitor 'from elsewhere' than with local initiatives" like, for example, the multilayered performances within Carnival celebrations in Cuba and throughout the African Diaspora (Sarduy 2001, 170; Hill 1993, 218). In these situations the original intention and intensity of the music/dance is lost or watered down, usually to entertain wealthier outsiders.

The creation of new dance spaces with cover charges in dollars, such as the famous Palacio de la Salsa, La Casa de la Música, La Cecilia, Café Cantante, and Café Mi Habana that are enjoyed by tourists and nationals with access to dollars, creates "complexes of yearning." Cuban dancers yearn for those places that are much too expensive for the majority and where the better orchestras play most frequently in order to earn money, but where the total musical event is not as good. In these dollar venues, the artistic demand responds to the economic plan of the country by promoting tourism. Thus the other performances of the same bands in *bailes públicos* at La Piragua or La Plaza de la Revolución are attended by a great deal of people who are avid for music and motivated by the natural desire to dance. Access to dollar venues is contin-

16. La Charanga Habanera plays for a private wedding, 2003.

gent upon employment in the tourist sector, income from remittances of family members abroad, or *el negocio*, participation in the informal and illicit economy. The "haves," who are able to attend dollar venues for leisure, are usually white Cubans, which dovetails with common ideas about public dances that are frequented only by blacks and mulatos.

Once I attended a private wedding of a Spanish businessman and a Cuban bride, which was held at the garden of La Cecilia, a restaurant and dollar-only concert venue. The wedding featured a live performance by one of Cuba's most popular bands, La Charanga Habanera. It was the absolute opposite of the public dance. I have a photo with just one couple dancing to the music, which is totally different from La Tropical, La Piragua, or even La Casa de la Música. The flavor (*el sabor*) was missing. The bandleader said of the groom who was trying to imitate his dancing, "He has a lot of heart, but no rhythm." This is not an example of the dancing public that best promotes the evolution of Cuban dance music, because he and Cubans like him do not feel the music or dance it well. The example points to the importance of Afro Cuba and the incompleteness of Cuba without it.

Middle Ground: La Tropical

La Tropical beer factory was founded in 1891. In 1904 it began hosting events to promote beer sales in a type of garden called Jardines de la Tropical. The garden was designed by Catalán architects in the spirit of Gaudí with riverside pavilions that blended Moorish cupolas with tropical jungle motifs (Cluster and Hernández 2006, 152). It holds about 5,000 people. From 1904 to 1940, Spanish societies had parties there where they danced to traditional rhythms from the mother country as well as to Cuban ones like danzón, habanera, and vals tropical (Orejuela 1998, 10–11). By the 1920s, La Tropical was already a must-see destination for tourists who were interested in Cuban music. These dances maintained and reaffirmed Spanish culture on the island. They also provided a space for cultural mixing as poor recent immigrants from Spain, who lived in areas of Havana alongside blacks and mulatos, brought influences from those sectors to the Spanish dances. By the 1940s, Jardines de la Tropical became one of a limited number of social venues where almost all segments of Havana society met (Cluster and Hernández 2006, 152).

In the 1940s, the president of the beer factory decided to widen his market by catering to blacks and mulatos, who were mostly rum drinkers due to their historical proximity to the cane fields. From then on La Tropical became a key center for Afro-Cuban popular music and dance; it was even called *el catedral del baile* (the Cathedral of Dance). While Spanish societies continued to use La Tropical on Sundays, black and mulato musicians like Arsenio Rodríguez, Chapottín, Fajardo y sus Estrellas, Sonora Matancera, Dámaso Pérez Prado, Benny Moré, and many others made their reputations there during the rest of the week. Starting in 1954, a new stage called Salón Rosado was added, which was used for night dances, while the older Jardines de la Tropical were used for matinee functions (Orejuela 1998, 15–16).

"Promoters" who belonged to Afro-Cuban societies organized most events at La Tropical. They put on dances named after popular songs (e.g., "El Cerro tiene la llave," Cerro has the key) or organized them by themes (like "white suit" or "guayabera" dances). These events tapered off throughout the 1960s as Afro-Cuban societies were dissolved. (In fact, the craze over Mozambique, el pilón, and other dances of the 1960s took place mostly at Salón Mambí, which opened its doors in 1962 inside a different cabaret called Tropicana.) Events came to be organized

17. Salón Rosado de la Tropical, 2006. The signs reads, "No se acepta divisa"—No foreign currency accepted.

by the National Institute of the Tourist Industry; for example, it organized an important festival in 1961 called "Papel y Tinta" (Paper and Color), with the participation of extraordinary Cuban stars, like El Benny, Orquesta Aragón, and others (Orejuela 1998, 17).

In 1968, La Tropical, like most popular venues, was shut down for economic reasons (scarcities of food, drink, electricity, amplification) and also because the gatherings of young people got a bit too worked up and turned into riots (Leymarie 2002, 151). Throughout the 1970s it was used instead for *fiestas de quince* (coming-of-age parties for Cuban girls), events organized by university organizations, and so forth. The closing of La Tropical, despite the opening of Salón Mambí, is signaled by many as an important cause for a malaise in Cuban dance music throughout the 1970s into the 1980s. (This occurred in spite of the popularity of groups like Irakere and Los Van Van.)

In 1985 Salón Rosado reopened its doors. The "same blacks that had danced at La Tropical since the 1940s, those who had danced at the Mambí in the 1970s" came back. Within just a few years, the upstart movement timba was cultivated at La Tropical with its roots in *rumba* and *son* (Orejuela 1998, 17–18).

Lacking other dance spaces to go to, young people in Havana without re-sources to attend expensive venues that charged in dollars crowded the dance floor at Salón Rosado Benny Moré de la Tropical. Dances with Los Van Van, La Revé, Adalberto Álvarez, Irakere, NG La Banda, La Cha-ranga Habanera, El Médico de la Salsa, Issac Delgado, Paulito F.G., and Manolito Simonet, among others, have marked a "golden age" for La Tropical, [the] indisputable incubator for this musical movement. (Ore-juela 1998, 18)

Juan Formell, founder of Los Van Van, says the following with re-spect to perceptions of La Tropical and its role in Cuban culture.

It's true that today a popular dance can become a regrettable social fact, because people go with a different mentality. There is more violence and rows are formed; they throw beers and light flares; and that's no longer the spirit of the public dance where one went in search of diversion, friends, and possible love connections. But the solution taken was the easiest one, not the best: to close the dance spaces. Because if in a place like La Tropical, where five thousand people fit, Orquesta Revé or Adal-berto play and eight thousand show up that is not bad, and I wish so many people attended all cultural activities. What happens is that only five thousand people can enter the dance and the others who cannot have nowhere else to go and are thirsty for music, and that's where the *molote* begins, the discomfort, and the protests that there are brawls and shout-ing, and it all ends in the closure of the place. Imagine, in the nineteenth century there were fifty dances daily although many of them were pri-vate, it's clear, and now we are struggling to have one. (Padura 1997, 100)

The crowd and the events at La Tropical, an "intermediary dance space" or middle ground, are similar to the public dance because the cover charge for the main dance floor is very small. Usually it costs be-tween ten pesos (*moneda nacional*) to dance with a decent band, and twenty-five pesos to enjoy one of the country's elite groups like Los Van Van or La Charanga Habanera, even though these shows are sometimes free in observance of a national holiday or important celebration. Many of the same people who go and enjoy public dances also go to La Tropi-cal. Inside La Tropical, the dance space is divided in two zones: one zone is very large and has a very popular feeling to it (*de pueblo*); it is located on the ground level extending from the stage back to the beer vendors and restrooms. The other zone, called Salón Protocolo, is smaller and lo-

18. Inside La Tropical, 2006. The dance floor is empty, closed for repair.

cated up above on a mezzanine level, where admission is charged and refreshments are purchased in dollars. Tourists are found on the upper
level, curious to experience the famous Tropical "thermometer of Latin
music." Some Cubans dance on the upper level also, either having been
treated to a night out by foreign friends or having saved up to go. The effect of looking out over the main dance floor is one of connection and
disconnection. The lower portion is like the molote of the public dance;
it is the place that is considered the thermometer of salsa and also a place
of "possible conflicts." Standing on the ground floor main dance space,
"Jenny" from Los Van Van told me, "[This] is where all those without
twenty-five bucks to pay a cover charge come to dance." She acknowledges occasional violence but emphasizes that she mostly sees "people
dancing, sweating, enjoying music together" (see also David Turnley's
2002 documentary film *La Tropical: The Best Dancehall in the World*).

Conclusion

Through a survey that I distributed among people in Havana and also
through interviews that I conducted, I learned that a preference exists

for dollarized dance spaces like La Casa de la Música and La Cecilia, even though respondents had rarely, if ever, been there. Also, a strong contempt exists for the public dances at La Piragua or La Plaza de la Revolución even when respondents had never attended one of these either. The public dance is considered a space of conflict, "massive bad taste" (*chusmería masiva*) and "maximum vulgarity," with mobs of drunks, blacks, and noisy music; "a place where you have to watch out" (*de cuidado*). One young lady from the Superior Institute of Art said, "People who are educated or have a certain intellectual level don't go because they know that the worst of the worst of the worst go to these events."

On the contrary, in the majority of the encounters that I had people thought that La Casa de la Música and La Cecilia are pleasant places to dance and enjoy popular Cuban music, due to the ample air-conditioned space and the tranquility they provided. Many persons had never been in the dollar dance spaces for lack of resources and refused to go to public dances. It appeared to be an economic problem that impeded the entrance in the dollar locales (although some considered that La Casa de la Música was in "thinly veiled bad taste" and therefore they did not go), while in the case of the public dances, people's refusal to attend apparently was due to some negative experience or the teachings of their families or of the society itself.

Only a few university students and professionals responded positively, that they saw no problem in attending a public dance, because, in their words, "We are young too and we must have fun." From my own personal experiences in Havana, I know, for example, that it is difficult to find a young lady (no matter what neighborhood she is from) that will accept an invitation to La Tropical or to a public dance; in fact, invitees have become angry that I even brought such names up![4] So, where do the multitudes that populate these festivities come from?

It seems that the real incidents of violence that happen at public dances, together with what remains of prejudice, rejection, and fear of blacks or of the so-called lower classes, make it so that many Cubans want nothing to do with *bailes públicos*, at least officially. This is similar to white Cuban women who say that they aren't interested in black men (never!) but who can be seen creeping in dark company. There is a sense that some Cubans will never admit that they enjoy these venues. Educational campaigns on television, such as those used to combat drug abuse and environmental pollution, could help to rectify inappropriate behaviors and stop the all-too-common negative attitudes toward (and crude remarks about) the public dance. This, combined with the review of film footage from dances to be shown on television, as suggests Formell, and as was done, for example, with the end-of-the-summer dances in La Plaza de la Revolución in 2003, could help the situation.

The most beautiful thing about the public dance is that no matter how rich or poor, black or white, high or low class, whether student, scientist, jinetero, or unemployed citizen, everyone can enjoy Cuban music—already the product of a long history of transculturation, the continuous process that is Cuba at its best. When a Cuban does this with good intentions, always using caution, yet without the fear caused by prejudice, he or she participates positively in the continued transculturation and creation of the Cuban nation. As Fidel Castro has said earlier, the fight against discrimination would be "against ourselves" countering tendencies and habits that seem natural and correct although they are not. To reject the public dances instead of seeking ways to reclaim them for the benefit of all would be a true pity, as much for the Cuban nation and the harmony among its various sectors, particularly in these times of change and social hierarchization, as for the music itself, the prize of Cuban cultural patrimony.

Adalberto Álvarez says, "The baile público is the thermometer of popular dance music. So, (without it) how do we try out what we are doing with the dancer? How do you know if your music really moves people?" (Padura 1997, 180). These issues must be considered as Cuba reinserts itself into the international music market and the question again arises, Who is the music for? Clearly it is for everyone, for the whole world, but surely it must be for Cubans first, as part of a unification and improvement project for its people. With fewer activities like the public dance, violence in the city may increase. Without the cathartic relief of the dance, the frustrations of everyday life may be too much to bear and drive people mad. From what I have learned, almost everyone concurs that there should be more public dances or affordable venues where popular bands can play. As a researcher of Cuban music from the outside and a lover of it from deep within, I hope that my observations and criteria do not offend and that a way can be sought to rescue the image of the public dance so that this space can accomplish its function, that of a crucible in the ongoing process of transculturation, which is Cuban culture. In terms of intense heat and interaction through music, the public dances at La Piragua, La Plaza de la Revolución, and so on reign supreme. After them, La Tropical provides the richest environment for cultivating Cuban music/dance. Dollarized clubs like La Casa de la Música, La Cecilia, Café Mi Habana, and others come in last place in terms of dynamic engagement or involvement. Within the dollarized dance spaces, matinee concerts are better than night concerts.

The mapping of Cuban society at the baile público places emphasis on *landscape and geographic space,* which are also central to the maroon aesthetic. The social pyramid is inverted within the public dance. For a moment, blacks become dominant as they dance in the *molote*— the rugged, difficult to access space, in the forest (Irakere), at the heart of the music. Just as blacks absconded to the hills to create self-determined communities by raiding and improvisation—thereby preserving and extending Afro Cuba and remaining in conflict and complicity with the wider society—so do the dancers in the molote. The critical and pivotal influence that blacks secure during the public dance is not totally fleeting. As the "joy train" rolls on, their music and dance expressions obtain a modicum of power, and Cuban blacks influence government policy (toward recording, tourism, touring, etc.) and attract and access international markets and international visitors, thereby extending the discourse of Afro Cuba.

CHAPTER 6
Around the Iroko Tree: Fieldwork in Cuba

> My success as an ethnographer necessitated a continued negotiation of role
> expectations based on my light pigmentation, my femaleness, my middle
> class status, and my American citizenship.
>
> —FAYE HARRISON (1990, 98)

In the photograph that opens this chapter, I walk with several other
people around an *iroko*—la ceiba or silk cotton tree—located near the
main cathedral in one of the oldest parts of La Habana Vieja. The ritual
happens every year on November 16 in honor of Agayú, who is syncretized as San Cristóbal de La Habana, and entails a small coin offering
at the foot of the tree and making seven rounds of it while touching the
trunk firmly. Agayú is the ever-burning fire at the center of the earth
and the cracks (volcanoes) that allow this type of energy to surface; it is
a portal between worlds. Agayú is said to carry people across great divides and obstacles (Edwards and Mason 1985, 49). For Cubans and
other Caribbean people, the iroko symbolizes a link with the ancestors
and things African.[1] One can only imagine how many millions of souls
have circled the ceiba. They retrace the steps of the ancestors and pre-
pare ground for future generations. Their palms press against the bark:
the spiritual home base and source of vital force (*aché*). This ritual is
analogous to my fieldwork experience. In the very act of taking to the
field, I retraced the steps of many anthropologists who did so before
me—from Lewis H. Morgan, Bronislaw Malinowski, Robert Lowie, Al-
fred Kroeber, Margaret Mead, St. Clair Drake, Zora Neale Hurston,
Claude Lévi-Strauss, to Clifford Geertz and John Langston Gwaltney—
using their tools, now refashioned, to do ethnography, part of the work
of representing culture. That is to humbly enter a community, interact
and learn through participant-observation, actively wait to understand,
or in Franz Boas's words "come to terms" with a given culture, and run
away from and into myself.

Melville Herskovits, Lorenzo Turner, William Bascom, Fernando

19. Iroko, 2002.

Ortiz, Lydia Cabrera, Pierre Verger, Katherine Dunham, Pearl Primus, Gonzalo Aguirre Beltrán, Sydney Mintz, Robert Farris Thompson, and others traveled along the Atlantic continuum as researchers before me. As an African (American) on the path, seeking to establish an academic voice, I was accompanied especially by Dunham, Hurston, and Primus. Just as "hot rhythm" and "cool science" battled for possession of Dunham and Primus who used their fieldwork as raw material for dance creations, they also vied for Hurston whose meticulously collected folklore became the metaphors, allegories, and performances in her novels (Hurston 1990b, 294). This combination of art and social science continues through me as I perform ethnography and envision the diaspora through the lens of my camera.

In the photograph of the ceiba, a man looks off into the distance, perhaps at those next to perform the rite, for on this day people arrive constantly and wait in line. All that he sees is connected to the tree and to the ancestors through his hand and his very gaze. My own eyes stare into the camera. My presence represents a present (now) that links the past and future to Africa. African Americans and Cubans are family, connected to each other by what we have of Africa within us, and by our similar, often interconnected histories. My gaze marks the ethnographic moment; the time I spent in Havana and have recounted in this volume. My gait has the seriousness of the new initiate, not the swagger of the adventurer. I have come to honor and comprehend something of the connection between black U.S. Americans and black Cubans.

I agree with Pearl Primus that honesty and love are the most essential ingredients of any successful approach to fieldwork. About her fieldwork experience in Africa, Primus writes:

> I am fortunate to be able to salvage the still existent gems of dance before they, too, fade into general decadence. In many places I have started movements to make the dance again important. Ancient costumes were dragged out, old men and women—toothless but beautiful with age—came forth to show me the dances which will die with them. (Martin 1963, 185)

She expresses the sad heaviness of ethnographic fieldwork—a "rescue" enterprise of missionary zeal and valiant, yet hopeless, effort, since everything, even culture, must die or at least change.

On another melancholy note, Lévi-Strauss feels himself "maimed," a perpetual outsider who endures a "chronic rootlessness" because he cannot refuse this work, which has, in a sense, chosen him. "Like mathematics or music, anthropology [characterized by fieldwork] is one of the few genuine vocations. One can discover it in oneself, even though one may have been taught nothing about it" (Lévi-Strauss 1992, 55). Boas, in the introduction to Hurston's *Mules and Men*, describes an important key to her work and ethnography in general as "gaining confidence" from a given community (Hurston 1990a, xiii). What he calls her "lovable personality" and "revealing style" are really her skill as a guide along the paths of the diaspora.

My own motivation to do anthropology—which, as a cultural anthropologist, I consider inseparable from ethnography—came from a desire to write about African and African American culture "now," before it became history, and thus the province of historians who often lie. According to John Henrik Clarke, "most Western historians have not been willing to admit that there is an African history to be written about, and that this history predates the emergence of Europe by thousands of years" (1970, 3). Ivan Van Sertima notes, for example, the "attempt, deliberate and sustained over the centuries [by historians and other scholars], to deny the contribution of the black African to ancient Egyptian civilization" (1976, xvii). Basil Davidson cites a "new racism" in scholarship beginning in the early nineteenth century, which "was consistently nourished by . . . [European] imperialism" (quoted in Van Sertima 1995, 6). Carter G. Woodson observed that "the philosophy and ethics from our [U.S.] educational system have justified slavery, peonage, segregation, and lynching" (2005, xii). He continues, "The same educational process which inspires and stimulates the oppressor . . . depresses and crushes . . . the spark of genius in [black people] by making [them] feel that [their] race does not amount to much and never will measure up to the standards of other peoples" (xiii; see also Melville Herkovits's *The Myth of the Negro Past*). Like Frantz Fanon, I felt the need to "prove the existence of black civilization at all costs" (Fanon 1967, 34). Ignoring that anthropologists lie too or that our discipline could be "just another way to call me a nigger" (Gwaltney 1980, ix), I decided never would I allow them (whoever they were) to say that mine were a people without history or culture.

I agree with Gonzalo Aguirre Beltrán, a student of Herskovits, who contrasted historical and ethnographic study respectively as research into the "past" and "present," and recognized the benefits of combining these approaches (Beltrán 1989, 10). I agree also with Lévi-Strauss that anthropology is "a form of history, linking up at both ends with world history and my own history" (1992, 58). Like Hurston in *Mules and Men* or Ruth Behar in *Translated Woman*, I have attempted through fieldwork to effect a genuine reconciliation between my self and my past (Hurston 1990a, xvi; Behar 1993, 321). Looking at Cuba has been a way of better understanding myself as an individual with scholarly and artistic aspirations in relationship to an evolving culture and history of the African Diaspora. I feel the immediacy of the ethnographic project. As the song goes, "Now's the time" always.

Fieldwork is a "fuzzy liminal space" where tension between wealth and poverty, black and white, foreign and local are rehearsed again and again (Jackson 2001, 9). Just as I observed how *los especuladores* exemplified "identity fashioned in the crucible of behavior" (Jackson 2001, 171), as an anthropologist in the field—where self and Other clash and converse (Clifford 1988, 8)—I too would have to perform (Jackson 2001, 184). I lived for extended periods in the neighborhoods of Pogolotti and Los Sitios, at the Supercake building in Centro Habana, and on Calle 25 in El Vedado. I conversed with musicians, musicologists, and all types of students and lovers of Cuban music, not to mention of course the many friends and other citizens who are the average Cuban. As a child of Eleguá, I observed and participated everywhere I could: on street corners, in *callejones* (alleyways), brothels, museums, at CDR meetings, tourist banquets, clubs, street parties, libraries and archives, during Carnival, in the homes of important artists and intellectuals, in government offices, on beaches, and so on. In Victor Turner's words, I engaged in "disciplined abandonment" (1982, 100).

In what follows I describe my experiences in different spaces—religious, musical, academic, dance, and everyday spaces—to show how my identity as an African American man from the middle class conducting fieldwork in Havana highlighted important realities about social relations in contemporary Cuba.

Everyday Spaces

When I arrived in Havana in 2002, my long dreadlocks greatly affected people's perceptions of me. Most did not like my hair at all: "Why don't you cut that stuff off!?" Kids called me *el güije*, after a supposedly humorous character on Cuban television. He has dark skin, wild, dreadlock-like hair, speaks *bozal* Spanish, and wears tattered caveman clothes. I found out later that this was a caricature of a figure from Afro-Cuban mythology. In the collection *Afro Cuba*, Jesús Cos Causse's poem brings out the deeper concept of the güije.

> The *güijes* slept from Africa to Cuba
> and only awoke when they heard
> the drums. They came through
> storms and crossed the seas in the face
> of Caribbean hurricanes. That's why they
> are children of the rains and live in the waters. They
> say a slave tired of being a slave opened
> the jars and the *güijes* escaped, this the
> cane field knows, and so does the moon
> of that night the slave was seen to open
> the jars and the *güijes* came out, while he sang
> a freedom song. (Sarduy and Stubbs 1993, 61)

My experiences spanned a gamut between the oppression and rejection that blacks face and the unity and magic of collective identity and struggle.

Cosas de la Vida

Anthropologist Faye Harrison discusses how her African Diaspora aesthetic, including braids and African garb, affected people during her fieldwork in Jamaica. In her experience, her hair for the most part set people on edge and made her a bit suspicious. In my experience, a woman did not hesitate to tell me, "This is the first time ever in life I met a handsome black man [*negro bonito*]!" This was already a slap in the face of the race; but on top of that, she had actually met me before. On our first encounter, however, I wore dreadlocks, and she, like most folks, had hated them. Some thought they were novel or cool (*on me*, not in general), but most folks agreed they should be cut and replaced with some other style.

During a morning jog along the Malecón, a police officer sized me up and took my exercise for a getaway; as I began to run, he nearly ran after me to request documents. I let my annoyance show and we began to converse/argue about racism in Cuba. He claimed it was gone, had been defeated, look how much Cubans of color can do, look at how *your* (U.S.) government and police treat blacks!

"But why did you stop me, isn't it obvious I'm jogging like everyone else?"

"You looked suspicious. How was I to know you hadn't stolen something?"

Police stop blacks more often than whites on the street to produce ID and check them out. This scrutiny was even more intense for a black man with locks. Only a few, usually artists or people who had traveled outside of Cuba, could appreciate my aesthetic and endeavored to discover what I was like inside. Later in my stay I cut my hair to see if it made a great difference, which it did not. At times I was taken for a student from the Caribbean or Africa, but almost never was I accepted as an African American researcher. It was as if no one could conceive of it; that identity slot did not exist. This despite the work of Hurston, Dunham, Harrison, Daniel, and other scholars of color in the region, and despite the presence of black American medical students on the island. Sometimes after days of interaction with a group of people someone would ask, "So, what part of Oriente [eastern Cuba] are you from?" and when I responded that I was from the United States they would say, "Yankee-land? Yeah right! Where are you *really* from?"

As happens often in academic and other white-collar spaces, I was stopped at the entrance to the Museum of Music by a white gentleman who asked, "And what did you want, sir?" A young Afro-Cuban man who also works at the Museum had been watching, and immediately his eyes met mine—he too had experienced that moment many times. Inside the museum I watched the late Gregorio Hernández Ríos "El Goyo" present on the role of *el barracón* or slave quarters in the syncretized creation of "Afro-Cuban culture." I was surprised to see him there because he was renowned as a *rumbero*, a musician not an academic, and I felt how his presentation shocked the scholars who were present—mostly white anthropologists, musicologists, and ethnomusicologists—into silence. He talked of his experiences as a black man in 1950s Cuba, going to prison for fighting to defend his honor, as a way of understanding or approximating the experience of the slave in the barracón. In nonacademic language, subtle yet very clear in its intent, he compared enslaved blacks during colonial times to jailed blacks during the Republican era, and, without addressing it directly, sounded a strange note about the status of Afro-Cubans today. Due to my own experiences and those of others, I wondered if the electric silence that filled the room was not caused by realities of how black experiences in Cuba have changed and simultaneously remained similar.

Por Proxeneta/For Being a Pimp

After cutting my hair, I was to observe a concert by La Charanga Habanera at Café Mi Habana in Hotel Capri. While waiting outside, a friend asked me to do him the favor of escorting a young woman who would not be allowed to enter alone, due to certain rules in place to control prostitution. In the back of my mind I worried that this might cause some problem, but I agreed. Once inside I was interacting and talking with other musician friends, enjoying beer and the deejayed music before the show. There was a strange German youngster who talked only of Karl Marx. As he droned on ignoring the music, a huge bouncer approached me (sports jacket too short and all) and asked, "Where's the girl?" I responded "I don't know," and since he didn't move on I continued, "Maybe she went for water or to the restroom." He became visibly angry now, and I began to speak in English, since I was always told that nothing could ever happen to a tourist in Cuba. "Don't speak to me in *American*," he said in Spanish, "you are more Cuban than I am!"

It occurred to me that he was reading the situation all wrong. Before

I could explain, I was picked up under each arm by two guards, the doors and velvet partitions were opened, and I was tossed into the driveway, confused for a *proxeneta* or a pimp. Only later, accompanied by an important bandleader and with documents from the Ministry of Culture and the Fernando Ortiz Foundation, was I allowed to come back to the club. This story brought tears of laughter to the entire staff at the Foundation, where I was a guest researcher. The particular kind of confusion that it exemplifies was certainly responsible for their suggestion that I research and write a piece on public dances in Havana, which are considered dangerous. After all, I was more Cuban than them.

This brings up the question of "going native," always a concern for ethnographers, as it bodes the end of scientific knowledge. Bronislaw Malinowski suggested that ideal participant-observation takes place at the boundary between complete integration and academic distance, where the ethnographer can perceive and consider even the *imponderabilia* of the community under study but maintain enough perspective to effectively analyze it/them. Considering the merits and dilemmas of identification as a source of knowledge, Renaldo Rosato invokes Dorinne Kondo, a Japanese American ethnographer whose own image reflected in a mirror—transformed into that of a typical Japanese woman—surprised and frightened her (Rosaldo 1989, 180; Kondo 1990). Kondo became dizzy with fear that she had lost herself or remade herself too well, attempting to understand the community she was studying. My own "near-native" identity was responsible for the club incident and was jarring in a way similar to Kondo's experience. Events like this one taught me about perceptions of blacks in Cuba, gave me a clearer idea of what really does happen in certain music/dance spaces, and gave me greater impetus to ascertain motivations for these perceptions and behaviors.

Conversation with Eduardo Rosillo

Everyday and academic spaces and their happenings flow into musical ones. I met Eduardo Rosillo in Santiago de Cuba, and later I tracked him down for an interview at his home in Havana. He is a well-known and very knowledgeable radio personality (Radio Progreso) and also a historian of Cuban music. He talked a lot about the flow between society, necessity, and music. A memorable example that he offered was the story of Arsenio, *el ciego maravilloso*, Arsenio Rodríguez. Arsenio was blinded by a kick to the head from a horse that ruined his optical nerves. Relocated from Matanzas to Güines, he began to learn how to play the tres; one day they started calling him *el Diablo* (the devil) because he played the strings with his feet. Later on when he perfected this style, he began to use the name himself.

Rosillo says that Arsenio incorporated the tumbadora, or conga drum, into the *conjunto*[2] format for social, not musical, reasons. The rowdy members of his band would often leave him stranded after gigs—to go drink and party. To avoid this, he hired a family member, someone he could trust, who only knew how to play congas. When Antonio Arcaño heard the new sound, he added the conga drum to his own *charanga*-style orchestra, which altered that musical format forever. (All of this according to Rosillo is from firsthand accounts.)

Only with the conga drum could the so-called *nuevo ritmo* be developed, which made way for the mambo and chachachá to evolve from danzón. That is to say, without Arsenio's social dilemma, these hugely important rhythms would not exist. One day in Los Angeles, California, Arsenio said to Dámaso Pérez Prado, "Tú sabes que yo inventé el mambo" (You know that I invented mambo), to which Prado responded, "Sí, but it's me making the money off of it!" In our interview Rosillo emphasized that in popular music there is no "invention," everything flows and emerges from sociocultural necessities.

Religious Spaces

Even though Santería religious music and culture were not the main focus of my research, they are an important part of Cuban life, and, thereby, they figured also as part of my personal journey in Cuba. In addition, in these religious and cultural spaces, I learned about myself and perceptions of me. I learned about the religion first through my friend's mother, who later became my *madrina*, my godmother or tutor in the ways of Yoruba descendants in Cuba. She was not at all mercenary in her treatment of me. I say this because, just like Christians pass the collection plate, Lucumí communities of Cuba must deal with economics too, and sometimes this aspect can overshadow the spiritual, especially when foreigners (*yumas*) and their money are concerned. I underwent a rite of passage called *kariocha* in which I was consecrated as a devotee of the deity Ochun.[3] This involved seven days of intense ritual activity, involving dozens of functionaries and musicians who contributed their *aché* to various phases of the process in the form of knowledge and hard work. Animal sacrifices were made; special meals were prepared; oral and drum liturgies were recited in order to bind the spirit of the river to my head.

I know that the priests and ritual specialists who were called upon for the various ceremonies I experienced were always glad to see me. Since I was from up North there would be better pay and better refreshments (from the dollar store) for all involved. In this way global economics touches spiritual belief and practice; the same global dynamics that affect the dance spaces that have been discussed throughout this book come to bear also on Cuban religious spaces. On one hand, I was isolated by my North American origins and money; they constituted barriers that made it difficult for me to trust people and also to win people's trust. On the other hand, because of my African roots, my skin color, and my ability to dance and drum, I could sometimes outperform my nationality and class limitations. At those times I became one more strong arm, another voice calling down orisha. These moments allowed me to embody the Afro-Cuban essence that I talk about as being preserved and perpetuated in timba and the dance spaces of Cuba.

Blurring Gender

In addition to other symbolic meanings, the Yoruba orishas are archetypes of maleness and femaleness. For example, Changó, "un negro tiposo" always "en fiesta o con una buena negra" (Fernández 1997, 32)—a big black man, always partying with a fine black woman—represents "total maleness" (Edwards and Mason 1985, 55). The rain is thought of as his potent semen, and even his female children are called "sons" (Edwards and Mason 1985, 55). Ochun, conversely, is consummate femaleness, "as famed for giving children to her worshippers as she is for her beauty" (Bascom 1984, 90). The orishas are not one-dimensional, however. They also model alternative interpretations of gender. Changó's male children wear their hair braided in a women's style called *agogó* to honor him (Fernández 1997, 32). One of Ochun's many praise-names is *obá* or king. In her avatar known as *pasanga*—prostitute or adulteress (Mason 1992, 318)—she explodes notions of passive female sexuality by using sex to gain power and control in the world (Bascom 1984, 98). The orisha Oyá is described as a comely woman, who "grows a beard (becomes more fierce than a man) on account of war" (94). Traditions that describe orishas Oduwa, Olokun, and

Osumare as *male and female* are maintained side by side (Mason 1992, 240; Mason 1996, 2; Bolívar 1990, 99).

My experience among the drummers of Añá and in the wider religious community taught me more about gender roles in Cuba. I felt a great sense of camaraderie and fraternity within the battery of drummers that adopted me. Like Changó, the owner of the drums, omo Añá are men's men, tempered with fire and rum. They lead a bohemian lifestyle in which women are one of the rewards of their trade (which in other ways is not lucrative).[4] A female devotee (preferably consecrated to Ochun) serves the drummers during the ritual meal that precedes any major drumming ceremony. Traditionally, women do not play batá drums in Cuba, and if they do learn, as some have, they definitely do not play batá drums consecrated with Añá.[5] Women are encouraged to keep a respectful distance from the drums during ritual celebrations. They are allowed to salute the drums but are discouraged from lingering too close for too long, and sacred drummers, like babalawos, must not be homosexual.

At the same time men embody female orishas like Ochun and Yemayá, and women embody male orishas like Ogun and Changó. Many homosexual men participate in the religion as "horses" through which the deities manifest a physical presence among the worshippers (see Matory 1988, 1994 for an in-depth discussion). Felix "el pato" was famous for becoming possessed by Changó, giving penetrating *consejos* to believers, and performing unbelievable feats like smearing bubbling *amalá* porridge on his face (Carlos Aldama, interview, 2004). In some cases the possession state is feigned. Here it seems that men imitate the orishas, and in doing so freely engage in female behaviors, which are otherwise not possible in the social context. This appropriation of sacred space to express cross-gender impulses through performance reflects both the gender blurring within the Yoruba tradition that nourishes Cuba *and* the particular macho orientation and rigidity of sexual roles on the island (see Allen 2011 for an in-depth look at black erotics and sexuality in contemporary Cuba).

Different Worlds

A wonderful level of acceptance and fellowship was the norm for me in religious settings. Still, the fact of my North American-ness, which was tied to stronger economic possibilities and a history of exploitation and control over Cuba, was always present. On one occasion, when I had planned a *toque* (ritual drumming ceremony) for my godfather, I was accused by *las malas lenguas* (community gossips) of wanting to document the festivities for later sale or other vile mercenary purposes. This was not the case, but it highlights the reality of a split between North and South, and the fact that I am able to bear off their lives, their *aché*, as data, while the members of this community are mostly forced to stay (Behar 1993). Once on the U.S. side of the border, in possession of knowledge and translated stories, I have more access to venues in order to spread them and benefit from the process. I am a professor largely because of what I learned from people in Cuba who may never have access to the world I live in. Pedro Sarduy and I took a photo together after a joint interview with a musician in Havana, and he commented that we were much alike: we favor each other, and our research interests in Afro Cuba were similar. But there was also a big difference. "You are American and I am from the Third World," he said.

Sarduy was reminding me that, as an ethnographer conducting fieldwork, I was "somewhat innocent and somewhat complicit" (Rosaldo 1989, 69) as a positioned subject from the semiaffluent, professional class of the most powerful nation in the world, despite the fact that as a black man I was also engaged in the process of cultural reconstruction and healing that is under way throughout the African Diaspora. Just as when Katherine Dunham takes over her hosts' quarters in Accompong and even has a servant so that she might study them comfortably, my work was motivated by anti-imperialist, pan-African fervor *and* facilitated by well-known structures of domination (Dunham 1946, 7). In Cuba, I was reminded in both overt and subtle ways of my identity and position. The world system that aided my presence among Cubans is also (at least partly) responsible for their long-term hardship and a devastating current crisis (Rosaldo 1989, 86). What anthropologist Fernando Coronil has called the "geopolitics of empires" was brought home to me time and again (1995, xvi), for example, by the American flag on Cuban bodies.

Star-Spangled Cuba

For at least two centuries the United States and Cuba have had an intimate and complex relationship marked by inequality and exploitation at many turns, but also, undeniably, by mutual attraction. Cuba's na-

20. Abrazo/Embrace, 2003.

tional hero and poet, José Martí, lived for many years in the United States and from here theorized Cuba's independence from Spain. "America" extracted sugar from the Pearl of the Caribbean and left in exchange poverty and illiteracy due to poorly distributed wealth. Baseball has been a better gift and is cherished in Cuba as the national sport; ballplayers even escape from the island for a chance to compete and earn in the majors. Hemingway was an adopted son of Cuba. However, the U.S. government is perpetually at odds with Fidel Castro and the Cuban Revolution, a battle that has entailed armed invasion, terrorism, counterintelligence, propaganda, trade embargoes, travel restrictions, and daredevil emigration. Simultaneously, the two neighbors are locked in an embrace of shared historical experience, music, dance, and images, representations of self and the Other. To see the flag of the United States of America in Cuba is ironic, surprising, and yet makes perfect sense. Stories of the long embrace of Cuba and the United States, in which I am implicated, are told in the colors of the flag and through the eyes of the people, questioning me according to my various identities: Black, North American, anthropologist, dancer, photographer . . . *cubano* (?)!

Historian Louis Pérez Jr.'s book *On Becoming Cuban* examines the process by which contact with the North shaped Cuban culture and national identity. According to him, by the late nineteenth century Cubans were already very familiar with what was becoming known as the "American way of life." It was normal for Cubans to have traveled or lived in the United States, to use American goods and technology, and to envision their own future linked to that of the United States, a kind of big brother to the north, a modern alternative to their Spanish colonial past. In 1898, at the start of the American century, the U.S. military intervened in the Cuban independence war against Spain, just as the Cubans were about to claim victory and sovereignty, and immediately began to increase North American economic and political control, as well as cultural influence on the island. During Cuba's Republican era, "so thoroughly had North American forms penetrated the structural order of daily life that it was often impossible to make sharp distinction between what was properly 'Cuban' and what was 'North American'" (Pérez 1999, 12). However, as North American market culture proved unable to meet Cuban aspirations, the affinity for North American people and ways was increasingly matched by the uneasy feeling "that the potential and the promise of nationality—of being Cuban—was within reach if only the 'weight' of North American hegemony could be lifted" (12). A passionate love/hate relationship was developing, which would express itself in all its irony starting with the Cuban Revolution of 1959.

Considering the harsh policy of the U.S. government toward Cuba it is no big surprise that at different times the American flag has been officially banned and/or strongly discouraged in Cuba. It could not be worn on clothing at work, government officials and their families could not have it in their homes, and so on. In Havana there is a billboard along the Malecón, the poetic boulevard along the sea, that depicts Cuban soldiers clad in green army gear jeering across the ocean at a monstrous Uncle Sam complete with a red, white, and blue top hat, and fangs. The board reads: "Capitalists, we are not afraid of you!" This is the kind of representation of the old Stars and Stripes that is expected because from a certain Cuban viewpoint, the U.S. flag represents not only the long-standing connection between our two countries but also the American desire to control Cuba, as expressed in the Platt Amendment, the Bay of Pigs invasion, the U.S. trade embargo and travel restrictions, the Helms-Burton Law, and so forth. Anthropologists are also present in Uncle Sam's monstrous shadow, implicated as we are in the imperialist colonial encounter, appropriating and attempting to subordinate and control through knowledge. This valence on the meaning of the flag brought me discomfort on many occasions; the colors burned, for example, when I was in Havana as President George W. Bush launched his attack on Iraq.

Among people in the streets these days, however, our star-spangled colors are being represented on hats, handkerchiefs, T-shirts, underwear, dresses, tattoos, and so on, worn in a different spirit. Instead of confrontation, people seem also to express identification with aspects of U.S. culture, like sports or music, and sometimes even infatuation with the capitalist way of life or the concept of "freedom," represented by the flag or images of the U.S. greenback. For some, the flag represents their connections to visitors from the United States who have brought needed or desired gifts. These are connections that have been forged in peace, not aggression; hope and humanity, not imperialism or treason. These were more hopeful reminders for me that the ethnographic project—if inextricable from unequal power dynamics—is also a tool to "make oppression morally unacceptable and human emancipation politically conceivable" (Rosato 1989, 181).

Cuba's recent action of removing the U.S. dollar from the Cuban economy—legal tender alongside the Cuban peso for the last ten years—

21. Vestido/Dress, 2003.

heightens the drama of all representations of North American influence on the island. As the United States occupies Iraq and Afghanistan, seemingly setting the stage for another American century, the creative and fiercely independent Cubans, linked historically and culturally as they are to the United States, are in a unique position to comment on the American way—even through the spy glass of Anthropology—through symbolic representations like the flag.

Mistaken Identity

As I negotiated my own identity through dress and speech, I noticed how important these kinds of serious identity performances were all around me. I was fascinated by how much people questioned my identity in Cuba. Why so much doubt, suspicion, and surprise? Was it only with me or did everyone experience this? I do not know anyone else who has had the same problem (see Mark Sawyer 2006). I heard of and saw some cases where Cubans assumed different-national identities in order to *resolver*, or do whatever needed to be done. For example, a dark skinned man with braids successfully turned Bahamian, though he spoke almost no English, and a lighter fellow became Italian simply by adjusting the accent of his Spanish. Though I have seen scams in a lot of places, never had I experienced anything like this. Fanon discusses a similar situation.

> I have known—and unfortunately still know—people born in Dahomey or the Congo who pretend to be natives of the Antilles. . . . This is because the Antilles Negro is more "civilized" than the African. . . . I was talking recently with someone from Martinique who told me with considerable resentment that some Guadeloupe Negroes were trying to "pass" as Martinicans. But, he added, the lie was rapidly discovered, because they are more savage than we are; which, again, means they are further from the white man. (1982, 26)

Assuming another identity—whether Bahamian, Italian, Spanish, Puerto Rican, or Dominican—is an attempt to signal and wield increased power in relation to other Cubans, and to get closer, as it were, to depositories of economic or at least symbolic power (located in nations and languages). Are some Cubans so desperate to be around (*rela-*

cionarse con) foreigners that they pretend to be foreigners themselves? The most skilled impersonators avoid the stigma of *jinetero,* or hustler, by simply disappearing among the tourists. This kind of cleverness is related to the challenges of Cuban life during the 1990s special period up through the present. My own position/identity was highly contested because people expected that I was bluffing; I was a Cuban trading on the power/access associated with English language, U.S. nationality, and assumed wealth.

La Lanchita de Regla

Like many, I always tossed a coin into the water as I rode the tugboat across the Bay between Havana and Regla. Usually the boat was full and there were bicycles and people of all hues, shapes, and sizes. The ride inspires a meditative mood, and most riders watch the water in silence. The day before yesterday three men who kidnapped one of these tugboats and headed for the United States were executed by firing squad, damned in the end because the United States refused to help (as they were still in Cuban territory) and the Cuban government refused to give them fuel to continue. They were apprehended, and we all thought they would be put in jail forever *y punto* (period). That would be it. But the reality was different. They were executed and quickly, only two days after their capture. Now they're telling me that there have been protests here near Coppelia and on the Island of Youth, which is closed off now, no entrance or exit. They say they are yelling "¡Abajo Fidel!" The kidnappers had been killed so quickly, though they had not injured anyone, and only wanted to leave Cuba and go to the United States. This struck an odd note with many. I've seen nothing of this on the news where the events were relayed with great pride as a matter of necessity. Yaneisy tells me that the mother of one of the kidnappers has called Fidel a terrorist. Surely the United States and some of their follower nations will do the same as well. Some people called the spring of 2003, when these events took place, *la primavera negra* (the Black Spring).

La Gua Gua

The Cuban soul reveals itself often on the bus. During the sometimes-long waits for *la gua gua,* people form orderly lines and ask *¿Quién es el* *último?* (the person after whom they should board the crowded bus). Sometimes these "lines" become chaos when the bus arrives. On board people are encouraged to press on as far as they can to make room for as many passengers as possible. A stranger lucky enough to get a seat will offer to hold an old lady's package or a young man's backpack to make the ride easier. There was no machine, but an actual person collecting fares and directing traffic onboard. Only he or she could decide who might be the last person to fit on the bus.

Once a friend from Guantánamo who was visiting home from the States rented a school bus and a large group of us (maybe twenty-five people) drove to the beach, passing along the barbed-wire borderline of the U.S. Naval Base to reach there. They warned that if you cross over you could be shot. After a lovely day, all set to return home, we discovered that the bus was stuck in the sand. Every attempt to move out lodged the bus in deeper. Everybody got off and we men tried to dig us out to no avail. We regrouped and tried again, with still no luck.

After a while the women and the children joined in, using pots and pans (empty now of the *congrí*, spaghetti, and *ensalada* we dined on all day) to dig away sand. The children tossed in pieces of wood and stones for the tires to grip. Then together we pushed with all our might, and for a long moment it seemed impossible. Impossibility was transformed and the bus was lifted. We roared in one voice as *la gua gua* cleared the dune and took the road. No one said "Viva la Revolución" (Long live the Revolution), "Patria o Muerte" (Homeland or Death), "Venceremos" (We will win), or any slogan, but there was an energy, a look in everyone's eyes that seemed to express the positive human spiritual gifts of the Cuban Revolution, mainly faith and dogged determination. They probably didn't even all agree about many aspects of the Cuban social experiment called the Revolution, but they had nonetheless all been shaped by it. The spirit of the Cuban people and La Revolución are very much alive! When my friend, la guantanamera, left Cuba that trip she cried and cried.

Around the Iroko

Once, during Carnival in Santiago at about 4:00 a.m. several friends, drummers all, approached me while partying on Paseo Martí in the barrio of Los Holmos and invited me to join them for a *toque de santo* in Guantánamo. We went, played batá drums and sang in honor of the orishas, and returned early the next morning to find the carnival revelers we had left still at it. On another occasion we took a longer trip from Santiago to Holguín, further west but still part of Cuba's eastern region. As the ten of us mounted buses and cars along the way I noticed names from Compay Segundo's famous song "Chan Chan," from the Buena Vista Social Club. We were following his musical path: "De Alto Cerro voy para Marcané, llego a Cueto y voy para Mayarí."[6] The photograph, Iroko, which begins this chapter, alludes not only to the footsteps of ethnographic forebears but also to the many paths and people I followed and learned from in Cuba. It suggests cycles that allow us to depart and return to find that the music, the ceremony, the (re)search continues through and beyond us.

As an ethnographer in Cuba I endeavored to understand "how people grapple with uncertainty and confusion, how meanings emerge through talk and collective action" in the context of contemporary dance music and dance spaces (Emerson, Fretz, and Shaw 1995, 4). It has been a great surprise and satisfaction to see the reaction of Cuban people (and people who know Cuba) to my images and writing about the island. They are touched and inspired by certain "truths" they say I have captured. The task of ethnographic fieldwork is to create a bridge among people through scientific inquiry and empathy. Part of this empathy is what Harrison calls "the ability to see out of more than one eye." She challenges anthropologists with multiple consciousnesses and vision to take active roles in the struggle for a decolonized society and science of human kind. My goal too is to "enlist anthropological analysis into the struggle for Caribbean transformation" (Harrison 1991, 90–91).

CHAPTER 7
Conclusion: Keep Dancing

Afro Cuba is the product of a history that is both ugly and beautiful. Since colonial times, the aim of Afro-Cubans has been to gain recognized positions within Cuban society and to act as full members of it. To survive along the way, they took refuge in cabildos, mutual aid societies, public civic celebrations, and religious worship, encouraging unity and cultural counterattack against their oppressors. They expressed themselves at times through newspaper publications or through left-wing political organizations. In the process, a distinct Afro-Cuban culture developed, gifted with a popular imagination that was capable of substituting elements and adjusting philosophical values to new social situations with great improvisational virtuosity.

As the spaces mentioned above were closed, new ones have developed where the discourse of Afro Cuba is carried on. This book has shown that timba music and places where it is performed are spaces where the discourse of Afro Cuba continues. Timba, a maroon music, has tapped into the spirit of struggle while remaining tied to—even complicit with—dominant forces within and beyond Cuban society. By looking at the experiences of black Cubans and exploring the notion of Afro Cuba, timba's evolution and achieved significance can now be understood in the larger context of Cuban culture. In timba (lyrics and sound) and in various dance spaces where it is performed, race, gender, and class issues are worked out to its hectic, polyrhythmic beat.

In Cuba, the sounds and performance strategies of Africa have blended with musical crosscurrents from Europe, Asia, the United States, Latin America, and the Caribbean, exemplifying Amiri Baraka's notion of the "changing same." Fernando Ortiz affirms that Cuba would not be Cuba without *el negro*. Still, the initial rejection of various mu-

22. Guarachando (Dancing & Being), 2003.

sical styles by mainstream society—followed by eventual acceptance—shows the precarious and marginalized historical position of blacks in Cuba. Rumba, danzón, son, chachachá, Mozambique, and timba have all been marked with the stigma of "chabacanería," but the same dances have also been accepted later as *muy cubano*—valuable aesthetically, culturally, and economically.

Drawing on African-Caribbean musical concepts like collective participation, call-and-response, and improvisation, timba articulates the tensions in Cuban society during the special period. In this context, the especulador has embodied the ideals of some Cubans (especially Afro-Cubans) in the form of a cultural type or performance. *Especulación* blends musical and nonmusical performance. At concerts musicians sing about wealth and display it to their audiences; the audiences "wear" their ideas of wealth and desire, which are represented by fashion, gesture, and so on. Flashy dress, bluffing, big spending, and machismo are significant symbolic responses that Cubans have to the current national situation. The performative dialectic between reality and illusion dramatizes the Afro-Cuban struggle for equality and opportunity, which is yet to be wholly fulfilled.

By using the term *Afro Cuba*, I do not promote "notions of essence and identity that ultimately restrict and confine black cultural production" (hooks 1994, 47). Instead, I suggest a notion that "acknowledges a common thread through an infinitely wide range of manifestations" (47). Black Cuba is distinct yet at one with Cuba. By the same token, it is bound also within the wider African Diaspora. My identity as an African American, man, anthropologist, dancer, *omo Añá*, santero, and photographer definitely shaped my experience in Cuba—blocking some paths, while opening others.

The majority attendance of blacks at public dances and the opposite scene at La Casa de la Música and other dollarized spaces reveal disparities of opportunity that are based on color and which remain as challenges to contemporary Cuba. They also represent hope as locations for potential social transformation, through personal, community, and national identity formation in the context of popular music and dance.

This ethnography of contemporary Cuba follows the research of scholars of race, gender, and class in Cuba within the specific context of Cuban music and dance spaces. It tells what Afro-Cuban voices, instruments, and performing bodies have to say about contemporary Cuba, which is itself in dialogue and struggle with the outside world. I echo Paul Gilroy in signaling the "power of music in developing black struggles" and the need to analyze lyrical/musical content and form as well as the social context.

Particularly important contributions of this work include the discussion of a maroon aesthetic extended beyond the colonial era to the context of contemporary society; deep description of the dance spaces of Cuba (*bailes públicos*, La Tropical, *el molote*, and others); and the examination of the performance of identity and desire through the character of "the especulador." The work is part of a new generation of scholarship of Cuban culture since the fall of the Soviet bloc, taking its place alongside works like Sujatha Fernandes's *Cuba Represent!* (2006), which considers how Cuban hip-hop reinterprets notions of what is "revolutionary" in the Cuban context.[1] It also complements works focused on dance (and other) spaces of social transformation throughout the African Diaspora like Donna Hope's *Inna di Dance Hall* (2006), about reggae and urban culture in Jamaica.

By reading timba lyrics, considering its sound and performance, and analyzing the self-performance of individuals who are influenced by them—in both musical and nonmusical contexts—I have shown how Afro-Cubans are and have been reacting to and actively shaping the social, political, and economic moment in which they are living. Through various kinds of performance around timba, they fashion ways to *escape* perceived inferiority and unattractiveness, and reverse their historical marginalization in Cuban society. In this way timba is maroon music in contemporary Cuba. Through dancing and being—creating, dancing timba music as well as performing the self according to specific strategies in various spaces—Afro-Cubans extend a historical identity into the future, which is in dialogue and tension with the wider Cuban society. Timba is without a doubt rebel music/dance in a renegade stance.

Epilogue: Remembering Manolín

Since my last visit, the buildings had endured three more years of rain, wind, sun, and the strain of life, and the people were stretched thin. I realized the seriousness of the promise/prophecy of the Cuban Revolution and redemption. It was as if the place is being ground down almost to dust. Nothing but spirit remains. Life goes on. The drum speaks, babies are born, quinceñeras, velorios, la pincha, la rumba, la novela all continue. Cubans are incredibly resilient and patient. Some say "Cuba no cambia" (Cuba doesn't change), but things do shift.

The major debate in Cuba while I was there in 2006 was about the future of the country without Fidel. The phrase "eternal comandante de la revolución" struck me because it says that Fidel will be present always through his ideas and the system he has set in place, even when he is physically no more. Most people were shocked when he turned over power to his brother, and they seemed genuinely afraid of what will happen when Fidel dies. Some conjectured about whether he was already gone. Some celebrated in the exclusive areas of Havana with champagne and cell phone calls to Miami. *"Estamos en tiempos de cuento,"* they said. These are storybook times. Most agreed that things would definitely *not* get out of control, *que estaba todo pensao*, especially with iron-fisted Raúl at the helm. There would be no all-out chaos. There were more guardias throughout Havana. Whereas before a single officer may have stood at the crossroads of 23 and L Streets, now each of the four corners was manned with multiple guards. Army reserves were activated to defend Cuba in the event of a U.S. attack.

Fidel was mostly absent from the television screen but omnipresent in the street on posters, banners, book covers, and billboards. "Vamos bien" (We're fine) was one billboard I remember. The image of an old but vital Fidel proclaimed his eternal presence, in spite of physical frailty and even beyond death. What did come on television was footage from the various rallies held throughout the island to show support for Fidel and wish him a speedy recovery, as well as to demonstrate strong patriotism and commitment to continuing the revolution no matter what, with or without Fidel. The people spoke passionately (even if scriptedly) about how el pueblo cubano has learned its lessons well and is prepared to carry on. Federations, unions, and individuals are ready to fulfill their responsibilities to the patria. A rumbero from Santiago de Cuba, a member of the group Yoruba Andabo, sang, *"Yo soy hijo de Fidel, yo cumplo con mi deber"*—I'm a son of Fidel, I fulfill my responsibility.

In the Santería community there were many more babalawos (priests of Orula, the divination deity) than I'd ever noticed before. Often there were more of them than santeros (priests of other orishas) at toques. I heard people say that since they were a source of income, initiations into Ifá, Santería, and the sacred batá drum tradition of Añá were becoming less exclusive and more common. Some said it doesn't cost as much as it used to: "Qualquiera con quatro pesos (anyone with a little money) can become a babalawo." Initiations bring material and economic, as well as spiritual well-being, so initiators are not turning folks away. I saw *iyanifá* (women priestesses of Ifá) for the first time in Cuba. Many, especially young people, seemed to be making ocha *para especular.*

In the mid- to late 1990s, Manolín traveled the world electrifying dance floors with his timbero style, while remaining based in Havana. His stint living and performing in the United States inspired the song "Ya tengo amigos en Miami" (I already have friends in Miami) on his 1997 disc *De buena fe* (In Good Faith). This song did not sit well with Cuban officials in the context of hostile U.S./Cuba relations, though fans on the island were not opposed to it. After remaining for a time in the United States he returned to Cuba and attempted to make things work there, but he was not successful. As a result of his first visit to Miami he was censured on Cuban radio. He says that the Cuban government was "unable to understand [his] position" and even told him that he would have to stop performing as El Médico, to instead be a backup singer for an unknown salsa band called Fiebre Latina (Castro 2001, 1).

After a year and four months back in Cuba, Manolín relocated definitively to the United States "for my daughter, my music and my ambition to take my music to the farthest corners of the earth . . . and to break taboos" (Castro 1999, 2). After struggling for several months to gain permission to do a television program in Mexico, he made his way to Atlanta, Georgia, where he turned himself over to immigration officials and was jailed for a week while his case was sorted out. He realized full well that he was by no means assured success as a musician in this new country: "[The United States] is a very difficult market, and it means starting over from scratch" (Castro 1999, 2). Speaking of his fans in Cuba he said, "Thank you very much, because I owe it all to them . . . everything that I am today, and the fact that I have come here does not mean that I have abandoned them. I have them here with me— they are the ones who give me strength. Someday I hope they will understand and feel proud of me."

El Médico has released just one studio album since his move to the United States, entitled *Tal como soy* (As I am) from 2003. This production was a total departure from his timba recordings of the 1990s. The slow tempo and absent polyrhythm of the songs highlight the fact that Manolín was never a great vocalist. For fans that expected another stroke of timba genius this production was certainly a disappointment. Still, I remained a hopeful fan.

At the end of my visit to Havana in 2006, I received an e-mail invitation to a concert by Manolín, El Médico de la Salsa with the Timba All-Stars in San Francisco. Upon returning to California, I went to the show and had a surprising experience. Manolín, whom I had never seen live in Havana because his shows were always sold out, even if they cost thirty dollars (an extremely expensive ticket), was performing to a small audience of not-so-enthusiastic fans. Instead of a fine suit he wore a very regular long-sleeved T-shirt, jeans, and sneakers. It was like surprising the little ordinary man behind the mask in Oz, or learning the truth about Santa. The larger-than-life timba all-star, who made so much magic, seemed only common, humbled, cheapened.

Maybe this was the last show on the last night and he was tired, but the energy was low. Manolín seemed bored with what he was doing, as he sang only the hits from ten years ago. To me, he represented the threat to the Revolution posed by the special period and recovery measures, that hedonistic musical moment when things transitioned closer to capitalism for a time. Cuba had survived the crisis, moved on, and could now jeer at Manolín as the well-known Havana billboard jeers at Uncle Sam: "*¡Señores capitalistas, no les tenemos absolutamente ningún miedo!*" (Capitalists, we are not afraid of you!). He also represented Cuba itself, so tired. *La guerra cansa*, war is tiring—even wars of ideas.

23. Te fuiste/You left (Remembering Manolín), 2003.

The exciting initial burst of timba onto the scene as a fresh approach to Cuban dance music is done. The basic elements of a style or subgenre have been set and are referenced by all kinds of musicians in and outside of Cuba. In a popular *paladar* (restaurant run out of the home) in Centro Habana there was a mural that featured some of Manolín's most famous lyrics.

Tú te fuiste, y si te fuiste perdiste . . .
Yo no, yo me quedé
Guarachando

You left so you lost . . .
I stayed here
Grooving (dancing and being)

In 1995, when this song ("La bola") was wildly popular in Cuba it spoke of lost love, but in veiled speech it spoke to those who left the island as political dissidents or in search of economic opportunity, especially the thousands of *balseros* who left in 1994. The lyrics become ironic and strangely nostalgic when we consider that Manolín has since left himself (Castro 2001). In the mural, these lyrics are the backdrop against which people eat and converse. El Médico is gone but not totally forgotten. He has marked Cuban music and society. Similarly, though timba is relatively less hot today than in its golden-era boom of the 1990s, it is still a major part of Cuban life. In restaurants, homes, clubs, weddings, public dances, and so on, Cubans work out who they are and who they aspire to be, to the timba beat. There is some question, though, as to whether or not timba can thrive outside of Cuba, even in places like the San Francisco Bay Area; Lima, Peru; Cali, Colombia; and Rome, Italy, where large communities of fans dance timba. Can bands made up of expatriate Cubans and others create new timba music that expresses the life and times of the host locations, rather than relying on timba classics or current hits from Havana? Separated from the neighborhoods of Havana and the unique chemistry of that translucent city, even El Médico, with his tongue of fire, may find himself with nothing meaningful or magical to say—tongue-tied.[1]

Back in the United States, faced with the task of writing about Cuba, I understand even more the delicate task of representing culture. At a recent exhibit of my photographs called *Cuba en colores*, I met an American woman who is an advocate for Cuban sovereignty, has

24. Cuba postcard with Changó symbols.

25. Manolín, El Médico de la Salsa.

founded an organization based on U.S.-Cuba relations, and travels regularly to the island. As we spoke about the debates on race included in my book, she became very angry that certain authors' ideas were included. To her, any "negative" portrayal of Cuban society was not only a disservice to the country's noble, largely successful social project but a betrayal. I can hear the warnings of Cuban friends who advised me to avoid polemical issues or direct criticism in order to preserve my ability to travel to Cuba—one wrong word and I might be out.

I feel the danger of being too critical and betraying the openness Cuba showed me; however, if I remain silent about the inequality of blacks, the story is incomplete, and I betray my pact with informants, anthropologists, and others interested in a society without race as a determinant of life possibilities and status. The pact entails that I (as scientist and griot) will honor and further the (Afro) Cuban tradition of struggle—also our time, interviews, books, and so on—by documenting and analyzing culture, and helping to create more space for Afro-Cuban voices to speak and be heard. This way Cuba and even the world could benefit. In Ruth Behar's words, "there is danger in speaking and in being quiet" (1998, 5).

Because of its history of struggle and its current positioning vis-à-vis the United States and other world powers, Cuba inspires much passion.

This may increase in the near future. Fidel Castro's transition out of power opens up new possibilities for political reform on the island. At the same time, the aftermath of the George W. Bush administration may also bring changes in U.S. policy toward Cuba, as a more progressive leader, President Barack Obama, takes the helm. Both of these "new beginnings" have refocused attention on Cuba and intensified debates among those interested in Cuba's fate. Whatever happens, representing Cuban culture—like creating it—will likely remain an intricate dance fraught with political and emotional consequences. Future research along the lines of this book will show how music and dance reflect and affect change in the context of ongoing social transformation. May Changó and all the orishas guide my steps and those of the researchers that follow.

Appendix 1: Timba Timeline

1954   Stadium Tropical (later Salón Rosado de la Tropical) is born as an important dance space that would become the "thermometer of salsa music," comparable to the Palladium in New York, a crucible of popular music and dance. It was used for night dances while the older "gardens" (Jardines de la Tropical, dating back to 1904) were used for matinee functions.

1959   Fidel and his revolutionary armed forces triumph and take Havana in January.

1960   Law no. 890 nationalizes many privately owned businesses in Cuba (October 13). Washington cuts off normal diplomatic relations with Havana.

1962   Total trade embargo is imposed (February 27).

Escuela Nacional de Arte (ENA) is created. The school produces musicians of world-class technical and expressive skill.

Salon Mambí opens at the old Tropicana nightclub. It is one of the very few dance spaces functioning during the mid- to late 1960s and 1970s in Havana.

1963   Benny Moré, El bárbaro del ritmo, the king of popular dance music in Cuba, dies (February 19). His career marked the development of danzón, son, mambo, and chachachá, all of which are sources of timba.

1964   Cuban record company EGREM (Empresa de Grabaciones y Ediciones Musicales) is formed.

1967   Orquesta de Música Moderna is founded by the National Council for Culture (which later becomes the Ministry), under the direction of saxophonist Armando Romeu. This group spawns musicians that later join or found other bands of great importance in the development of timba (e.g., Chucho Valdés, who created Irakere).

1968   Musicians become employees of the state, organized and contracted as members of booking agencies (*empresas de espectáculos*). All places serving alcohol, including dance spaces like La Tropical, are closed down for at least one year, a blow that slowed the development of popular music. Still, this same year the group Elio Revé y su Changüí is born.

Pablo Milanés, Silvio Rodríguez, Eduardo Ramos, and Noel Nicola—all singers from the Nueva Trova Movement—join Grupo de Experimentación Sonora (Sound Experimentation Group). This collective developed the song of social protest and experimented with advanced techniques of composition and performance, sowing seeds that would blossom on the cutting edge of Cuban music's future—Irakere, Afro-Cuba, Síntesis, and others.

1969   Juan Formell founds Los Van Van after a brief stint with Elio Revé.

1970   José Luis Cortés joins Los Van Van where he plays flute and sax, composes, and arranges.

1971   Congress on Education and Culture takes place. The interest of Cuban youth in foreign music is an issue of concern.

1972   Nueva Trova becomes an officially sanctioned movement under the sponsorship of the Communist Youth Union.

1973   Anglo-American pop and folk music is banned from radio airwaves for approximately one year. Pianist Chucho Valdés founds Irakere.

1976   Ministry of Culture is created under the new socialist constitution.

1977   Jazz Cruise to Havana brings renowned North American jazz musicians, like Dizzy Gillespie, Earl Hines, and Stan Getz, to play in Cuba.

1978   Orquesta Son 14 is born under the direction of Adalberto Álvarez.

Irakere tours the United States and plays the Newport Jazz Festival.

1979   A concert at Karl Marx Theater in Havana features musicians from United States, including salsa artists Rubén Blades, Héctor Lavoe, and Roberto Roena. The cool reception by the Cuban audience suggested that people wanted to hear rock and jazz, not reformatted son (i.e., old Cuban music).

1980   José Luis Cortés leaves Los Van Van to join Irakere.

First-ever Festival Jazz Playa takes place (to become famous Cuban jazz festival).

1983   Oscar D'León performs in Havana, reigniting the dance music scene on the island.

1984   Adalberto Álvarez relocates to Havana and founds Adalberto Álvarez y su Son.

1985   El Salón Rosado de la Tropical reopens its doors.

1988   José Luis Cortés together with several other daring musicians founds NG La Banda (New Generation Band).

Berman Amendment to embargo regulations allows "informational materials" including films and sound recordings from Cuba to enter the United States for the first time in decades.

1989   The Soviet bloc falls and the so-called special period in Cuba starts, during which timba assumes a clear shape and personality.

Cubartista, a highly bureaucratic booking agency managing foreign engagements of Cuban musicians, is dissolved and replaced by Artex, another state-owned but more independent agency.

Pianist Juan Carlos Alfonso—after being a composer, arranger, and musician with Revé—founds his own group Dan Den.

José Luis Cortés and NG La Banda tour the neighborhoods of Havana (something that had never been done) in what was called "gira por los barrios."

1991   First Festival of Dance Music takes place in Havana.

Cuban television program *Mi salsa* (My Salsa) starts, featuring Cuban dance music.

In October Communist Party membership opens up to revolutionary Christians and other religious believers.

1992   The Cuban Constitution changes to reflect that the state is now "secular" rather than "atheist."

After stints with various groups (among them Opus 13 and Dan Den) Paulo Fernández Gallo founds his own band, Paulito F.G. y su Élite.

Torricelli Bill is passed in U.S. Congress, strengthening the trade embargo against Cuba.

A second incarnation of La Charanga Habanera launches under the direction of David Calzado, with a new style that helps to define the timba movement.

El Salón Rosado becomes El Salón Rosado Benny Moré de la Tropical in honor of the great singer.

1993   The dollar is legalized in Cuba and becomes an important if polemical reality in the day-to-day life of the Cuban people.

Musicians are authorized to negotiate their own contracts and recording deals with foreign companies.

La Casa de la Música and El Palacio de la Salsa open up in Havana, beginning a golden age of timba music and dance. Manuel Simonet, pianist from Camagüey, founds Manolito Simonet y su Trabuco.

1994   Manolín, El Médico de la Salsa records his hit song "Una aventura loca" (A crazy adventure), first in a long list that would mark a special moment (some would say an extended ecstasy) in Cuban dance music.

Street riots in Havana lead to the balsero crisis in which 35,000 Cubans leave the island.

1995   Lazarito Valdés debuts his group Bamboleo at Festival Jazz Plaza.

1996   Manolín makes a successful tour of Europe, marked by send-off and welcome-home concerts at La Tropical, both of which are legendary.

The Helms-Burton Law tightens embargo against Cuba.

1997   La Charanga Habanera is sanctioned and punished with a year's silence for a performance considered too vulgar. Elio Revé dies and his son Elito assumes leadership, making the group's sound more contemporary and entering the timba arena.

1998   Varadero '98, takes place, a concert that brought together the stars of timba under the leadership of Juan Formell, Adalberto Álvarez, José Luis Cortés, David Calzado, Paulito F.G., Manolín, El Médico de la Salsa, and Issac Delgado.

Abdala, a six-million-dollar, world-class recording studio, is built in Havana.

2000   Juan Formell y Los Van Van win their first Grammy award for the disc Llegó Van Van/ Van Van Is Here, a mix of Cuban rhythms with a strong dose of timba.

2001   Pianist, composer, and arranger César "Pupy" Pedroso leaves Los Van Van to form his own group, Pupy y los que son, son.

Manolín defects to Miami.

2003   Manolín releases pop/ballad album entitled *Tal como soy* (As I am).

2006   Manolín gives a concert in San Francisco, California.

Appendix 2: Interviews

Abreu Hernández, Luis. Percussionist, Los Papines.

Aldama, Carlos. Batá drummer. San Leandro, CA. 2004.

Alén, Olavo. Musicologist.

Armas Rigal, Nieves. Dance historian.

Batá, Carmen. Professional percussionist. July 26, 2002.

Betancourt, Joaquin. Violin, producer. September 15.

Calderón de Armas, Rafael. Dancer, repairman.

Carión Blanco, Maibelys. A young professor of folkloric dance at ISA.

Casanella, Liliana. Philologist and journalist.

Driggs, Yoel "Showman." Percussionist, singer.

Duarte, Tirso. Singer, Charanga Habanera, Pupy y los que son son.

Fabré, Cándido. Singer. Santiago de Cuba. July 27.

Fajardo, Pedro. Violin, Los Van Van. November 21, 2002.

Fernández Gallo, Paulo (Paulito F.G.). Singer, director, Paulito F.G. y su Élite.

Galindo, Aramis. Singer.

Linares, María Teresa. Musicologist.

Luna, Boris. Keyboard, Los Van Van.

Padura, Leonardo. Writer.

Pedroso, César "Pupy." Composer, director of Pupy y los que son, son.

Petineaud, Jorge. Musicologist.

Pina, Edmundo "Mundele." Trombone, drum machine, Los Van Van.

Revé, Elio. Director of Elio Revé y su Charangón. Santiago de Cuba. July 25.

Revé, Oderquis. Director.

Rivera, Mario "Mayito." Singer, Los Van Van.

Rosillo, Eduardo. Radio host.

Rubalcaba, Gonzalo. Pianist, Ann Arbor, Michigan. 2001.
Simonet, Manolito. Piano, director of Manolito Simonet y su Trabuco.
Valdés, Armando. Community organizer.
Valdés, Lázaro. Piano, director of Bamboleo.
Valdés, Yenisel "Jenny." Singer, Los Van Van. June 10.
Zaldívar, Rolando. Radio host (Disco Fiesta 98). August 12.

Except where indicated, all interviews were conducted by the author in
Havana in 2003.

Notes

Preface

1. The *batá* are a trio of hourglass-shaped, double-headed talking drums, originally from the city-state of Oyo in Yorubaland, adapted and preserved in Cuba.

Chapter 1

1. *Son* is a musical and vocal style of dance music considered one of the basic, most important genres of Cuban music. Its structure has Bantu African as well as Spanish elements mixed in a Cuban way with rhythmic turns, choruses, percussion, and guitar tones. It is danced in closed partner position. The musical ensemble to play it classically includes *tres* (guitarlike instrument with three pairs of strings) or guitar, sometimes accompanied by marimbula (large wooden box with metal keys to pluck; a big thumb piano), güiro, clave, and bongó. It was born in eastern Cuba at the end of the nineteenth century in towns like Guantánamo, Baracoa, Manzanillo, and Santiago de Cuba. It became the most authentic expression of the humble sectors of the Cuban social, economic, political structure (blacks and mulatos). Throughout the twentieth century, composers like Ignacio Piñeiro and Arsenio Rodríguez, and performers like trumpeter Felix Chapottín and singer Benny Moré helped to establish son as music of national and international popularity and influence (Orovio 1992, 455–60). Son was the main ingredient in New York salsa of the 1970s and continues to be a major touchstone for contemporary musicians in Cuba and elsewhere.

2. Some of the known maroon communities include those of eastern and western Jamaica; the Paramaka, Saramaka, Matawai, and Kwinti of Suriname; the Aluku of French Guiana; the Palenqueros of Colombia; the Garifuna of the Atlantic coast of Central America; the maroons of the Costa Chica region of Mexico; the quilombos of Brazil; the cimarrones of Cuba; and the Seminole maroons of Oklahoma, Texas, Mexico, and the Bahamas (Agorsah 1994, 2). Con-

temporary music/dance styles from these areas also merit investigation as extensions of the maroon aesthetic.

3. Except for figures 24 and 25, all are photographs taken by the author.

Chapter 2

1. The idea of lower-class blacks being more culturally invested in music and dance is reiterated throughout this entire volume, by my informants and by many writers. It may seem stereotypical and implausible, but there is something to it. In Cuba, "popular music has long been dominated by people of color" because music was considered an unstable, even immoral line of work. According to Alejo Carpentier, the scarcity of musicians and the need for music made it impossible to discriminate against blacks in this profession, even within the Catholic Church (Carpentier 1946, 38). Throughout the colonial period, much, if not most, of the European military and religious music on the island was performed by blacks and mulatos. By 1831 there were three times more black musicians than whites (Leymarie 2002, 10). "Blacks and mulatos filled the working class positions of street vendors, tailors, cooks, silversmiths, *musicians*, stevedores, etc. that upper-class whites found demeaning, and lower-class whites were unable or unwilling to do" (Cluster and Hernández 2006, 50; emphasis added). According to Helio Orovio, "For many years almost all [professional] musical activity was carried on by blacks" (1984, 181). This strong identification of blacks with music does not, however, imply lack of ability, interest, or achievement in other areas.

2. This is by no means true for all styles of Cuban music. Others genres like rumba and comparsa are "creolizations" of primarily African musical traditions, which were influenced by Spanish music and culture in Cuba.

3. Adjustments have been made by Cuban groups based on encounters with music from other parts of the African Diaspora as well. For example, Edmundo "Mundele" Pina, trombonist from Los Van Van, says that they incorporated synthesizers to augment what had been a "soft" charanga sound in order to compete with French Caribbean bands like Kassav (interview, 2003). Of course, hip-hop influenced their incorporation of the electronic drum pad.

4. Many of the genres from which timba borrows have themselves been rejected by some as immoral, inelegant, degenerate, or even anti-nation. Tango, cumbia, reggae, merengue, samba, son, and hip-hop have each come to be recognized as signature rhythms of their respective nations (Savigliano 1995; Wade 2000; Cooper 2004; Austerlitz 1997; Pacini-Hernández 1995; Guillermoprieto 1995; Moore 1997; Rose 1999).

5. *Changüí* is a variant of *son* from Guantánamo in eastern Cuba and is considered to be one of the oldest forms of *son*. A *charanga* is an orchestra format that developed at the start of the twentieth century primarily to play *danzón*. Originally, flute, violin, piano, upright bass, timbal, and güiro made up the typ-

ical group. Later conga drums, two more violins, and three singers were added. This augmented charanga format is considered to be the standard for playing *chachachá* (Orovio 1992, 132, 133).

6. The classic tumbao for *son* progresses harmonically I-IV-V-IV-I or alternately I-II-VI-V-I (Fabián 1997). Rhythmically, emphasis is placed on the "and" of the second and fourth beats (Moore 1997).

7. *Dancehall* is a form of popular music that developed in Jamaica in the 1980s as an evolution of reggae, characterized by explicitly sexual or violent lyrics and computerized rhythm tracks.

8. *Soca* is a Trinidadian music style originating in the 1970s as an evolution of calypso incorporating electronic music and geared primarily to dancing at fetes and during Carnival parades.

9. *Comparsas* are neighborhood-based music groups that perform in carnival processions; *comparsa* is also another name for the *conga* rhythm that they play.

10. In the Cuban context the term *African* refers to manifestations of black culture "informed by ancient African organizing principles" that crossed the Atlantic from the Old World to the New (Thompson 1984, xiii). Sometimes these cultural patterns are identifiable as derived from specific ethnic groups or sometimes only recognizable as a general "Negro type" (read Afro-Cuban) (Bastide 1971, 8, 10), which is the result of transculturation among original African ethnic groups, Europeans, and Asians on Cuba (Ortiz 1995). In both cases creation is based largely on a common "understanding, attitude of mind, logic and perception" (Mbiti 1969, 2) shared by the various African ethnic groups who were introduced on the island and used by them to adapt to new circumstances (Brandon 1997; Herskovits 1990; Ortiz 1951).

11. These so-called figures of synthesis create art that is not centered in the reinterpretation of some form but is rather the gelling of various influences and tendencies, and for this reason they are unique, singular cases. Neither is it possible to consider perpetuating their style, because their accomplishment implies rupture, climax, and end. Theirs is a paradigm that invalidates continuation and demands search in new creative directions, not better or worse, but certainly different (Orejuela 1999, citing Leonardo Acosta in *Benny Moré* [Havana: Perfil Libre de Amin Nasser, UNEAC, 1985]).

Chapter 3

1. The Yoruba cultural area covered present-day Nigeria and the east of Benin, as far as the kingdom of Ketu. The Arará were from the kingdom of Allada, in the south of Dahomey, near the slaving port of Ouidah. The Bantu (Congo in Cuba) inhabited the south of Cameroon, Gabon, the Congo (formerly Congo-Brazzaville), Burundi, Rwanda, Congo-Zaire, and Angola, as far as the north of Namibia. Calabar (source of Carabalí culture in Cuba) stretched between Nigeria and Cameroon, from the coast to Lake Chad (Roy 2002, 12; see also Brandon 1997).

2. "The creolization process has affected all groupings to such a degree that it is difficult to talk of any form of racial purity, whether in physiological or socio-cultural terms. Nonetheless . . . strong racial differences . . . must be recognized and respected as such" (Sarduy and Stubbs 1993, 14).

3. Mexican philosopher José Vasconcelos wrote of a "fusion and mixing of all peoples" out of which would emerge "the definitive race, the synthetical race, the integral race, made up of the genius and the blood of all peoples and [there-fore] more capable of true brotherhood and true universal vision." Also called Latin American exceptionalism, it suggests too that race relations in Latin America are more harmonious than in Anglo America, especially the United States: "the ethnic barricading of those to the north in contrast to the much more open sympathy of those to the south" (Vasconcelos 1979, 18–21).

4. Sarduy believes that Moore's intense feelings about racism's persistence in Cuba are due in large part to his upbringing in Camagüey, a particularly racist portion of the island, and the only heartland of Black Nationalism in mid-twen-tieth-century Cuba. According to Sarduy, "[Moore's] experience of race there, and his early, fleeting firsthand acquaintance with revolutionary Cuba (1962–1964 were the only years he returned to live and work in Cuba) are clearly what fueled his extrapolation of race suppression ever since in Cuba" (Sarduy and Stubbs 1993, 24).

5. In this view, any attempt to criticize continued racial inequality within the revolutionary-socialist society is viewed as an act of the ideological enemy working against the nation (Martínez 2007, 158). Its effect can be similar to that of the "black peril," as it unfairly poses reasonable aspirations (like equality) as attacks against the nation.

6. Historian Tomás Fernández Robaina cites the closing of Afro-Cuban clubs, though coherent in terms of the ideology of the times, as a shortsighted error by the revolutionary leadership that hindered the struggle toward equality for blacks in Cuba (interview, 2003).

7. I saw this in Salvador da Bahia, Brazil, as well. Black Brazilians talked often of being the only black at a nice restaurant or the only black resident in a chic neighborhood, for example.

Chapter 4

1. As in many places, men in Cuba occupy the dominant position vis-à-vis women, who historically take on a passive role. Though this is changing, the im-age of the especulador is firstly male. Although women can use the self-repre-sentations that signal the especulador, men are first associated with the charac-ter, just as they are associated first with wealth, breadwinning, and freedom to craft and represent the self.

2. In 2004, the dollar was again removed from the economy. A "convertible peso" colloquially referred to as *el chavito* replaced it, equal in exchange value

to the dollar against the Cuban peso. In this way, the dual system remains in place.

3. Impromptu showdowns in timba echo verbal duels from several Cuban and other African Diaspora musics: rumba columbia and punto guajiro in Cuba, hip-hop "battles" in the United States, dancehall reggae "sound clashes" in Jamaica, and a modality of Brazilian samba called "partido alto."

Chapter 5

1. A *bajichupa* is a lightweight top (literally "pull down and suck," from Spanish *bajar y chupar*).

2. El Palacio de la Salsa club is now defunct and has basically been replaced by La Casa de la Música, which I focus on as a dollarized dance space.

3. Yenisel "Jenny" Valdés is the first woman to sing as a permanent member of Los Van Van. Before this, she was also the first woman to sing with NG La Banda.

4. My being from the United States may have affected their reactions also; I may have been expected to take them somewhere "better."

Chapter 6

1. Katherine Dunham documents that in Jamaica British officials negotiated and signed a peace treaty with Cudjoe, leader of a rebel community of escaped slaves, under a silk cotton tree (1946, 13).

2. A *Conjunto* is a type of orchestra format that developed in the 1940s to play *son*, *bolero*, and *guaracha*. Usual instrumentation includes piano, upright bass, bongó, conga drums, guitar, and four trumpets, sometimes with maracas and clave (Orovio 1992, 116).

3. In Cuban Lucumí, *kariocha* means to "put orisha on the head." In Spanish and English this becomes *hacer santo* or *make saint*. *Saint* in this case refers to the Yoruba orishas (see Mason 1992, 21–32; Hagedorn 2001, 212–19, for descriptions of the ritual process).

4. See *Carlos Aldama's Life in Batá: Cuba, Diaspora, and the Drum* (Vaughan and Aldama 2012) for an in-depth discussion of batá and the life experiences of ritual drummers in Cuba.

5. In Santiago de Cuba I interviewed Carmen Batá who claims to be the first woman batá drummer in Cuba. She is quick to clarify that she does not play consecrated drums. (The drums she plays, "son aberikulá, no tienen nada de fundamento": the drums are unconsecrated and have not been prepared for use in sacred rituals.) She says she would be interested to play in ritual settings but would probably have to wait until she is much older. She had heard tell of an older, postmenopausal woman who played consecrated batá in Matanzas (interview, 2003). See Hagedorn 2001, 20–21, and Sayre 2000 on women drummers.

6. From Alto Cerro I go to Marcané, I arrive at Cueto and from there go to Mayarí. This is a route from Santiago to Holguín in eastern Cuba.

Chapter 7

1. For more perspectives on Cuba during the special period, see also ¡Venceremos? The Erotics of Black Self-Making in Cuba by Jafari Sinclair Allen and Cuba in the Special Period: Culture and Ideology in the 1990s by Ariana Hernández-Reguant.

Epilogue

1. An article about Issac Delgado's defection from Cuba in 2007 mentions Manolín among Cuban musicians, particularly timberos, whose careers "flopped" upon relocating permanently to the United States (Levin 2007).

Glossary

aché—the power to make things happen

agogó—African bell, musical instrument; also braided hairstyle worn in honor of orisha Changó

agromercado—state-sponsored farmers market

aguardiente—firewater, strong alcohol

ahínamá—common colloquial expression meaning "it's just right, keep it right there"

alabao—part of a common saying, "alabao sea el santísimo," let God be praised, an expression of surprise

amalá—ritual dish of cornmeal porridge prepared for Changó

apagón—planned or unplanned blackout caused by energy shortages

aplatanao—cubanized, a foreigner made "Cuban"

asere—colloquial for buddy, friend, derived from "I salute you" in the language of the Abakuá secret society

babalawo—high priest in the Yoruba tradition, diviner par excellence

baile de maní—Congo-derived fight-dance contest in which male contestants form a circle and take turns trying to fell each other with punches amidst dance and improvised song

bajichupa—garment, light strapless top worn by women (baja y chupa, pull down and suck)

barbudo—bearded Cuban revolutionary fighters

barracón—holding cells from which slaves were sold; also housing for blacks on plantations both during and after slavery (barracoon in English)

batá—trio of hourglass-shaped, double-headed talking drums of the Yoruba people preserved in Cuba

batey—the sugar mill grounds, compound

bonkó—Afro-Cuban word meaning friend or brother

candela—literally fire; for anything or person "to be (ser) candela" signals mischievousness carro particular—taxi that goes up and down main thoroughfares in Havana, usually old model American cars

casabe—a dry, round bread/cracker baked originally by Taíno natives from the ground root of the yucca plant

casino—salon dance popularized in Cuba in the 1950s that remains popular today, Cuban salsa dance

chabacano/a—low class, vulgar

champola—horn passages in timba music

Changó—Yoruba deity of thunder, lightning, dance, drum, and male virility

changüí—musical style, ancestor of the son rhythm, from eastern Cuba

chardo/a—black person

chavito—Cuban "convertible pesos" equivalent to the U.S. dollar (slang term)

chequendengue—flavor, style (see also *sandunga*)

choteo—ironic, distinctly Cuban humor

cimarrón—runaway slave, maroon

clave—rhythmic pattern that guides most Afrocuban music

conga—procession rhythm and happening from eastern Cuba (especially Guantánamo and Santiago)

congrí—dish of rice cooked with black beans

conjunto—band consisting of piano, upright bass, bongó, conga, guitar, four trumpets, and three singers, which developed in the 1940s and mostly played son, bolero, and guaracha

consumir—to consume, to partake in a restaurant or bar

cubanía—cubanness

cubanidad—cubanness

cuenta propia—entrepreneurial business (literally "on one's own")

dar coco—divination ritual with coconuts

derecho—money earned for any service within the context of Afrocuban religion or music

dicharacho—a slang word or phrase

diplotienda—stores for foreign diplomats in Cuba (before legalization of the dollar), accepting only foreign exchange currency

discofiñe—discotheque where popular music is played for the dancing enjoyment of children

discotemba—discotheque for middle-aged dancers (see temba)

divisa—foreign exchange currency (U.S. and Canadian dollars, Euros, etc.)

ebbó—sacrifice in Yoruba tradition

efun—white powder used in Lucumí (Yoruba) religious practice

egun—ancestor

ekelekuá—a kind of Afro-Cuban version of "oopsy daisy" or "there we go"

estribillo—choral refrain, in dialogue with improvised verses from a solo vocalist

farándula—music/club scene, fans, directors, band members, managers, a subculture with its own norms and laws filin—from the English *feeling*, this style was characterized by emotive, jazz-style singing

fiñe—child

fula (fulankere)—slang for "bad," used also to denote U.S. dollars; in the nineteenth century it also meant gunpowder, something explosive

guagua—bus

guaguancó—midtempo variant of rumba in which male and female pairs perform a dance of attraction and repulsion, characterized by the males' possession gesture called *vacunao*

guajiro—country person, farmer

guaposo—tough guy, gangster

guaracha—genre of dance music, similar to son, dating back to the nineteenth century

güije—black monster

habanero/a—a person from Havana

invento—illegal business

iyesá—refers to a Yoruba subgroup brought in large numbers from West Africa to Cuba, and to specific drums and drum rhythms they use on the island

jinetero/a—literally "a horse jockey," used to refer to male and female hustlers who make their living off of tourists (also *jinetear*, the verb)

maferefun—Yoruba for "give praise to . . ." used to express thankfulness or reverence to the orishas

Malecón—Havana's oceanfront promenade

mambí—Cuban soldier in the Cuban Independence War of 1895

mambo—Afro-Cuban musical genre, and horn lick within musical lexicon of timba

mano de orula—"Hand of Orula," an initial step of initiation into Yoruba religious practice in Cuba

mestizaje—race mixing

modupe—thank you, I appreciate . . . (Yoruba)

moforibale—literally "I scrape my head on the ground" (I prostrate myself), traditional Yoruba greeting used to show respect to elders

molote—crowd, festive commotion

montuno—middle section of dance number in which chorus alternates with improvisations by a lead singer

moreno/a—black person

niche—black person

Obatalá—Yoruba deity, eldest of all orisha

Obba—Yoruba river deity, wife of Changó

Ochun—Yoruba river deity, wife of Changó

odu—a figure in Yoruba divination (whether Ifá or diloggun)

orisha—cultural hero, venerated ancestor, or force of nature

ossode—a reading by a babalawo through Ifá divination

pachanga—style, also a specific rhythm and dance from the 1960s and also a party

pachanguita—simple Gilligan-style hat popular at the start of the twenty-first century in Cuba

paladar—restaurant run out of a home, serving typical Cuban cuisine (*comida criolla*)

palestino—refers to Cubans from the east (*Oriente*) who are often illegally resident and socially scorned in the capital

pardo—black person

pato—homosexual man

patois—creole language, lingua franca in Jamaica, W.I.

pepe—a john or a soft touch (slang)

pesao—a jerk, unpleasant person

pincha—work or job (slang)

repartero—poorly educated, low class, also refers to hardcore timba dancers and fans

reparto—refers to outlying, marginal neighborhoods of Havana like Mariano, Pogolotti, and Mantilla

resolver—to hustle or handle emergent situations by any means necessary

rumba de solar—popular gathering, party around rumba music

sandunga—flavor, style, feeling

sello—literally stamp, original characteristics of particular musical groups

shopping (la)—dollar-only stores

solar—lower-class housing, tenement building with shared patio

soneo—improvisation by a solo vocalist in call-and-response dialogue with a chorus

soukous—popular music of the Democratic Republic of Congo and Congo West Central Africa

swing—style, elegance, charm

tajona—dance from eastern Cuba in which participants dance around center post, intertwining colorful streams of cloth as they go.

temba—a middle-aged person, male or female (slang)

to' e' mundo—colloquial Cuban pronunciation of "todo el mundo," everybody

toque de santo—religious party usually incorporating batá drums

trapichear—to work in the black market (from trapiche, sugar-crushing machinery)

vacunao—pelvic thrust, male gesture symbolizing sexual possession from rumba guaguancó

wanikiki—money (slang)

warriors—Eleguá, Ogun, Ochosi three important orishas of the Yoruba pantheon worshipped in Cuba

wemilere—Yoruba religious party with drumming

yambú—slow, old form of rumba (along with guaguancó and columbia)

References

Acosta, Leonardo. 1982. *Música y descolonialización*. Havana: Editorial Arte y Literatura.

Acosta, Leonardo. 1989. *Del Tambor al sintetizador*. Havana: Editorial Letras Cubanas.

Acosta, Leonardo. 1998. "La timba y sus antecedentes en la música bailable cubana." *Salsa Cubana* 2, no. 6: 9–11.

Acosta, Leonardo. 2004. *Otra visión de la música popular cubana*. Havana: Editorial Letras Cubanas.

Agorsah, E. Kofi, ed. 1994. *Maroon Heritage: Archaeological, Ethnographic, and Historical Perspectives*. Barbados: Canoe Press.

Alén, Olavo. 1999. *From Afrocuban Music to Salsa*. Havana: Center for the Investigation of Cuban Music.

Allen, Jafari S. 2011. *¡Venceremos? The Erotics of Black Self-Making in Cuba*. Durham: Duke University Press.

The American Heritage Dictionary. 1992. 3rd ed. New York: Houghton Mifflin.

Aparicio, Francis. 1998. *Listening to Salsa: Gender, Latin Popular Music, and Puerto Rican Cultures*. London: Wesleyan University Press.

Armenteros Mejuto, Zoe. 1997. "Una descarga con Juan Carlos Alfonso." *Ritmo Cubano, revista de la casa discográfica de la EGREM*.

Askew, Kelly. 2002. *Performing the Nation: Swahili Music and Cultural Politics in Tanzania*. Chicago: University of Chicago Press.

Austerlitz, Paul. 1997. *Merengue: Dominican Music and Dominican Identity*. Philadelphia: Temple University Press.

Balbuena, Bárbara. 2003. *El casino y la salsa en Cuba*. Havana: Editorial Letras Cubanas.

Barclay, J. 1993. *Havana: Portrait of a City*. London: Cassel.

Barnet, Miguel. 1981. *La fuente viva*. Havana: Editorial Letras Cubanas.

Barnet, Miguel, and Esteban Montejo. 1994 [1968]. *Biography of a Runaway Slave*. Willimantic, CT: Curbstone Press.

Bascom, William. 1984 [1969]. *The Yoruba of Southwestern Nigeria.* Long Grove, IL: Waveland Press.

Bastide, Roger. 1971. *African Civilizations in the New World.* New York: Harper and Row.

Béhague, George H., ed. 1994. *Music and Black Ethnicity: The Caribbean and South America.* Miami: North-South Center, University of Miami.

Behar, Ruth. 1993. *Translated Woman: Crossing the Border with Esperanza's Story.* Boston: Beacon Press.

Behar, Ruth, ed. 1998. *Bridges to Cuba/Puentes a Cuba.* Ann Arbor: University of Michigan Press.

Behar, Ruth. 2002. *Adío Kerida, Goodbye Dear Love: A Cuban-American Woman's Search for Sephardic Memories.* Documentary film. Women Make Movies.

Behar, Ruth. 2007. *An Island Called Home: Returning to Jewish Cuba.* New Brunswick, NJ: Rutgers University Press.

Bello, Roberto. 1997. "El Salón Rosado de la Tropical: El imperio de la salsa." *Musicalia* 2, no. 1 (January–March).

Beltrán, Gonzalo Aguirre. 1989 [1946]. *La población negra de México.* Veracruz: Universidad Veracruzana.

Benítez-Rojo, Antonio. 1996. *The Repeating Island: The Caribbean and the Postmodern Perspective.* Durham: Duke University Press.

Benmayor, Rina. 1981. "La Nueva Trova: New Cuban Song." *Latin American Music Review* 2, no. 1 (Spring).

Bilby, Kenneth. 1985. "The Caribbean as a Musical Region." In *Caribbean Contours,* edited by Sidney W. Mintz and Sally Price. Baltimore: Johns Hopkins University Press.

Bilby, Kenneth. 1994. "Maroon Culture as a Distinct Variant of Jamaican Culture." In *Maroon Heritage: Archaeological, Ethnographic, and Historical Perspectives,* edited by E. Kofi Agorsah. Barbados: Canoe Press.

Bolívar, Natalia Aróstegui. 1990. *Los orishas en Cuba.* Havana: Ediciones Unión.

Brandon, George. 1997. *Santeria from Africa to the New World: The Dead Sell Memories.* Bloomington: Indiana University Press.

Braun, Theodore A. 1999. *Perspectives on Cuba and Its People.* New York: Friendship Press.

Brock, Lisa, and Digna Castañeda Fuertes, eds. 1998. *Between Race and Empire: African-Americans and Cubans before the Cuban Revolution.* Philadelphia: Temple University Press.

Brown, David. 2003. *Santería Enthroned: Art, Ritual, and Innovation in an Afro-Cuban Religion.* Chicago: University of Chicago Press.

Browning, Barbara. 1995. *Samba: Resistance in Motion.* Bloomington: Indiana University Press.

Burton, Richard. 1997. *Afro-Creole: Power, Opposition, and Play in the Caribbean.* Ithaca: Cornell University Press.

Cabrera, Lydia. 1986 [1957]. *Anago: Vocabulario Lucumí (el Yoruba que se habla en Cuba).* Miami: Ediciones Universal.

Cantor, J. 1998. "The Sound of Change." *Miami New Times.* October 16.

Carpentier, Alejo. 1946. *La música en Cuba.* Mexico City: Fondo de Cultura Económica.

Casanella, Liliana. 1998. "Textos para bailar: ¿una polémica actual?" *Salsa Cubana* 2, no. 7.

Casanella, Liliana. 2000. "Mujer . . .mucho más que una musa inspiradora" (segunda parte). *Música Cubana* 5:54–57.

Casanella, Liliana, and Taidys García. 1999. "La música bailable y su incidencia en el habla popular cubana." *Actas* (volumen II), IV Simposio Internacional de Comunicación Social, editado por el Centro de Lingüística Aplicada. Editorial Oriente y Consiglio Nazionalle delle Richerche, 968–74.

Castro, Jacira. 1999. "Manolín, El Médico de la Salsa Interview #1." www.salsapower.com.

Castro, Jacira. 2001. "Manolín, El Médico de la Salsa Interview #2." www.salsapower.com.

Castro Ruz, Fidel. 1983. "Quizás el más difícil de todos los problemas: la discriminación racial. 25 de marzo de 1959." *El pensamiento de Fidel Castro Tomo I, Volumen 2,* 395–97. Havana: Editora Política.

Chambers, Iain. 1986. *Popular Culture: The Metropolitan Experience.* London: Methuen.

Chavarría, Daniel. 2005. *Príapos.* Havana: Editorial Letras Cubanas.

Chernoff, John Miller. 1979. *African Rhythm and African Sensibility: Aesthetics and Social Action in African Musical Idioms.* Chicago: University of Chicago Press.

Chomsky, Ava, Barry Carr, and Pamela Maria Smorkaloff, eds. 2004. *The Cuba Reader: History, Culture, Politics.* Durham: Duke University Press.

Clarke, John Henrik. 1970. "Introduction." In *Introduction to African Civilizations,* edited by John G. Jackson Jr. Secaucus, NJ: Citadel Press.

Clifford, James. 1988. *The Predicament of Culture: Twentieth Century Ethnography, Literature, and Art.* Cambridge: Harvard University Press.

Cluster, Dick, and Rafael Hernández. 2006. *The History of Havana.* New York: Palgrave Macmillan.

Cooper, Carolyn. 2004. *Soundclash: Jamaican Dancehall Culture at Large.* New York: Palgrave Macmillan.

Coplan, David B. *In Township Tonight: South Africa's Black City Music and Theatre.* New York: Longman House.

Coronil, Fernando. 1995. "Introduction to the Duke University Press Edition, Transculturation, and the Politics of Theory: Countering the Center, Cuban

Counterpoint." In *Cuban Counterpoint: Tobacco and Sugar*, edited by Fernando Ortiz. Durham: Duke University Press.

Crowell, Nathaniel Hamilton, Jr. 2002. "What Is Congolese in Caribbean Dance." In *Caribbean Dance from Abakuá to Zouk: How Movement Shapes Identity*, edited by Susanna Sloat. Gainesville: University of Florida Press.

D'Amico-Samuels, Deborah. 1991. "Undoing Fieldwork: Personal, Political, Theoretical, and Methodological Implications." In *Decolonizing Anthropology: Moving Further toward an Anthropology of Liberation*, edited by Faye V. Harrison. Washington, DC: American Anthropological Association.

Daniel, Yvonne. 1995. *Rumba: Dance and Social Change in Contemporary Cuba*. Bloomington: Indiana University Press.

Daniel, Yvonne. 2005. *Dancing Wisdom: Embodied Knowledge in Haitian Vodou, Cuban Yoruba, and Bahian Candomblé*. Chicago: University of Illinois Press.

Daniel, Yvonne. 2010. "The Economic Vitamins of Cuba: Sacred and Other Dance Performance." In *Rhythms of the Afro-Atlantic World: Rituals and Remembrances*, edited by Mamadou Diouf and Ifeoma K. Nwankwo. Ann Arbor: University of Michigan Press.

Davidson, Basil. 1980 [1961]. *The African Slave Trade*. Boston: Little, Brown.

de Certeau, Michel. 1980. "On the Oppositional Practices of Everyday Life." *Social Text* 3:3–43.

De Frantz, Thomas F., ed. 2002. *Dancing Many Drums*. Madison: University of Wisconsin Press.

de la Fuente, Alejandro. 2001. *A Nation for All: Race Inequality and Politics in Twentieth Century Cuba*. Chapel Hill: University of North Carolina Press.

de la Hoz, Pedro. 1997. "Adalberto Álvarez: en el alma de los bailadores." *Tropicana Internacional* 3:2–6.

Del Pino, Amado. 1997. "De frente al público: Paulito F.G." *Revolución y Cultura* 36, no. 5: 22–24.

Depestre, Rene. 1984 [1977]. "Hello and Goodbye to Negritude." In *Africa in Latin America*, edited by Manuel Moreno Fraginals. New York: Holmes and Meier.

Diouf, Mamadou, and Ifeoma K. Nwankwo. 2010. *Rhythms of the Afro-Atlantic World: Rituals and Remembrances*. Ann Arbor: University of Michigan Press.

Drewal, Margaret Thompson. 1991. "The State of Research on Performance in Africa." *African Studies Review* 34, no. 3: 1–64.

D'Rivera, Paquito. 1998. *Mi vida saxual*. San Juan, Puerto Rico: Editorial Plaza Mayor.

DuBois, W. E. B. 1994 [1903]. *The Souls of Black Folk*. New York: Dover.

Dunham, Katherine. 1946. *Katherine Dunham's Journey to Accompong*. New York: Henry Holt.

Dunham, Katherine. 1983. *Dances of Haiti*. Los Angeles: UCLA Press.

Dunham, Katherine. 1994 [1969]. *Island Possessed*. Chicago: University of Chicago Press.

Edwards, Gary, and John Mason. 1985. *Black Gods: Orisa Studies in the New World*. Brooklyn: Yoruba Theological Archministry.

Emerson, Robert M., Rachel I. Fretz, and Linda L. Shaw. 1995. *Writing Ethnographic Fieldnotes*. Chicago: University of Chicago Press.

Esquenazi Pérez, Martha. 2001. *Del areíto y otros sones*. Pp. 27–28. Havana: Editorial Letras Cubanas. The author cites Fray Bartolomé de Las Casas, *Historia de las Indias*. Madrid: Imprenta de Miguel Ginesta, 1975.

Estrada, Alfredo José. 2007. *Havana: Autobiography of a City*. New York: Palgrave Macmillan.

Fabián Sardiñas, Mario. 1997. "Tumbao en son montuno y guajira." *Tropicana Internacional*. no. 4.

Faget, Senobio. 1999. "Benny Moré: La informalidad o el turno del ofendido." *Salsa Cubana* 3, no. 9: 28–30.

Fanon, Frantz. 1982 [1952, 1967]. *Black Skin, White Masks*. New York: Evergreen Press.

Feijóo, Samuel. 1986. *El son cubano: poesía general*. Havana: Editorial Letras Cubanas.

Feinsilver, Julie. 1989. "Cuba as a World Medical Power." *Latin American Research Review* 24, no. 2: 1–34.

Feinsilver, Julie. 1994. "Cuban Biotechnology: A First World Approach to Development." In *Cuba at a Crossroads: Politics and Economics after the Fourth Party Congress*, edited by J. F. Pérez-López. Gainesville: University Press of Florida.

Fernandes, Sujatha. 2006. *Cuba Represent! Cuban Arts, State Power, and the Making of New Revolutionary Cultures*. Durham: Duke University Press.

Fernández Robaina, Tomás. 1994. *El Negro en Cuba 1902–1958: apuntes para la historia de la lucha contra la discriminación racial*. Havana: Editorial de Ciencias Sociales.

Fernández Robaina, Tomás. 1997. *Hablen paleros y santeros*. Havana: Editorial Ciencias Sociales.

Ferrer, Ada. 1999. *Insurgent Cuba: Race, Nation, and Revolution, 1868–1898*. Chapel Hill: University of North Carolina Press.

Ferriol Muruaga, Angela. 1998. "Política social cubana—situación y transformaciones." *Temas* no. 11.

Formell, Juan. 2002. "Solo soy un Van Van." En Revista *Universidad Para Todos: Música y músicos cubanos*.

Formento, Manuel Castro. 2002. *La dolarización, el ALCA, y la unión monetaria en America Latina*. Havana: Editorial Ciencias Sociales.

Fraginals, Manuel Moreno. 1978. *El ingenio: Complejo económico social cubano del azúcar*. 3 vols. Havana: Editorial de Ciencias Sociales.

Fraginals, Manuel Moreno. 1984 [1977]. *Africa in Latin America*. New York: Holmes and Meier.

Friedman, J. 1991. "Consuming Desires: Strategies of Selfhood and Appropriation." *Cultural Anthropology* 6, no. 2: 154–63.

Gandoulou, Justin-Daniel. 1989. *Dandies à Bacongo. Le culte de l'élégance dans la societé congolaise contemporaine*. Paris: L'Harmattan.

García Luis, Julio. 2001. *Cuban Revolution Reader*. New York: Ocean Press.

García Meralla, Emir. 1997. "Timba brava." *Tropicana Internacional* 4:47–48.

García Meralla, Emir. 1998. "Son de la timba." *Salsa Cubana* 2, no. 5: 18–19.

Gilroy, Paul. 1993. *The Black Atlantic: Modernity and Double Consciousness*. Cambridge: Harvard University Press.

Gomez, Michael A. 1998. *Exchanging Our Country Marks: The Transformation of African Identities in the Colonial and Antebellum South*. Chapel Hill: University of North Carolina Press.

Gondola, Ch. Didier. 1999. "Dream and Drama: The Search for Elegance among Congolese Youth." *African Studies Review* 2, no. 1 (April).

González, Elmer. 1996. "Salsa nueva o salsa nueva: en el color está la clave." *91.9 la revista que suena* 13 (Oct.–Nov.).

González Bello, Neris. 1999 (inédito [unpublished]). *Juan Formell y Los Van Van: 30 años de historia y vigencia en el contexto cultural cubano*. Trabajo dc Diploma, Instituto Superior de Arte. Havana, Cuba.

González Bello, Neris, and Liliana Casanella. 2001. "Gozando y a lo cubano con la Charanga Habanera." *Salsa Cubana* 5, no. 16.

González Gutiérrez, Alfredo. 1998. "Economía y sociedad: los retos del modelo económico." *Temas* no. 11. Havana.

Green, Richard. 2002. "(Up)Staging the Primitive: Pearl Primus and 'The Negro Problem' in American Dance." In *Dancing Many Drums*, edited by Thomas F. De Frantz. Madison: University of Wisconsin Press.

Guillén, Nicolás. 2002a. "Sones y soneros." *Nicolás Guillén: Prosa de prisa (1929–1985) Tomo I*. Havana: Ediciones Unión.

Guillén, Nicolás. 2002b [1964]. "Tengo." *Obra Poética Tomo II*. Havana: Ediciones Unión.

Guillermoprieto, Alma. 1991. *Samba*. New York: Vintage Press.

Gutiérrez, Pedro Juan. 2002 [1998]. *Dirty Havana Trilogy*. New York: HarperCollins.

Hagedorn, Katherine J. 2001. *Divine Utterances: The Performance of Afro-Cuban Santería*. Washington, DC: Smithsonian Press.

Harrison, Faye V. 1991. *Decolonizing Anthropology: Moving Further toward an Anthropology of Liberation*. Washington, DC: American Anthropological Association.

Hazzard-Gordon, Katrina. 1990. *Jookin': The Rise of Social Dance Formations in African-American Culture*. Philadelphia: Temple University Press.

Helg, Aline. 1995. *Our Rightful Share: The Afro-Cuban Struggle for Equality, 1886–1912*. Chapel Hill: University of North Carolina Press.

Henry, T. 1998. "¡Timba, timberos!" *Salsa Cubana* 2, no. 5: 22–23.

Hernández-Reguant, Ariana, ed. 2009. *Cuba in the Special Period: Culture and Ideology in the 1990s*. New York: Palgrave Macmillan.

Herskovits, Melville J. 1990 [1941]. *The Myth of the Negro Past*. Boston: Beacon Press.

Hill, Donald R. 1993. *Calypso Calaloo: Early Carnival Music in Trinidad*. Gainesville: University Press of Florida.

hooks, bell. 1994. "In Our Glory: Photography and Black Life." In *Picturing Us: African American Identity in Photography*, edited by Deborah Willis. New York: New Press.

Hope, Donna P. 2006. *Inna di Dance Hall: Popular Culture and the Politics of Identity in Jamaica*. Mona: University of the West Indies Press.

Huizinga, Johan. 1971 [1955]. *Homo Ludens*. Beacon Press.

Hurston, Zora Neale. 1985. *Spunk: The Selected Short Stories of Zora Neale Hurston*. Berkeley: Turtle Island Foundation.

Hurston, Zora Neale. 1990a [1935] *Mules and Men*. New York: Harper Perennial.

Hurston, Zora Neale. 1990b [1938]. *Tell My Horse*. New York: Harper Perennial.

Jackson, John G., Jr. 1970. *Introduction to African Civilizations*. Secaucus, NJ: Citadel Press.

Jackson, John, Jr. 2001. *Harlemworld*. Chicago: University of Chicago Press.

Jones, Le Roi [Amiri Baraka]. 1967. *Black Music*. New York: William Morrow.

Kapcia, Antoni. 2005. *Havana: The Making of Cuban Culture*. New York: Berg Press.

Keil, Charles. 1966. *Urban Blues*. Chicago: University of Chicago Press.

Kondo, Dorinne. 1990. *Crafting of Selves: Power, Gender, and Discourses of Identity in a Japanese Work Place*. Chicago: University of Chicago Press.

Kutzinski, Vera M. 1993. *Sugar's Secrets: Race and the Erotics of Cuban Nationalism*. Charlottesville: University of Virginia Press.

León, Argeliers. 1985. *Del canto y el tiempo*. Havana: Editorial Pueblo y Educación.

Lévi-Strauss, Claude. 1992. *Tristes Tropiques*. New York: Penguin Books.

Levin, Jordan. 2007. "Cuban Salsa Star Follows His Heart, Dream to the U.S." www.popmatters.com.

Leymarie, Isabelle. 2002. *Cuban Fire: The Story of Salsa and Latin Jazz*. New York: Continuum Press.

Linares, María Teresa. 1970. *La música popular*. Havana: Instituto del Libro.

López, Rigoberto. 1997. *Yo soy del son a la salsa*. Documentary film. Havana: ICAIC.

Lowie, Robert H. 1959. *Robert H. Lowie, Ethnologist: A Personal Record*. Berkeley: University of California Press.

Loyola Fernández, José. 2000. "Salsa, son, y ritmo." *Música cubana*, no. 5, S: 5–15.

Manuel, Peter. 1995. *Caribbean Currents: Caribbean Music from Rumba to Reggae*. Philadelphia: Temple University Press.

Marful, Pablo Riaño. 2002. *Gallos y toros en Cuba*. Havana: Fundación Fernando Ortiz.

Martin, John. 1963. *John Martin's Book of the Dance*. New York: Tudor.

Martínez, Ivan-Cesar. 2007. *The Open Wound: The Scourge of Racism in Cuba*. Kingston, Jamaica: Arawak.

Mason, John. 1992. *Orin Orisa: Songs for Selected Heads*. Brooklyn: Yoruba Theological Archministry.

Mason, John. 1996. *Olóòkun: Owner of Rivers and Seas*. Brooklyn: Yoruba Theological Archministry.

Matory, James Lorand. 1988. "Homens Montados: homossexualidade e simbolismo da possessão nas religiões afro-brasileiras." In *Escravidão e Invenção da Liberdade*, edited by João José Reis. São Paolo: Editôra Brasiliense.

Matory, James Lorand. 1994. *Sex and the Empire That Is No More: Gender and the Politics of Metaphor in Oyo Yoruba Religion*. Minneapolis: University of Minnesota Press.

Mazurre, Ileana, and Aaron Vega. 2000. *Van Van: empezó la fiesta*. Video documental. ICAIC y Primer Plano Films Group S.A.

Mbiti, John S. 1969. *African Religions and Philosophy*. London: Heinemann Press.

McCoy, Terry, ed. 2003. *Cuba on the Verge*. New York: Bulfinch Press.

Mesa-Lago, Carmelo. 1981. *The Economy of Socialist Cuba: A Two-Decade Appraisal*. Albuquerque: University of New Mexico Press.

Mintz, Sidney. 1989 [1974]. *Caribbean Transformations*. New York: Columbia University Press.

Mintz, Sidney W., and Sally Price, eds. 1985. *Caribbean Contours*. Baltimore: Johns Hopkins University Press.

Moonsammy, Patricia. 2009. "Rapso Warriors: Poetic Performance, Revolution, and Conscious Art Music in Trinidad and Tobago." Dissertation, University of Michigan.

Moore, Carlos. 1988. *Castro, the Blacks, and Africa*. Los Angeles: UCLA Center for African-American Studies.

Moore, Carlos. 2007. *Racismo e Sociedade: Novas Bases Epistemológicas para Entender o Racismo*. Belo Horizonte: Mazza Edições.

Moore, Robin. 1997. *Nationalizing Blackness: Afrocubanismo and Artistic Revolution in Havana, 1920–1940*. Pittsburgh: University of Pittsburgh Press.

Moore, Robin. 2006. *Music and Revolution: Cultural Change in Socialist Cuba*. Berkeley: University of California Press.

Morejón, Nancy. 1988. *Fundación de la imágen*. Havana: Editorial Letras Cubanas.

Morejón, Nancy. 2003. "Afro-Cuban Identity: Cuba and the Afro-Cuban Essence: A Metaphor?" In *Cuba on the Verge*, edited by Terry McCoy. New York: Bulfinch Press.

Moreno, Isidro. 1999. "Festive Rituals, Religious Associations, and Ethnic Reaffirmation of Black Andalusians: Antecedents of the Black Confraternities and Cabildos in the Americas." In *Representations of Blackness and the Performance of Identities*, edited by Muteba Rahier. London: Bergin and Garvey Press.

Nettleford, Rex. 1993. *Inward Stretch, Outward Reach: A Voice from the Caribbean*. London: Macmillan Caribbean.

Orejuela, Adriana. 1998. "La Tropical. Bitácora de la música popular cubana del siglo XX." *Clave*. Año 4. Número 1. Volumen 5 (Segunda época). Pp. 10–19.

Orejuela, Adriana. 1999. "Benny Moré: Una figura de síntesis." *Salsa Cubana* 3, no. 9: 22–25.

Orovio, Helio. 1984 [1977]. "Music and Dance in Cuba." In *Africa in Latin America*, edited by Manuel Moreno Fraginals. New York: Holmes and Meier.

Orovio, Helio. 1992. *Diccionario de la música cubana*. Havana: Editorial Letras Cubanas.

Orovio, Helio. 1998. "Rumba en la salsa, pop, folk y timba." *Salsa Cubana* 2, no. 5: 14–17.

Orozco, Danilo. [Unpublished.] *Nexos globales desde la música cubana con rejuegos de son y no son*. Havana: Ojalá.

Ortiz, Fernando. 1924. *Glosario de afronegrismos*. Havana: Imprenta "El Siglo XX."

Ortiz, Fernando. 1992 [1921]. *Los cabildos y la fiesta afrocubanos del Día de Reyes*. Havana: Editorial de Ciencias Sociales.

Ortiz, Fernando. 1993a [1950]. *Wilfredo Lam y su obra*. Havana: Publicigraf.

Ortiz, Fernando. 1993b [1951]. *La Africanía de la música folklórica de Cuba*. Havana: Editorial Letras Cubanas.

Ortiz, Fernando. 1993c [1951]. *La música y el teatro de los negros en el folklore de Cuba*. Havana: Editorial Letras Cubanas.

Ortiz, Fernando. 1994 [1951]. *Los tambores batá de los yorubas*. Havana: Publicigraf.

Ortiz, Fernando. 1995a [1940]. *Cuban Counterpoint: Tobacco and Sugar*. Durham: Duke University Press.

Ortiz, Fernando. 1995b [1986]. *Los negros curros*. Havana: Editora Universitaria.

Ortiz, Fernando. 1996 [1916]. *Los negros esclavos*. Havana: Editorial de Ciencias Sociales.

Pacini-Hernández, Deborah. 1995. *Bachata: A Social History of a Dominican Popular Music*. Philadelphia: Temple University Press.

Padura Fuentes, Leonardo. 1997. *Los Rostros de la salsa*. Havana: Ediciones Unión.

Pagano, César. 1984. "El Carnival de Barranquilla" (de la columna La Clave Latina). *El Tiempo* (Bogotá). February 26.

Parenti, Christian. 2003. "Post-modern Maroon in the Ultimate Palenque." In *The Cuba Reader: History, Culture, Politics,* edited by Ava Chomsky, Barry Carr, and Pamela Maria Smorkaloff. Durham: Duke University Press.

Pérez, Hugo. 2003. "Chucho and El Tosco: The Babalawos of Cuban Music." In *Cuba on the Verge,* edited by Terry McCoy. New York: Bulfinch Press.

Pérez, Louis A., Jr. 1999. *On Becoming Cuban: Identity, Nationality, and Culture.* New York: Ecco Press.

Pérez de la Riva, Juan. 2000. "El culí en el medio económico y social cubano." *Catauro, Revista cubana de antropología* 1, no. 2 (July–December).

Pérez-Stable, Marifeli. 1999. *The Cuban Revolution: Origins, Course, and Legacy.* Oxford: Oxford University Press.

Perna, Vicenzo. 2005. *Timba: The Sound of the Cuban Crisis.* London: Ashgate.

Portuondo Linares, Serafín. 2002 [1950]. *Los independientes de color.* Havana: Editorial Caminos.

Price, Sally, and Richard Price. 1999. *Maroon Arts: Cultural Vitality in the African Diaspora.* Boston: Beacon Press.

Pype, Kitrien. 2007. "Fighting Boys, Strong Men, and Gorillas: Notes on the Imagination of Masculinities in Kinshasha." *Africa* 77, no. 2.

Quintero Rivera, Ángel. 1998. *Salsa, sabor y control: Sociología de la música 'tropical.'* Havana: Fondo Editorial Casa de las Américas.

Quiroga, José. 2005. *Cuban Palimpsests.* Minneapolis: University of Minnesota Press.

Rahier, Jean Muteba. 1999. *Representations of Blackness and the Performance of Identities.* London: Bergin and Garvey Press.

Retamar, Roberto Fernández. 2000. *Todo Caliban.* Havana: Editorial Letras Cubanas.

Riaño, Pablo. 2002. *Gallos y toros en Cuba.* Havana: Fundación Fernando Ortiz.

Rivera, Raquel Z. 2003. *New York Ricans from the Hip Hop Zone.* New York: Palgrave Macmillan.

Rivera, Raquel, Wayne Marshall, and Deborah Pacini-Hernández. 2009. *Reggaeton.* Durham: Duke University Press.

Roberts, John Storm. 1999 [1979]. *The Latin Tinge.* New York: Oxford University Press.

Robinson, Eugene. 2004. *Last Dance in Havana: The Final Days of Fidel and the Start of the New Cuban Revolution.* New York: Free Press.

Rodney, Walter. 1982 [1972]. *How Europe Underdeveloped Africa.* Washington, DC: Howard University Press.

Rogozinski, Jan. 2000. *A Brief History of the Caribbean: From the Arawak and Carib to the Present.* New York: Plume.

Rosaldo, Renato. 1989. *Culture and Truth: The Remaking of Social Analysis.* Boston: Beacon Press.

Rose, Tricia. 1998. *Black Noise: Rap Music and Black Culture in Contemporary America.* Hanover: Wesleyan University Press.

Roy, Maya. 2002. *Cuban Music: From Son and Rumba to the Buena Vista Social Club and Timba Cubana.* Princeton: Markus Weiner.

Royce, Anya Peterson. 1982. *Ethnic Identity: Strategies of Diversity.* Bloomington: Indiana University Press.

Sahlins, Marshall. 1993. *Waiting for Foucault and Other Aphorisms.* Charlottesville: Prickly Pear Press.

Saney, Isaac. 2004. *Cuba: A Revolution in Motion.* Blackwood, Nova Scotia: Fernwood Publishing.

Santiesteban, Argelio. 1997. *El habla popular cubana de hoy.* Havana: Editorial Ciencias Sociales.

Santos Gracia, Caridad, and Nieves Armas Rigal. 2002. *Danzas populares tradicionales cubanas: contenido, movimiento y expresión.* Havana: Centro de Investigación y Desarollo de la Cultura Cubana Juan Marinello.

Sarduy, Pedro Pérez. 2001. "These Things Happen in My Country." In *Cuban Festivals: A Century of Afro-Cuban Culture,* edited by Judith Bettelheim. Princeton: Markus Weiner.

Sarduy, Pedro Pérez, and Jean Stubbs, eds. 1993. *Afrocuba: An Anthology of Cuban Writing on Race, Politics, and Culture.* New York: Ocean Press.

Sarduy, Pedro Pérez, and Jean Stubbs, eds. 2000. *Afro-Cuban Voices: On Race and Identity in Contemporary Cuba.* Gainesville: University Press of Florida.

Sarusky, Jaime. 1999. "José Luis Cortés: Entre el barrio y Beethoven." *Revolución y Cultura,* no. 4.

Sarusky, Jaime. 2005. *Grupo de Experimentación Sonora del ICAIC: Mito y Realidad.* Havana: Letras Cubanas.

Savigliano, Marta E. 1995. *Tango and the Political Economy of Passion.* Boulder, CO: Westview Press.

Sayre, Elizabeth. 2000. "Cuban Batá Drumming and Women Musicians: An Open Question." *Center for Black Music Research Digest* 13, no. 1: 12–15.

Scarpaci, Joseph L., Roberto Segre, and Mario Coyula. 2002. *Havana: Two Faces of the Antillean Metropolis.* Chapel Hill: University of North Carolina Press.

Scott, Rebecca J. 1985. *Slave Emancipation in Cuba: The Transition to Free Labor, 1860–1899.* Princeton: Princeton University Press.

Scott, Rebecca J. 2005. *Degrees of Freedom: Louisiana and Cuba after Slavery.* Cambridge: Belknap Press.

Sloat, Susanna, ed. 2002. *Caribbean Dance from Abakuá to Zouk: How Movement Shapes Identity.* Gainesville: University of Florida Press.

Slobin, Mark. 1993. *Subcultural Sounds: Micromusics of the West.* Hanover: University Press of New England.

Smith, Ronald R. 1994. "Arroz Colorao: Los Congos de Panama." In *Music and*

Black Ethnicity: The Caribbean and South America, edited by Béhague. Miami: North-South Center, University of Miami.

Stewart, Gary. 2000. *Rumba on the River: A History of the Popular Music of the Two Congos*. New York: Verso.

Stolzoff, Norman C. 2000. *Wake the Town and Tell the People: Dancehall Culture in Jamaica*. Durham: Duke University Press.

Suárez, Norma, ed. 1996. *Fernando Ortiz y la cubanidad*. Havana: Ediciones Unión.

Sublette, Ned. 2004. *Cuba and Its Music: From the First Drums to the Mambo*. Chicago: Chicago Review Press.

Tabares, Sahily. 1997. "Paulito F.G.: El bueno soy yo." *Salsa Cubana* 1, no. 2: 26–29.

Thompson, Robert Farris. 1984. *Flash of the Spirit: African and Afro-American Art and Philosophy*. New York: Vintage Books.

Turner, Victor. 1982. *From Ritual to Theater: The Human Seriousness of Play*. New York: Performing Arts Journal Publications.

Turner, Victor. 1986. *The Anthropology of Performance*. New York: Performing Arts Journal Publications.

Turnley, David. 2002. *La Tropical: The Best Dancehall in the World*. Film. Arts Alliance America.

Van Sertima, Ivan. 1976. *They Came before Columbus*. New York: Random House.

Van Sertima, Ivan, ed. 1995 [1989]. *Egypt Revisited*. New Brunswick: Transaction Publishers.

Vasconcelos, José. 1979 [1925]. *The Cosmic Race/La Raza Cósmica*. Baltimore: Johns Hopkins University Press.

Vaughan, Umi, and Carlos Aldama. 2012. *Carlos Aldama's Life in Batá: Cuba, Diaspora, and the Drum*. Bloomington: Indiana University Press.

Verdery, Katherine. 1996. *What Was Socialism and What Comes Next?* Princeton: Princeton University Press.

Wade, Peter. 1997. *Race and Ethnicity in Latin America*. London: Pluto Press.

Wade, Peter. 2000. *Music, Race, and Nation: Música Tropical in Colombia*. Chicago: University of Chicago Press.

Waxer, Lise, ed. 2002. *Situating Salsa: Global Markets and Local Meaning in Latin Popular Music*. London: Routledge Press.

Woodson, Carter G. 2005 [1933]. *The Mis-Education of the Negro*. Drewryville, VA: Khalifah's Booksellers.

Index